# LEAVE US ALONE

# LEAVE US ALONE

*Getting the Government's Hands*
*Off Our Money, Our Guns,*
*Our Lives*

## GROVER NORQUIST

WILLIAM MORROW
*An Imprint of HarperCollinsPublishers*

HarperCollins books may be purchased for educational, business, or sales promotional use. For information please write: Special Markets Department, HarperCollins Publishers, 10 East 53rd Street, New York, NY 10022.

FIRST EDITION

Designed by Lovedog Studio

Library of Congress Cataloging-in-Publication Data has been applied for.

ISBN: 978-0-06-113395-4

08  09  10  11  12  WBC/RRD  10  9  8  7  6  5  4  3  2  1

*For my Mom and Dad,*
*Carol and Warren Norquist*

# CONTENTS

PART III: THE BATTLEGROUND

# PREFACE

A sculptor was once asked how he created a marble statue of Zeus. The sculptor explained that first you get a big block of marble and then you simply remove the bits that don't look like Zeus.

In writing this book, I first decided what book I did not wish to write. I chose not to write another book entitled *The Other Team Sucks* or *My Team Is Going to Win Come Heck or High Water, So Get Used to It*. Others have done fine work here. Such books do serve to rile up the troops, preach to the choir, and make oneself feel better after a well-turned rant.

Nor did I want to write a book about how my team is losing and Western civilization is slouching toward Sodom and there is simply nothing to be done.

One such book explaining the collapse of the modern Republican Party and conservative movement came out weeks before the revolution of 1994. Another book describing the permanent decline of the Democrat Party was published just before Bill Clinton was elected to govern with a Democrat House and Senate in 1992.

I also chose not to write a utopian book about how the world would be perfect if all my ideas were turned into law tomorrow. It was a while ago that I discovered that the world was not organized around what I wanted done. I was very disappointed. But unlike some, I was ten years old when this truth became painfully clear. It takes a great deal of hard work by millions of Americans to turn around the ship of state and keep it moving in the right direction for a generation. This book is about how the center-right can move America toward greater freedom and individual liberty, not just an assertion that we should.

I also worked hard to avoid writing a book that could be summarized as a "longer version of a good magazine article." There are many fine books on the market that take one interesting idea and put it on the literary rack and turn the wheel until toes and fingers have two hundred pages distance between them. I have written more than one hundred magazine articles and given hundreds of political speeches and created dozens of political meetings, coalitions, and campaigns. The lessons of success and failure, what works and what doesn't in real time are poured into this book.

Rather I have written a book that describes the two competing coalitions in American politics, how they are organized, what makes them stronger or weaker. What each can achieve and what they cannot do. And how you the reader may fit into the contest. These two competing political coalitions—descriptively titled the Leave Us Alone Coalition and the Takings Coalition—are at the heart of the center-right and the left, respectively.

To gain a deeper understanding of American politics—where it's been, where it is and particularly where it will be over the next half-century—it is more important to understand those coalitions than the parties themselves. This book was written to give you that understanding.

Returning to what this book is not, it is not a book about the 2008 presidential campaign or the strengths or failings of President Bush or Hillary Clinton. It is about the near and far future.

Nor is the book a reaction to Republican success in 2000 and 2004 or Democrat success in 2006. I do believe, as an analyst and a combatant, that if present trends continue, the center-right coalition will grow and strengthen while the left's strength ebbs. Of course, there are countertrends and a possible Democrat parry for every Republican thrust. Some of my optimism for my team flows from the fact that I intend to work hard.

Much has already been written about today and tomorrow. The demands of twenty-four-hour television and hundreds of political bloggers and columnists with contracts to write insightfully twice a week put great focus on every twist and turn, projecting small victories into lasting majorities and consigning each party to everlasting oblivion when they falter in one election. Will this back-and-forth dance continue? Will one party grow away from the other slowly and steadily or jump ahead in one big leap as one did following the Depression and in the elections of 1974 and 1994?

After describing the two coalitions, I discuss a series of economic, demographic, and political trends that will shape the relative strength of these coalitions over the next twenty-five years. And as an advocate for the center-right coalition in America that is organized around its desire simply to "be left alone," I have also described the center-right's opportunities and strengths and the order of battle for the next generation.

I do believe that the center-right coalition in American politics will triumph in the long unending struggle to define America. But there will be bad election years, disappointing candidates, bad breaks, and undeserved luck on both sides. There will be wars and recessions. There is nothing inevitable about our moving toward the city on a hill Ronald Reagan spoke of: a nation of individual liberty and economic prosperity that shares its vision of the good life through example, not empire.

We could fall backward and become like Old Europe trading freedom and opportunity for security and enforced leveling. But with hard work I believe we can and will continue the progress started by

Goldwater, Reagan, Gingrich, and the growing movement they represented and led.

This is also the time to thank those who have been a great asset in the writing of this book. First and foremost, my wife, Samah, for her support and forbearance of long and odd hours as I worked to write a book around the demands of running Americans for Tax Reform and the responsibilities of a benedict.

Adam Radman was invaluable as a researcher and editor and good company on weekends. Many of the activists I work with helped provide charts and examples that illustrate the sweep of American politics that I hoped to capture in words and numbers: Dan Clifton, president of the American Shareholders Association; Ryan Ellis, president of the Alliance for Worker Freedom; Chris Butler, the chief of staff for Americans for Tax Reform; and John Kartch, Sarah Smith, Carrie Hale, Sandra Fabry, Elizabeth Karasmeighan, Scott LaGanga, Jane Frazer, Kelsey Zahourek, Karri Bragg, Patrick Gleason, Derek Hunter, Brian Johnson, Brandi Kolmer, Megan McChesney, and Satya Thallam.

# INTRODUCTION: THE CONTEST FOR AMERICA—A NOTE TO THE READER

America will soon make a decision about its future. It will be a permanent decision. There will be no going back.

You can and will play a role in that decision. Your individual decision to engage or withdraw could change history for the better or worse.

Over the next decade America will make decisions that will set us on the path of Old Europe—trading liberty for security, dynamism, and growth for safety and managed decline—or recommit itself to pursuing a free and open society where there are no limits on what the individual can accomplish free of the politics of envy and leveling and control.

We will decide to live as independent adults, regaining our dignity and control over our lives and families, or we will come to be increasingly treated by the government as if we never left high school: coddled, protected, and caged. We will make this decision. No one else.

While there have always been those pushing for more government control of your life and others defending your autonomy and liberty, these two competing forces have never before been so clearly separated

out into the two major political parties and they have never been so
evenly divided.

This is new for America. Following the Civil War the central division
was largely regional. If a voter told you he was Republican, it didn't
tell you much about his views on taxes or foreign policy, but rather
that he was almost certainly born north of the Mason-Dixon Line.
Waves of immigrants would marble the country with Irish immigrants reacting poorly to mistreatment by Yankee Protestants and becoming Democrats. Italian immigrants running into Irish-American
dominance in cities often became Republicans. This was not a very
rational way to pick up teams in what was fast becoming the richest
and potentially most powerful nation in the world.

Because Northerners outnumbered Southerners, and the Republicans had the advantage of being the party of national unity, they
dominated Congress and the presidency from 1860 to 1930, with only
Democrats Grover Cleveland and Woodrow Wilson holding the presidency for a total of sixteen years and Congress falling into Democrat
control for only twenty-two of those seventy years.[1]

The Great Depression gave the Democrats their great opportunity,
and Franklin Roosevelt created a majoritarian Democrat party composed of Southerners, union members, Jewish and Catholic immigrants, and northern big-city political machines. He won over much
of the African-American vote just three generations away from slavery. Roosevelt greatly increased the size of government at all levels,
creating jobs for his political machine. Government spending at all
levels in 1932 was 14.9 percent of GDP. It rose to 22.2 percent by 1952
and 30.2 percent by 1980.[2] Taxpayers supported 4,150,000 government workers in 1940; 6,589,000 in 1952; and 16,201,000 in 1980.[3]
Unions were granted sweeping powers to force workers to pay dues to
keep their jobs. FDR's coalition dominated American politics for sixty
years. Laws were changed, structures created and funded to keep the
ruling party entrenched. Republicans could occasionally win the
presidency in response to Democrat corruption and/or entanglement
in foreign wars such as Korea and Vietnam. But from 1930 to 1994,

the Democrats controlled the House of Representatives for all but four years: 1946–1948 and 1952–1954.[4] The Senate was Republican for only twelve of those sixty-four years.[5]

It was during the lifetime of Ronald Reagan that the modern Republican Party was transformed from a regional party of the North lamely waiting for the natural governing coalition to get in trouble and throw an election away to an internally consistent party that could command 60 percent of the vote in presidential elections. It is the party and movement created by Ronald Reagan that captured the House and Senate in 1994 and won the presidential elections in 1980, 1984, 1988, 2000, and 2004. Republican strength at the national level was matched with Democrat weakness. The Democrats have failed to win 51 percent of the votes cast for president since the Lyndon Johnson landslide victory over Barry Goldwater in 1964. Why did the Democrat hegemony falter? What is the nature of this Reagan Republican coalition? How was it created? Why does it hold together? Is it now waxing or waning in strength? Will the Republican Party run the country twenty-five years from now? Why does it behave as it does? Today, one team promises that if they gain control of the presidency and the Congress that they will, as an opening bid, raise taxes by three trillion dollars over the next decade, a $3,000 tax hike per taxpayer each and every year. They have proposed new government spending of over two trillion dollars. They would have the government control your health care, how much energy you can use, how it will be produced, and the size and make of your automobile. They would also determine much of your future and your children's future by racial quotas and require you to pay $500 in dues to labor-union leaders to keep your job. They have strong opinions on what and where you can eat, smoke, or drink. The other team is committed to opposing those efforts and enacting additional tax cuts that reduce taxes by two trillion dollars over the same period.

George Wallace said in 1968 that there is not a dime's worth of difference between the two major parties. Today, when America decides between Republicans and Democrats in just the election of 2008, it sees several trillion dollars worth of difference. Over the years to come the difference grows in size and scope.[6]

And while the two parties are pulling in diametrically opposed directions on every major issue of the day, they are more evenly matched in strength than ever before in history. The partisan vote for the presidency in 2000 and 2004 gave Republicans 112,496,775 votes and Democrats 110,024,225 votes. The two parties split the vote 50.5 percent to 49.5 percent. The total vote for Congress from 1994 to 2005 was equally close, with the total cumulative votes for Republicans of 288,674,630 and total cumulative votes for Democrats of 282,645,708 or 50.52 percent to 49.47 percent.[7] This evenly balanced struggle makes even a small political movement a possible tiebreaker.

In some European countries, if your political party gets 2 percent of the vote you might get to pick the next prime minister. In the United States, if your party gets 2 percent of the vote you are officially a nut. You may later become a successful talk-show host, but you do not get to ride in Air Force One.

In the private sector you can get rich winning 2 percent of the market for widgets. At the Olympics they give you a shiny bronze medal for coming in third. In politics there is no bronze medal. There is no silver medal. The guy who comes in second place is simply known as the loser. This means that small political movements or groups interested in specific issues join with others to create the two coalitions that support the two major American parties until one party wins a majority. And that means you and yours. The political and demographic trends in this book are not impersonal forces beyond your control. They include you and your efforts.

Modern technology expands what even one person can do to bring friends, co-workers, family, church members, classmates to the polls. It allows you to be politically active not only in your hometown but across town, in another city, or in another state.

The 2000 presidential election was decided by 537 votes in Florida.

You and the people on your cell phone's speed dial could have brought five hundred voters to the polls that day.

The evenly balanced stalemate will not continue.

The fork in the road for America is before us now. If nothing is done, even if no new taxes are raised, no new spending programs invented, the simple growth of federal government spending driven by the existing entitlement programs of Social Security, Medicare, and Medicaid, and the aging of the baby-boomer generation will drive federal spending from 20 percent of the economy to 40 percent by 2050. Add in state and local spending and if nothing is done we will in two generations have the government spending more than half of the nation's income. And since those on welfare or getting government paychecks are not exactly net taxpayers, if you are a taxpayer your cost of government will have to increase to become much more than half of your paycheck to make up for those who are net tax eaters.

Between 1960 and 2000, the federal government hovered around 20 percent of the economy. Through Republican and Democrat presidencies and Congresses there was little change. Because the baby-boomer generation will soon begin driving up the cost of Social Security and Medicare, simply continuing the status quo is not an option. Inertia will soon bring us to the level of government control of France or Sweden.

But there is an alternative vision. We can, and I believe, must, reform the government programs that unchanged will destroy our liberties even before they empty our wallets. We can reduce the size and scope of government at all levels to make all Americans freer, richer, and more independent of government at all levels. More independent of the annoying and intrusive handmaidens of big government: labor unions, trial lawyers, government contractors of the social-welfare complex, and the busybodies of the Nanny State.

The first two chapters describe and outline the relative strength of the two competing coalitions in American politics. You will see how you and your family can play a role in strengthening the forces fighting for a freer future. You will come to understand the nature and reasoning of those who push for higher taxes and more government control. And how they can be defeated, or better yet, convinced to switch teams.

There is a series of demographic and political changes taking place over the next several decades. Some threaten to push us toward a European social-welfare state. Here we see the growing number of Americans who receive some government "benefits," and the growth in government-sector employment and unionization. Examining the strength of those advocating more and more of yesteryear's failed efforts is not done to sow despair. Rather it is to understand the playing field. A man's got to know his limitations. Political movements must also heed Clint Eastwood's wisdom.

Some trends strengthen the advocates of limited government: Every additional American who owns shares of stock directly in a 401(k) is more concerned with a strong economy, property rights, and low taxes on businesses. The more Mormons and Orthodox Jews, the more Republicans. The cheerful trends are not to promote triumphalism or false optimism. Rather, they encourage us to be alive and alert to favorable waves to ride. Successful men and movements make their own luck building on such opportunities.

Some of these trends are set in stone, and those involved in politics have to plan around them—people born this year will be voting in eighteen years. Today's eighty-year-olds will not. Some political and demographic changes can be sped up or stopped. Here the strength of organized labor may continue to wane or laws could be changed to force more Americans into paying union dues.

The next several chapters outline the battleground between the two political tendencies. How strong are they in the House, the Senate, the contest for the presidency, and control of state governments. What is the role of the new media, the Internet, 500-channel television, and talk radio?

The final four chapters walk through the steps necessary to winning this fight. "What is to be done?" How can we change the direction of taxation and government spending? The two key levers of the power of the state over you and your family can and must be reduced and defanged. What can be done to strengthen liberty today, tomorrow, and in the next decade?

We know that America will decide in favor of one direction or the other during this generation of Americans. This book walks through the next several decades and you will see how and where you can best enter the fray. Liberty, a lasting liberty, can be won for America and, through our example, for the entire world. But history teaches us that liberty can be lost through inaction or good motives driving bad policy.

Together we can and will win America's future. If the Republican Party fully grasps the chemistry and the power of the Leave Us Alone Coalition and acts on that understanding, a long-term political victory of unprecedented dimension is possible. The Takings Coalition can lose. Permanently.

Imagine an America where taxes are low and getting lower. Where the news each year is that your property-tax bill is lower than last year, not higher.

Imagine a world where every American parent has full school choice. Whatever amount the city or state decides will be spent on education will be attached to each child and follow him or her to the school, public or private, of the parents' choosing.

Imagine an America where every teenager looks forward to saving 10 percent of his salary, not through a government program, but with a personal savings account that travels with him through life, from job to job, always under his control. Every young American would correctly look forward to amassing real wealth. Not just a promised pension.

Imagine an America where everyone who wishes to be an independent contractor rather than an employee has that right. He cannot be forced to join a union. He is free of federal and state labor laws. He is independent of those trying to "help."

Imagine an America where citizens have the right to carry a weapon for self-defense. Where criminals live in fear—not honest citizens.

Imagine an America where a person's property is sacrosanct. The government cannot tell you what to do with your home, your farm, your ranch, your property.

Imagine an America where the federal government taxes your consumed income one time at one single rate. And then leaves you and your money unmolested to save, invest, or spend as you alone see fit.

This is the American dream of the modern center-right movement, the Leave Us Alone Coalition, and in coming true, it would spell the absolute defeat of the modern left, the Takings Coalition.

What does the left offer to a self-employed citizen with an individual retirement account, a health savings account, a concealed-gun permit, and the ability to educate his own children in the school of his choice? That person does not ask the government for anything taken from anyone else. He cannot be threatened that if he doesn't let the government raise taxes he will be unemployed, he won't have a retirement, he won't have health care, and his kids will be stupid. He—or she—can look the world in the eye and tell it to go to Hades.

This book will show you how that vision of America can be realized.

# PART ONE

# THE TWO COMPETING COALITIONS

---

"I never said, 'I want to be alone.' I only said, 'I want to be left alone.'"

—*Greta Garbo*[1]


"A government that robs Peter to pay Paul can always depend on the support of Paul."

—*George Bernard Shaw*


"That is the problem with government these days. They want to do things all the time; they are always busy thinking of what things they can do next. This is not what people want. People want to be left alone to look after their cattle."

—*Obed Ramotswe, father of Precious Ramotswe,*
*head of The No. 1 Ladies' Detective Agency*

## CHAPTER ONE

# THE
# LEAVE US
# ALONE COALITION

What is today's center-right movement? What are the building blocks of the modern conservative movement that engulfs and buttresses the Republican Party, reinvented and restructured by the Reagan revolution? How has this movement grown and how is it held together? How is it able to vie for political power in America?

The center-right movement, the political movement created out of the defeated minority Republican Party of midcentury and sculpted by Ronald Reagan's political leadership and lifetime, is a coalition of groups and individuals that have one thing in common. They do not want the government to give them something. Or take something from others. On the key issue that motivates their vote, they want one simple thing from the government: They just want to be left alone.

They are taxpayers who want lower taxes. Businessmen and -women, entrepreneurs, investors who wish to run their own affairs without being regulated and taxed out of existence. Property owners who do not wished to be taxed out of their homes or property. Gun owners protective of their Second Amendment rights. Homeschoolers who are willing to spend the time and energy to educate their own children, asking only that the government leave them alone. Conservative

Catholics, evangelical Protestants, Orthodox Jews, Muslims, and Mormons, all members of the various communities of faith who wish to be left alone to practice their faith and pass it on to their children.

This movement is not simply a collection of unrelated interest groups in a marriage of convenience.

Pollsters can cajole citizens into answering twenty questions about twenty issues. But what matters in politics is the one issue that moves a citizen to vote for or against a candidate. The Leave Us Alone Coalition is brought together by many issues. Its members do not necessarily agree on some manifesto or confession of belief. There is no checklist where all members must agree on twenty articles of faith. Or ten. Or two. They find themselves shoulder to shoulder working together for the same candidates and over time the same party because on the issue that moves each of their individual votes—not necessarily on all or even most issues—what they want from the government is to be left alone.

Who are the members and leaders of the Leave Us Alone Coalition?

## TAXPAYERS

First and foremost they are taxpayers, those Americans whose primary vote-moving issue is keeping their taxes low. They believe the paychecks they earn belong to them. They react strongly to all efforts to raise their taxes. They have flowing in their veins the blood of the Sons of Liberty who created the American Revolution in response to direct taxation by the British Crown. More recently they reacted strongly to Democrat Walter Mondale's promise (threat) in 1984 that he would raise their taxes and to Republican President George H. W. Bush's breaking of his no-tax-hike pledge in 1990. In California in the 1970s, men like Howard Jarvis and Paul Gann and Lew Uhler led the fight against rising property taxes and ran Proposition 1 in 1970 and then Proposition 13 in 1978, which ignited the nationwide taxpayer revolt that swept Ronald Reagan into the presidency.

In 1980, Barbara Anderson led the taxpayer movement in unlikely Massachusetts that saw "Proposition 2½" passed by Bay State voters on the same night the state voted for Reagan. She remembers her Democrat parents, who owned a mom-and-pop hardware store, complaining about taxes and the arrogance of government in the same sentence. As a navy officer's wife, she saw federal government waste up close. As a young mother, she read about state and local government mismanagement while struggling to pay state and local taxes. Her second husband, who worked long hours of blue-collar overtime, described a proposed state graduated income tax as "the one where the harder you work the more they steal from you."

Then, in 1974, she heard a local official say about another property-tax increase: "Get used to it, folks; they're going up every year." She joined Citizens for Limited Taxation (CLT) as a volunteer that week, in rebellion against that attitude even more than the taxes themselves. She collected 4,800 signatures for a constitutional amendment initiative for tax limitation in Massachusetts.

She joined the staff of CLT in 1978. She later became the executive director on July 1, 1980, and ran the successful campaign for Proposition 2½, which cut property taxes in Massachusetts to 2.5 percent of fair market value, limited levy increases to 2.5 percent a year, and required a vote of the people in any town or city to raise additional property taxes over the limit. Proposition 2½ is a law, unlike California's famous Proposition 13, which is a constitutional amendment, but Barbara Anderson's force of personality and organized taxpayer movement have largely kept the legislature and several governors from messing with it.

Other Americans enter the taxpayer movement after having viewed the spending side of government and wondering if what we pay for is actually a net positive.

Jeff Ballabon, a New York–born young professional and now a conservative leader, was raised in a family that was generally supportive of the idea of a comforting welfare state. His personal turning point came when he was a young congressional staffer working for moderate John Danforth of Missouri. He attended a meeting on welfare reform and expressed what he thought was a commonsense observation that job training might help welfare recipients move from dependence to lives as independent actors able to provide for themselves and their families.

The room of largely Democrat staffers and welfare-rights activist organizers turned on him. Someone shouted, "You are stigmatizing nonwork." There was cursing and more shouting. Jeff and his heretical ideas were asked to leave the room.

"Walking back to the office and assimilating what I'd witnessed," Jeff recounts, "it became clear to me how their policies were focused entirely on maintaining political power over an enslaved class of the neediest people, destroying generations of Americans by enforced dependence. I was depressed, then angry, and finally determined to focus on freeing people from government ownership.

"I knew lots of decent, well-meaning folks, my parents included, were ardent supporters of welfare programs. That was because they viewed it as a backstop and just assumed that of course people are all doing their best to get away from welfare and get on their own two feet. They didn't see the corrupt politics of political slavery and couldn't imagine the psychological, emotional, and developmental damage done to the "beneficiaries" of the programs.

"From that point on, I guess I became a conservative. I viewed every domestic federal program with suspicion."

Some taxpayers have organized their town, county, city, or even state taxpayers' organization. Others simply vote for the candidate who will reduce their tax burden. These tax-motivated voters do not want taxes raised on others. They just want to be left alone.

Let's be clear. Not every taxpayer becomes a Reagan Republican. But those citizens whose vote is motivated by their tax burden and a desire to reduce it are charter members of the Leave Us Alone Coalition, and today they vote for the Reagan Republican candidates.

## BUSINESSMEN AND -WOMEN

A second group in the coalition is small-businessmen and -women, the self-employed, independent contractors, franchisees, and entrepreneurs who do not want their businesses overtaxed or regulated. They do not ask for favors from the government. They simply wish to be left alone. (There *are* businessmen who want the government to provide subsidies or to kneecap their competition—they are not part of this coalition. They bat for the other team.)

The rhetoric of the Democrats since the Great Depression is that government can or should "create" jobs, or "give" you a job. Jobs are, of course, not created by government. The government can take the money out of the real economy (defunding a job in the private sector) and drag the money into the government coffers and spend it to "create" a new job. This is the economic equivalent of taking a pail of water out of one side of a lake and walking around the lake—spilling some of the water—and then holding a press conference surrounded by cameras to be filmed pouring what is left in the bucket into the lake. "Vote for Fred, he is filling up the lake with water." Government cannot create. It can only take and relocate. It cannot give you anything, including jobs, which it didn't take by force in the first place.

Self-employed Americans, small-business owners, franchisees, and independent contractors best understand that jobs are created, not given. They have created their own job. They maintain it. They create jobs for others. They feel taxes and regulations intensely, not like the princess and the pea cushioned by a dozen mattresses, but more as the shoeless soldier at Valley Forge felt the frozen ground. Government cannot hide its rough edges, the true costs and damage done to the self-employed. The smaller the business, the more likely employees are to see the direct link between individual initiative and success and the dead hand of government and lower wages, lost days, and lost jobs.

Some eleven million households pay their taxes quarterly.[1] Their federal and state income tax burden is not hidden by the withholding of taxes from paychecks. Some Americans look only at their total take-home pay and overlook the FICA taxes and income taxes that come out of the paychecks. Those who pay their federal taxes quarterly vividly see and feel the cost of government and may better judge whether they are getting their money's worth.

Businesswoman and entrepreneur Kathy Gornik represents millions of Americans who vote to be left alone to run their own business. She was born in Cleveland to Yugoslavian immigrant parents,
who were Democrats. When she got out of school in Kentucky she
borrowed $20,000 from family and friends, and with a friend from
college, she started Thiel Corporation, producing high-quality audio
systems. Thiel now employs thirty men and women and exports to
thirty-two foreign countries.

She says she "detests" politics, but "politics loves me." Meaning
that government has a strong interest in the money she earns and
takes much of it. She says, "I just want to be left alone."

Theil is a subchapter S corporation, like 3.5 million others in
America, so Gornik writes four checks a year to the IRS. Their taxes
are not silently or "painlessly" removed through withholding.

There are millions of small businessmen and -women and self-
employed in America. The Census Bureau records 27 million businesses. Nineteen and a half million of them have no employees beyond
their owners, 5.3 million have twenty or fewer employees.[2] About
757,000 Americans run their own franchises, operating restaurants
like McDonald's, Subway, or Burger King, and services like Jiffy Lube
and Curves. There were an estimated 14.1 million direct sellers in
2005, including self-employed salesmen for Alticor (parent company
of Amway), Mary Kay, and Avon.[3]

Other Americans sell without working through a national network. More than seven hundred thousand Americans sell on eBay as
their primary or secondary source of income.[4] (Full-time eBay sellers
outnumber full-time steelworkers.)[5] They are, in effect, self-employed
independent contractors. They feel every tax. Democrats believe that
the hardworking man or woman working two jobs must want government help. That person specifically has gone to great lengths to
turn down the government's offer to "help" them outside of work.
The gulf between that hard worker and someone on welfare or the
possessor of a no-show, sometimes-show government job is greater
than the gulf between that worker and Bill Gates.

The state can offer little or nothing to these self-employed people and small-business employees other than the pain of taxation and the bother of regulatory burdens. Employees in large companies can be misled on the cost/benefit analysis of government. In the past the government could tax General Motors and hand each of the workers on the assembly line some little benefit. They would directly see the benefit and only indirectly feel the cost.

When a hundred workers are laid off by General Motors to pay the taxes for some new environmental fad or government spending program, who makes the connection? The politicians would claim the money was free, came from nowhere, had no cost, was being paid for by others—the big corporations. For the self-employed and small-business employee, politicians cannot loot the company and then pretend they are handing free stuff to employees/voters that came from nowhere. The cost of government is painfully transparent.

The costs of regulations imposed on small businesses by city, state, and federal governments are felt indirectly in higher prices by all Americans. The self-employed and small-businessmen feel not only the cost, but the hassle and humiliation of bureaucrats up close and personal, day after day. You and I visit the Department of Motor Vehicles every few years to renew a driver's license. A small-businessman must deal with dozens of agencies with the same power to withhold and delay and the same cheerful attitude and sense of urgency that we meet at the DMV.

As a result, the self-employed, small-businessmen, franchisees, direct sellers, and independent contractors tend to ask only to be left alone.

## THE SECOND AMENDMENT VOTER

Add to taxpayers and businessmen those voters whose primary vote-moving issue is the Second Amendment. There are ninety million gun owners in the United States and as many as twenty million hunters. Of course, not every hunter or gun owner is a member of the Leave Us Alone Coalition. Some hunters vote on an issue other than guns. But those gun owners who do vote on the Second Amendment are strong members of the coalition.

The gun issue has brought a surprising number of Americans into the Leave Us Alone Coalition. Witness Sandy Froman who might not have been expected to be "on the right" when she grew up in liberal San Francisco and went to Stanford University and Harvard Law School. A self-described five-foot-two Jewish woman, she was thirty-two, recently divorced, and living alone north of Los Angeles when a criminal tried to break into her home through her front door. A call to the police elicited the helpful advice that she go into her bedroom and lock the door. Neighbors did not respond. The police did not show up until the would-be intruder had given up and left.

Sandy had never fired a gun before. She did not grow up around guns. But as she cowered defenseless in her home, she "decided then and there I was never going to be that helpless again."

The next day she signed up for a gun-safety course at the local range and bought a Colt M-1911 pistol. "Buying that gun and becoming competent with it gave me confidence that I could defend myself," she said.

Sandy Froman also joined the NRA (National Rifle Association) that year. Eleven years later, in 1992, she was elected to the board of directors of the NRA in the same election that brought Charlton Heston to his historic five-year presidency. Then, in 2005, she was the second woman to be elected president of the NRA.

Americans who vote their Second Amendment rights as the "First Freedom" fit comfortably in the Leave Us Alone Coalition. They do not want anything from anybody. They simply wish to be left alone with their guns. They do not go door to door urging everyone else to own guns. They do not insist that fourth-grade students in public schools be taught books entitled *Heather Has Two Hunters*.

## HOMESCHOOLERS

The coalition has a small but powerfully motivated group of parents who have decided to educate their own children at home. They have declined the kind offer of the state to "educate" their children for free. One parent usually has to sacrifice the opportunity to work outside the home and give up one income in order to be both parent and teacher. This movement grew in response to unhappiness with the quality of public education and, for some, the concerns of religious parents about the increasingly secular school system.

Homeschoolers became a growing phenomenon and a political force largely through the leadership of Michael Farris, a lawyer in Washington State who was the son of a public-school principal. Farris had begun to educate his children in a local Christian private school when he met Raymond Moore, an early proponent of homeschooling, who made a simple argument, "People get their values from the people they are around."

Farris and his wife wanted their children to share their values, not someone else's, and so they began to homeschool in 1982. As word got around that a smart young lawyer was homeschooling his growing family, he was asked by more and more families to help them in arguments with local authorities who challenged their ability to homeschool. By 1983, Mike Farris founded the Home School Legal Defense Association and moved to the Washington, D.C., area to run this growing national association—the ACLU for homeschooling families. In 2000, Farris founded Patrick Henry College in Virginia as a university catering to students who were homeschooled.

Today homeschoolers are 1 or 2 percent of the population. They punch above their weight class, as they have been toughened up by defeating the teachers unions' efforts to criminalize homeschooling. Now an organized force, homeschoolers do not ask for anything from the government. They do not ask that their sacrifice be celebrated as an alternative lifestyle. They simply wish to be left alone.


## PROPERTY RIGHTS ACTIVISTS AND HOMEOWNERS

Property owners simply wish to be left alone in their homes, shops, farms, and ranches without the fear that the mayor might expropriate their land to give it to one of his favorite political contributors to build a shopping mall or sports stadium or because it rained last night and Al

Gore now claims their backyard as a wetland. This impulse has been organized into thousands of local property rights groups that arise when local, state, or even the federal government have threatened men and women who simply wish to be ignored by the state. This has become a national movement largely through the efforts of Chuck Cushman.

Cushman was raised a Democrat in California. In 1962, the federal government forced Chuck Cushman's father to sell his inholding— private property located within the Yosemite National Park. He was told to sell or lose his job. He sold. In 1970, Chuck purchased an inholding in Yosemite. When the feds came for his property and tried to pressure him and his neighbors to selling their land to the government, he chose to fight. He organized his fellow property owners in self-defense. They won and saved their entire town of Wawona. Chuck kept going. He organized his fellow inholders into the National Park Inholders Association. Chuck Cushman's defense of property rights was not only a national example that inspired thousands—he created a national network, the American Land Rights Association. Today Cushman helps organize, train, and coordinate the more than two thousand property-rights groups across the fifty states.

Cushman's more rural property-rights activists are joined by homeowners who wish to protect their homes from slow-motion expropriation through high property taxes, zoning changes, or high crime rates that drive down property values. Expensive and/or incompetent local government threatens to destroy the life savings of those whose largest investment is their home. These were the shock troops of the taxpayer revolt in 1978's Proposition 13.

## THE COMMUNITIES OF FAITH AND PARENTS' RIGHTS

The coalition also includes those Americans whose central concern is practicing their religion and raising their children in that same faith. They have been called the "religious right." This confuses the heck out of the establishment press that cannot understand how evangelical Protestants, both fundamentalist and Pentecostal, conservative Catholics, Orthodox Jews, Muslims, and Mormons can all cheerfully be in the same political movement. Shouldn't they be fighting each other? They do not agree on who gets into heaven. They don't have to. They realize that if they are to practice their faith their way they need to stand politically with others of different faiths who want the same freedom. They are political allies, even if the other fellow is going straight to Hades given his flawed understanding of scripture.

Religious differences used to drive voters of different faiths into different parties. Catholics and Jewish immigrants were made to feel unwelcome by Protestant Republicans. In 1928, Al Smith, the first Roman Catholic nominated to run for president as a Democrat, lost solid Democrat—and Protestant—southern states to Herbert Hoover.* As late as 1980 there were serious debates within evangelical and Pentecostal Protestant circles about how healthy or wise it was to be working side by side politically with those fellow Protestants whose theology was suspect.

Over the years the aggressively secular left has created a more ecumenical right.

No single religious denomination in America has ever been strong enough to dominate American politics. Each understood that. They now feel more threatened by a secular state ridiculing their faith and undermining their parental authority through government-run public schools that claim their children from kindergarten through state universities. The largest religion in America is Roman Catholicism with 25 percent of the population.[6] Baptists weigh in at 16 percent and Methodists at 7 percent.[7] In other nations where there is an obvious majority or minority—Hindus in India, Muslims in Saudi Arabia, Jews in Israel—one religion can impose its rule over an entire nation. The United States has enjoyed enough diversity that no one faith ever viewed itself as becoming dominant for political pur-

---

*These solid Democrat states included the southern states of Texas, Oklahoma, Missouri, Tennessee, Kentucky, West Virginia, Virginia, North Carolina, and Florida.

poses. When the American Constitution was formed, each Protestant denomination viewed a constitutional prohibition on a state religion to be their best bet. Now with the addition through immigration of more Catholics and Jews, Muslims, and the homegrown faiths of Christian Scientists and Mormons, there are greater numbers of religious minorities who fear not the state embracing a competing faith, but one imposing secularism.

The "religious right" is best understood as a parents' rights movement that fears state interference in the family just as small-businessmen fear regulatory burdens, and taxpayers fear the growing tax take and gun owners fear politicians calling for gun control. As a result, for each major religion, the more important that faith is to a person's life, perhaps best measured outwardly by how frequently one goes to church, synagogue, or mosque, the more likely one is to be a Republican. The more devout, the more likely a family is to be part of the center-right Leave Us Alone Coalition.

The 16 percent of Americans who attend church more than once each week voted 64 percent for Bush. The 26 percent of Americans who say they attend church weekly voted 58 percent for Bush. The 14 percent of Americans who attend church monthly voted 50 percent for Bush. The 28 percent of Americans who attend church "a few times a year" voted 45 percent for Bush and the 15 percent of Americans who "never" attend church voted only 36 percent for Bush.[8]

Polling shows this to be true of Catholics, Protestants, and Jews.

In 2004, Protestants who attend church weekly voted 70 percent for Bush, those Protestants who attend less often voted 56 percent for Bush. (White, evangelical, born-again—"religious right"—Protestants voted 78 percent for Bush over Kerry while all Protestants voted 59 percent for Bush.)[9]

Catholics who attend mass weekly voted 56 percent for Bush, and those who attend mass less often voted 49 percent for Bush.[10]

Rabbi Shmuel Bloom, the executive vice president of the Orthodox grassroots group Agudath Israel of America, said in 2004, "Almost 70 percent of Orthodox Jews, compared to 23 percent Conservative, and 15 percent Reform Jews, cast their votes for President Bush."[11]

One way to understand why the "religious right" usually finds itself comfortable in the Leave Us Alone Coalition is to remember how it came into being. Groups like the Moral Majority and the Christian Coalition did not bring evangelicals into the Republican Party in response to the 1962 ban on prayer in public schools or even the 1973 *Roe v. Wade* Supreme Court decision striking down state laws restricting abortions. The "religious right" was first visible in politics in the late '70s in response to threats from the Carter administration to withdraw the tax deductibility of contributions to Christian schools and to use the FCC's "Fairness Doctrine" to close down Christian radio stations. These threats may have been exaggerated. (William Murray, the son of the late atheist Madalyn Murray O'Hair, argues that the fear that President Carter's FCC was going to close down all Christian radio stations was close to a compete fabrication, but it reportedly generated more letters than the Vietnam War.) The sense of embattlement was real enough to move millions into politics.

One can get a better understanding of the "religious right" in America by examining the life and work of the man who truly brought it into being: Paul Weyrich.

Paul Weyrich was born in Racine, Wisconsin, where his father, a German immigrant, maintained the boiler at St. Mary's Hospital and was a Robert Taft Republican. Paul became a devout Catholic like his father and was motivated in politics by his faith. As a young Republican from the wrong side of the tracks, he says, he was a curiosity to the "country clubbers" who ran the local party.

He was the news director of WAXO in Kenosha, Wisconsin, when the Supreme Court banned prayer in government schools. He reached out to a Protestant minister, a Catholic priest, and a rabbi in criticizing the decision. He expected support from the Wisconsin Republican chairman Claude Jasper but, he recalls, Jasper "just about bit my head off," saying the party did not get involved in religious matters.

When Weyrich moved to Washington, D.C., he worked for Senator Gordon Allott of Colorado, but more important, he began to stitch together the various "wings" of the conservative movement into a coherent whole. He was present at the creation of the "religious right," the broad and ecumenical movement of evangelical Protestants and Roman Catholics. Weyrich explains, "What pushed the religious leaders into politics was not the ERA or abortion or other social issues. Rather it was Carter's attempt to regulate the Christian and parochial schools. This was the nexus between social conservatism and opposition to big government."[12]

The Christian right became politically engaged and organized in self-defense. It saw itself as besieged, under attack by the secular state. This point is often missed by some on the left who worry that it wishes to impose itself on others. It is also misunderstood by some self-appointed religious leaders who hope to march these Americans who organized themselves to be left alone out into offensive battle against various sinners.

These parents of faith will fight to control what is taught to their children in their schools. They will not cross the street to go after folks in San Francisco who behave oddly.

## THE OWNERSHIP SOCIETY

The growing investor class, those Americans who now own stock directly, increasingly through 401(k)s, individual retirement accounts, and mutual funds, also wishes to be left alone. Investors do not want their wealth damaged by taxes, inflation, labor unions, trial lawyers, or government abuse of businesses in which they own stock.

The expansion of the investor class, from 20 percent of households in 1980 to 50 percent of households in 2006, has begun to make clearer the connection between costs imposed on businesses and "benefits" flowing from government for employees of larger firms as well as the self-employed and small businesses.[13] What used to be taxes or regulatory burdens on "other people," "taxes on the big corporations" are now understood to be a government-forced withdrawal from every American's retirement savings: his or her 401(k) or individual retirement account.

How the growth of the investor class is changing American politics can be seen in the example of Steven Schier, the Congdon Professor of Political Science at Carleton College, in Northfield, Minnesota, a professor for thirty years. In his youth he saw himself as a beneficiary of government programs. "Almost a client," he says.

But unlike many professions, university workers have long had portable pensions since the creation of TIAA-CREF, which provides defined-contribution pensions like IRAs for a profession where scholars were expected to shift from one university employer to another with regularity. Industrial workers were expected to stay with one employer for their career. A century ago professors were understood to move frequently and to have the ability to understand investing for their retirement.

For years, Schier contributed 3 percent of his salary to his retirement fund while his employer, Carleton, invested 10 percent. Schier now adds another 10 percent from his salary each year into his 403b. So for thirty years now Schier has had at least 13 percent—and in recent years 23 percent—of his income saved in a portable pension. On average, every four to five years he has saved one year's salary. With interest buildup he now has many times his salary in his retirement fund.

Schier is now a proud and prosperous member of the investor class. Quietly, year by year, he has transformed from someone who might see himself as dependent to a man of independent means. Every tax, every regulation, every frivolous lawsuit is a direct attack on his wealth, his accumulated earnings, and his retirement. This professor is a businessman and investor.

## PUBLIC SERVANTS: THE POLICE AND THE MILITARY

The Leave Us Alone Coalition is not antigovernment. It simply wants properly limited government that plays a role in protecting the life, liberty, and property of citizens. This is why Republicans who oppose much of what the present federal, state, and local governments do tend to support the military and police. When soldiers or the police have their guns pointed outward toward foreigners who truly wish us harm or criminals who would rob us, they are the protectors of our liberty. This is why studies have found that the military itself is heavily Republican, as are many police. During the Cold War, those Americans who were most focused on the threat from the Soviet Empire and those fearful of crime were charter members of the Leave Us Alone Coalition and strong supporters of those parts of the government that provided that protection for all of us.

To distinguish between government workers who are likely members of our coalition and those on the other team, there are two simple tests. If the government employee in question is doing a job whose job description can be found in the Constitution, he or she is a strong candidate for the Leave Us Alone Coalition. Second, if an American who works for the federal, state, or local government can look in the mirror and confidently say, "If my neighbors knew my pay, benefits, and pension, the hours I work, and vacation days I take, they would cross the street and thank me for doing my job," then he or she will be comfortable with us.

But if that government employee would be embarrassed to let his taxpayer neighbors know his true pay, pension, benefits, and hours worked—then he should put out yard signs for the Democrat Party.

Those government employees who spend their days protecting the rights and freedoms of all Americans equally are natural members of the Leave Us Alone Coalition. The armed forces have protected us from and defeated British imperialism, German National Socialism, Japanese imperialism, and Soviet communism and kept us free. Soldiers, sailors, airmen, marines, and the National Guard know that Republicans and conservatives value their service. And if they forget who their friends are, some on the left helpfully chime in calling them "baby killers" "imperialists," and "Fascists." They are reminded by Bill Clinton who wrote of his "loathing" of the military. And in a widely publicized defining moment, in the first week of the Clinton administration, Army Lieutenant General Barry McCaffrey, the assistant to the chairman of the Joint Chiefs of Staff, said "good morning" to a young aide in the White House, who responded, "I don't talk to the military."[14]

Bill Clinton strengthened the sense of hostility and indifference to those government workers who protect us when he had publicly antagonistic relationships with the leadership of the CIA and the FBI director William S. Sessions.

Just before the 2006 election John F. Kerry played to this sense of Democrat disdain for the American soldier with his "botched joke" that was viewed as suggesting that only the dimwitted with few career choices get stuck in Iraq.

Our men and women in the armed forces are not an insignificant voting bloc. As of December 31, 2006, there were 502,466 men and women in the army; 345,566 in the navy; 178,477 in the Marine Corps; 345,024 in the Air Force; and 40,829 in the Coast Guard.[15] A recent study showed 75 percent of men and women in the army see themselves as Republicans.[16]

The police, prison guards, and much of the judicial system spend their time putting Democrats in prison for breaking into the houses of Republicans. They know their work protecting our lives and property is greatly appreciated by Republicans. And should the police feel insufficiently loved by the right, the left will push them away with national campaigns such as the one taking sides with the cop killer Mumia Abu-Jamal of Pennsylvania, who murdered police officer Daniel Faulkner. Cops tend to remember New York City Democrat Al Sharpton and Tawana Brawley. It was a while ago that the left gleefully referred to cops as "pigs," but not so long ago that police now retired and their sons and daughters now serving have forgotten who hates them. Today there are roughly 800,720 state and local police and 448,610 corrections officers.[17] It was the gun-rights movement that championed the legislation to allow police and retired police to carry their weapons across state lines so that every New York City policeman who lives in Connecticut or New Jersey does not commit a felony when he drives home with his service revolver.

## The Wednesday Meeting

The Leave Us Alone Coalition appears in the flesh every Wednesday in Washington, D.C., when 120 center-right activists meet from 10 A.M. to 11:30 A.M. in the offices of Americans for Tax Reform. There, activists from taxpayer groups, business groups, property rights groups, the National Federation of Independent Businesses, the 60 Plus Association, Citizens Against Government Waste, the American Conservative Union, the National Rifle Association, Eagle Forum, homeschoolers, Protestants, Catholics, Orthodox Jews, Muslims, and Mormons meet. Between twenty and thirty forward-looking presentations are made by the participants on what they and their groups are doing. No one tells anyone else what to do. They let everyone else know what they are doing. This is not a meeting for whining or criticism. Presentations are short, only a few minutes long. A great deal of paper is handed out, so anyone with lots to say can write it up and make copies. Bloggers and writers are invited to join on an off-the-record basis.

There are now similar meetings in forty-five state capitals and ten in "second" cities such as New York, Los Angeles, San Diego, and Albuquerque. The state and city meetings generally meet weekly when the legislature is in session and monthly when the legislature is out of session. All those who attend the state meetings are welcome to join and speak to the meeting in Washington when they pass through our imperial city. Over the years dozens of foreign guests have joined the meeting and have returned to their home countries and established Leave Us Alone Coalition meetings in a growing number of cities that now include Tokyo, London, Rome, Ottawa, and Brussels.

The stateside meetings are a physical representation of how the Leave Us Alone Coalition works to build and organize the center-right in America.

As I have mentioned, the groups and the movements they represent do not agree on everything. They do not agree on some ten-point manifesto. There is no statement of purpose. No votes are taken. They are all active because on their primary vote-moving issue they wish to be left alone and they recognize that—however benighted the other attendees of the Wednesday meeting or the conservative movement may be on a host of issues—they are not in conflict on their primary issues.

And so, if for one and a half hours each Wednesday the Christians can agree not to raise anyone's taxes, and the property rights activists can agree not to steal anyone's guns and the gun owners can refrain from throwing prophylactics at the Christians' kids—that is, if everyone can agree to keep out of the faces and pockets of everyone else in the room—then we can go forth and annoy the left for the rest of the week. This is a low-maintenance coalition. No one wants anything at the expense of anyone else on a primary issue.

## And vs. Or: Building a Movement

Perhaps the best way to understand how the Leave Us Alone Coalition works is through the serious lesson of a joke I first heard on the old Ed Sullivan TV show. It was about a businessman who had purchased fire and theft insurance for twenty years from his local insurance agent. One day his business burned to the ground and he went to his friend to collect his insurance money. The agent looked at the contract and up at his friend and back at the contract and said, "Oh, you should have had our fire *or* theft insurance."

In politics there is a great deal of difference between "*and*" and "*or*." The Venn diagram on the following page shows three circles. One represents all voters who vote on the gun issue as their primary vote-moving issue. The second circle represents those voters who cast their vote on the tax issue and the third circle is those voters who vote on a desire to be able to homeschool their children without government harassment. Now there are in real life as many circles as there are primary vote-moving issues. But for purposes of understanding the key distinction between "and" and "or" in politics, note that the deeply shaded area in the middle is that collection of voters who are protaxpayer, progun, *and* prohomeschooling. That is a very small zone compared to the larger area composed of those who are progun *or* protaxpayer *or* prohomeschooler. And the difference between "and" and "or" grows with the addition of other vote-moving issues: property rights, respect for one's faith and ability to pass it on to one's child, the investor class, etc. Each additional issue makes the "or" zone larger and the "and" zone smaller.

Now if you are planning to achieve political power by seizing the radio stations and the airports, you might be able to operate only with supporters in the "and" zone, but if you wish to win democratic elections with at least 51 percent of the vote it is easier if you are winning support from the larger "or" zone.

Phyllis Schlafly commented back in 1980 that she urged everyone to vote for the candidate of her choice for their own reason. It was not necessary for everyone to vote for Reagan in 1980 for the same reason. The were perhaps twenty reasons. And whichever one moved your vote was a fine and dandy reason. Political activists must resist the temptation to expect or demand that voters they speak with support their candidate for their reason.

When I was younger I would approach voters in 1980 and urge them to vote for Reagan because he was for lower taxes. When the

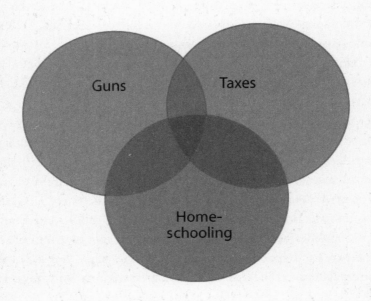

voter agreed, I would also urge them to vote for Reagan because he was good on guns. And I would proceed to go to other issues until I hit one the voter objected to.

One fish. One hook. It is not necessary or likely or even desirable to have a voter agree with your ten reasons for a correct vote. Once you have made the sale it is a waste of time to go on about other issues.

## THE COALITION HOLDS

From time to time, political pundits of the right and left point out some rip-roaring conflict within the Republican base and proceed to predict for the seventeenth time that the Reagan coalition will break into two or three pieces.

These predictions began back in 1980 when the *New York Times* noticed that people who go to church and people with jobs were both supporting Reagan. Surely they would soon be at each other's throats. They missed the fact that some folks both go to church and have jobs but more important, even if there were no overlap, each part of the coalition was there for its own reason independent of any other part of the coalition.

Yes, there are disagreements among members of the Leave Us Alone Coalition on many issues. Listen to talk radio. But the key question is always: Is this a conflict among coalition members on a primary vote-moving issue? Or it is a conflict on secondary, tertiary, or quaternary issues? (Or whatever fifth is?)

Pat Buchanan made just this error in his campaign in 1996 for the Republican nomination for the presidency. He correctly pointed out that polling of Republicans showed that 70 percent thought there were too many immigrants and 70 percent were skeptics of free trade with China.[18] Therefore he would run on these issues for the Republican nomination and win 70 percent of the vote.[19] But when he ran he never got more than 34 percent of any state's vote and won only 21 percent of the Republican primary vote. He tested his hypothesis again in 2000, avoiding the Republican primaries and running on the

Reform Party ticket, and won only 0.42 percent of the popular vote in the general election.[20]

When the Buchanan campaign pollsters asked what Republicans thought of immigration and trade with China they forgot to ask the second—and only important—question: And do you vote on this issue? As a member of the board of directors of the National Rifle Association, I can assure you that many NRA members have what I consider the oddest views on free trade with China. But they vote on guns.

I once had a lively conversation with a Palestinian American for fifteen minutes on his thoughts on who should run Hebron. At the end of the conversation he explained that he was a dues-paying member of the NRA and always voted guns. People often talk about subjects they don't vote on. Talk-show hosts get rich focusing on what Americans like to talk about and listen to. Political parties, candidates, and political movements live or die by focusing like a laser on those issues that move votes, not those that wag tongues.

Conversations, loud and boisterous, over secondary issues do not threaten the coalition. It is simply a reminder that if you intend to be the majority party in a nation of three hundred million souls there is not going to be unanimity. Political leaders manage such conflict, they do not eliminate it. If you want a political party where every member agrees on all major political issues of the day, then you have one of those Trotskyite parties in Britain with seven members. Fine size for a discussion group. Not a contender for power.

## A CENTER-RIGHT SUPERMAJORITY

And 51 percent is not enough. A governing majority movement must earn and deserve 60 percent of the vote in order to ensure winning 51 percent of votes counted. Why the large margin for error? Because there will always be candidates who forget to mention DUIs until the last weekend of an election; voter fraud; and handsome, competent

candidates on the other side who "steal" the votes of those who agree
with you on the issues but are voting for incumbency, personal friend-
ship, or a regional favorite.

You also need to earn 60 percent of the vote because a simple majority in the House and Senate is not enough to govern. You must
have sixty votes in the Senate to override a filibuster and enough votes
to maintain majorities in the House for specific legislation, not simply
leadership elections.

I describe Reagan Republicanism as both center-right and the
Leave Us Alone Coalition. Why? The phrase "center-right" is not a
sign that I am getting squishy in my old age. Rather it correctly cap-
tures two ideas. One, that the Reagan center-right movement is a
majoritarian movement. It is no longer a fringe movement of the
right, a once-minority faction of the then-minority Republican Party.
It encompasses a majority. I would argue that the center-right policies and candidates are supported by about 60 percent of voters when
we present our policies clearly with a competent candidate and campaign: Reagan in 1984, Bush and Perot against Clinton in 1992. And
center-right conveys that our policies cover both the right in American politics and much of the middle. In 1974–1978, when I was an
undergraduate at Harvard, I believed that the Soviet Union was both
evil and an empire. I believed socialism was a failed economic system
that led to poverty and lack of political freedom. I believed that inflation was caused by the federal government printing too much money.
I believed that murderers deserved to be executed. I argued that high
taxes slowed the economy and that welfare hurt the very people it was
supposed to help. In the 1970s, that made me a right-winger. Today I
could walk through Harvard Yard shouting these observations and be
met with yawns from students saying, "Tell us something we don't
know."

Over the years, Reagan Republicanism did not moderate. We did
not "move to the middle." The country saw the failure of the united
Democrat government under Lyndon Johnson and Jimmy Carter and
the contrasting success of Reagan's policies. Tax cuts led to economic

growth. The government stopped inflating the currency. The Soviet Union was defeated; socialism, the idea and practice, collapsed. Welfare reform first advocated by Reagan in 1971 was passed in the 1990s over Clinton's double veto and it worked. The failure of the left and the success of the center-right moved the nation toward us. Those once standing on the right were now standing dead center.

## TESTING THE THEORY AGAINST REALITY

Visualizing the framework of the Leave Us Alone Coalition allows one to understand what the Republican Party will do in its own self-interest, and what it cannot do and maintain its strength. The true test of a theory is whether it can explain the past and predict the future. Seeing the conservative movement and the Reagan Republican Party as animated by a broad coalition of groups and individuals that each wishes on its primary vote-moving issue to be left alone does that. A competent Republican leader will work to increase in number each of the moving parts of the Leave Us Alone Coalition. He or she will work to increase the number of self-employed, the number of gun owners, the number of homeschoolers, and the sensitivity of taxpayers to the tax burden by making it more transparent. He or she will never raise taxes; push gun control; attack private property, private schools, or homeschooling; raise taxes or regulations on small business or the self-employed; or insult people of faith.

The Leave Us Alone construct also informs political candidates. Candidates need to find and focus on the primary, vote-moving issue that attracts a voter. Each voter does not need four reasons to vote for you. One strong one will do. One fish, one hook.

Ronald Reagan in 1980 and George W. Bush in 2000 both stood in the center of the Leave Us Alone Coalition and spoke directly to each of its moving parts, assuring them that they would be left alone in the zone most important to them. George H. W. Bush made those commitments in 1988 and defeated serious primary and general election opponents. When Bush 41 broke his commitment to many of the members of the Leave Us Alone Coalition by supporting gun control, raising taxes in order to expand domestic spending, and enacting massive new regulatory regimes on business with the Clean Air Act and the Americans with Disabilities Act, he threw away the presidency he had inherited. Like a high school student bequeathed an expensive car, he had no idea how to maintain it. Bush's humiliating defeat in 1992 followed a presidency that successfully managed the collapse of the Soviet Union without a great deal of blood on the floor. Bush organized the entire world to push Saddam Hussein's Iraq out of Kuwait and did not get stuck occupying the place. Bush had achieved approval ratings as high as 90 percent. But there was a hole in the bottom of the boat—his tax hike and regulatory spree—and he lost to the "failed governor of a small state," Bill Clinton. But this presidential defeat was caused by Bush's mistreatment of the center-right, not the weakening of the coalition itself.

The coalition was still there. Add the Bush and Perot vote in 1992 and you have 57 percent of the vote. Clinton, representing the left, won only 43 percent of the vote in 1992. Many of Clinton's subsequent errors flowed from his believing the rhetoric of his supporters that his minority vote represented a "mandate" for the left's agenda. He ran promising change. America *did* want to change the government that under George H. W. Bush was raising taxes to spend more money and exploding the regulatory state. But Clinton did not want to change the government. He wanted to use the state to change America.

*Time* and *Newsweek* betrayed him by proclaiming that there was a national mandate for using the power of the state to change America into a social democracy through nationalizing 15 percent of the economy—doctors, hospitals, and health insurance.

Anyone who missed the creation and growth of the Leave Us Alone Coalition in the elections of 1980 through 1988 certainly got the message loud and clear in 1994. The Clinton administration threatened every single part of the Leave Us Alone Coalition in 1993 and 1994.

They passed the Brady bill and the assault-weapons ban threatening gun owners with future gun control. They raised taxes. On gasoline. On incomes. On Social Security benefits. Targeting small-businessmen and -women. Legislation was introduced that could lead to federal government control of homeschooling. They mistreated the military, politicizing appointments, playing social engineer with gays in the military, and moving toward allowing women in combat. They tried to nationalize all health care.

Every part of the coalition knew it could wake up any morning and read that the Democrat Congress and the Democrat president had agreed to pass legislation that attacked their central vote-moving concern. Republican House leaders Newt Gingrich and Dick Armey (R-TX) drafted a ten-point "Contract with America" that read like the list of grievances in the Declaration of Independence, reaching out to every threatened group in the country. And Americans responded with vigor.

On Election Day, November 8, 1994, nine million more Republicans went to the polls than did so in the previous off-year election of 1990. Republicans captured the House and Senate, gaining fifty-eight House Seats and nine Senate seats. They gained 10 governors and 505 state legislators.

In 1996, Republicans nominated a pre-Reagan presidential candidate, Bob Dole, who liked to tell the story of how he chose to run for local office as a Republican. He explained that when he learned there were more Republican than Democrat voters in his county he chose to be a Republican. Dole had distinguished himself as an opponent of supply-side tax reduction. He did not have an ideological bone in his body. He did not understand the nature of the modern Reagan Republican Party. In addition to the weakness at the top of the ticket, the Leave Us Alone Coalition victory in the 1994 congressional races meant that a Clinton presidency did not threaten many of its key issues. Congress would stop tax hikes, gun control, and new entitlement spending; regulations of private schools or homeschooling; overspending; and Clinton himself claimed to be chastened, saying in his 1996 State of the Union Address that he believed "the era of big government is over." A less threatened Leave Us Alone Coalition did not turn out with the urgency or numbers that it did in 1994. Still, it was enough to keep the House and Senate.

In 1998, Republicans ran a nationalized campaign, not on a Contract with America to protect the Leave Us Alone Coalition, but one to punish Clinton the adulterer. Republicans expected to gain seats in the House and instead lost five seats. Those who believe the Leave Us Alone Coalition is really a thinly veiled collection of Savonarolas might ponder that 1998 election that could not translate the widespread and real personal moral revulsion of how the president of the United States treated women into actual votes for actual congressmen.

In 2000, George W. Bush stood in the dead center of the Leave Us Alone Coalition and defeated a popular war hero, John McCain, who stood slightly off center due to his support for restrictions on political speech—campaign finance reform. And in November, in a time of peace and strong economic growth and up against a sitting vice president who had been training and preparing for this campaign all his life, was able to win an electoral vote majority despite the hiccup of the late-breaking DUI.

In 2002 and 2004, Bush ran as the champion of the Leave Us Alone Coalition, adding a defense against international terrorism to his quiver.

By 2006, the occupation of Iraq went from being seen as part of the war on terror designed to protect all Americans to an unending social-engineering experiment. The campaign was nationalized as a referendum on what was seen as Bush's vision of an occupation of Iraq without end. The Republicans were not campaigning for new or larger tax hikes. (They did call for extending the 2001 and 2003 tax cuts already in place, but this is the equivalent of turning in last week's homework a second time.) A number of personal scandals cost Republicans maybe six or eight seats in the House and two in the Senate.

In 2006, Republicans talked about their past accomplishments of

cutting taxes six times in six years. They wanted a thank-you vote.
But Americans do not cast their votes to say thank you. Every election
is about the future and there was no articulated argument "Vote Republican and we will do the following." No contract with America.
With one exception: Vote Republican and we will be occupying some
country called Iraq indefinitely.

Nor could the Leave Us Alone Coalition be rallied against the
threat of a Democrat Congress. Most Democrats ran promising not to
raise taxes. Forty ran with the endorsement of the NRA, swearing fe-
alty to the Second Amendment.[21] A number of tragic school-shooting
incidents in the summer and fall of 2006 could not coax Democrats
into calling for gun control. Some Republicans talked about how left-
wing Nancy Pelosi or Charlie Rangel was. But few Americans knew
who they were. (The Democrats couldn't campaign against Newt
Gingrich in 1994. He wasn't famous yet.) Highlighting Pelosi is a
strategy that may pay dividends in 2008 or 2010.

Had Democrats won House and Senate seats promising to spend
more, raise taxes, steal your guns, and impose secular values on your
children, then the Leave Us Alone Coalition would have been shown
to have turned out a minority vote. That is not what happened in
2006.

The Leave Us Alone Coalition structure of the modern center-right
has held together. It explains both election successes and failures over
the past twenty-five years. And understanding the coalition will allow
us to see what might happen in the next twenty-five years.

Many on the left violently object to the idea that the center-right is
a coalition of groups and individuals who vote together for the same
candidates because on the issue that moves their vote what they want
is to be left alone. Conservatives, they argue, or at least the religious
conservatives, want to legislate morality. They want to tell other folks
how to run their lives. They ask, "How in the world can a movement
that includes a strong right-to-life component be said to be a Leave Us
Alone Coalition? Pro-lifers who oppose legalized abortion are not
leaving us alone."

## WHAT ABOUT THE ABORTION ISSUE?

This is an adult question and its answer deepens one's understanding of the modern Republican Party beyond name-calling. There are in the Republican Party and the conservative movement both those who are pro-life and pro-choice on the issue of abortion. The key question driving the pro- and anti-legalized-abortion position for conservatives is "how many people are involved here?" If in the case of a pregnant woman, there is a mother and a baby, then there are two lives at stake and both deserve to be left alone. Both deserve to have their right to life protected. If, however, one believes that there is only one person involved, the woman, then the state has no legitimate interest in telling her what to do.

I do not know any conservatives who believe there are two persons involved in a pregnancy and it is okay to kill one of them. Nor do I know any conservative who believes that the woman is the only person involved and the state should force her to bear a child.

This allows both pro-lifers and pro-choicers to see themselves as wanting only to be Left Alone, and given their underlying beliefs, they are both right. The left and the Democrats make this a more divisive issue by not simply arguing for the legalization of abortion, but going further to demand that taxpayers be required to fund the abortions of others and that all health insurance include paying for abortions so that those morally opposed to abortion must fund the abortions of others. Those claiming to be "pro-choice" on abortion do not offer choice to those whose religious beliefs oppose financing abortions. The left further demands that parents should not have the right to even be informed if their daughter has an abortion. This is understandably seen as an attack on the family and parental rights.

The key political question here is whether this issue is the one that drives your vote. There are many Republicans who are personally pro-choice. They may wish the Republican Party were pro-choice. Some testify at GOP national conventions and have formed a national group called Republicans for Choice, led by Ann Stone. But by definition, if they have been voting Republican since *Roe v. Wade* in 1973, their vote and therefore their party identification are driven by an issue other than abortion. They may vote on taxes or guns, or national defense or crime.

## AND GAY RIGHTS?

Okay, what about gay rights? How can "gay bashing" conservatives be seen as "Leave Us Alone"?

Again, a serious question that deserves and requires a grown-up response. Republicans running for Congress win about one-quarter of the gay vote. Not only do many gays vote Republican, but there are gay Republicans who organize politically as gays. The Log Cabin Republicans are a national Republican group with over fifty state and local chapters with 20,000 members who are Republicans who are also gay. [22]

The Pink Pistols are a nationwide organization of gays who understand that gay bashing is less of a problem when gays own and know how to use guns. There are forty-eight Pink Pistol chapters.[23] One of the most memorable groups among the eighty-something organizations that combined in 1994 to defeat then-Speaker of the House Thomas Foley, who despite "representing" a rural Washington State district had supported gun control legislation, was "Queers with Guns." Concise. To the point. Descriptive.

It was the Republican Party that passed pension-reform legislation in 2006 that will allow gay couples to pass on defined-contribution pensions such as 401(k)s not just to spouses but to anyone they choose. It is the Republican Congress that has repeatedly voted to abolish the inheritance tax—a change that would particularly help gay couples. Rhetoric aside, the Democrats treat gays as they treat blacks, asking them to subsist on rhetoric while the Democrat Party continues to tax them and their lives on behalf of the paying clients—the labor unions, trial lawyers, and government employees.

So how do the Republicans win a quarter of the gay vote? Gay

Americans who simply want to be left alone recognize that the modern center-right movement has no agenda to outlaw homosexuality or use the power of the state to tax or attack gays as gays. Gay Americans who are also homeowners, businessmen, shareholders, gun owners or men and women of faith will find the modern left ready, willing and able to tax, regulate and attack them—not as gays—but as income earners, property owners, gun owners, etc.

And some gay political organizations go beyond wanting to be left alone to demanding that the government fund their organizations and arguing that the state should police speech they don't like.

But don't some religious conservatives argue that homosexuality is against the Bible? Yes. Everyone is free to believe and argue for what they believe—on their own time and their own dime. Even people you disagree with.

Being a charter member of the Leave Us Alone Coalition does not mean everyone else in the coalition agrees with you or even respects your choices or values. (Even though, in your case, of course, they should.) If you want everyone to like you, approve of you, or believe as you do—advocate for free love, believing Baptist or Cubs fan—you are free to go be a missionary for your views, spending your own money. The line is drawn at using the state and its power to force others to subsidize your views or to demand that they agree with you. In the bad old days the state would force you to attend the king's favorite church and believe as he did. That was wrong. It is also wrong when some groups want the government to use laws or the schools to tell others what to think or say. As we learned in grade school, there is no law requiring that others like us. Nor should there be.

The Leave Us Alone Coalition represents a majority of Americans. It holds together because while members vote on different issues, and hold often wildly conflicting views on secondary issues, they are not in conflict on their primary, vote-moving issues. They vote for candidates and parties that work to limit the size, scope, and cost of government to where the state protects the lives and property of its citizens and calls it a day.

CHAPTER TWO

# THE TAKINGS
# COALITION

It's time to meet the Takings Coalition.

These groups and individuals view the proper role of government as taking things from one group and giving them to someone else. Taking what? Money, property, power, and control. They start with money. Often for themselves. Who are they in favor of taking it from? You and me, the taxpayers.

Many of these folks will tell you they wish to be left alone in many areas of their lives. Yet they stand with the Takings Coalition because on their primary issue, their vote-moving issue, they want the state to take something from one group and give it to others.

Let's go around the table as the Takings Coalition gathers.

Seats are reserved for trial lawyers, labor-union leaders, government employees' unions, recipients of government grants, and the two wings of the dependency movement: those who are locked into welfare dependency and those who earn $90,000 a year managing this dependency and making sure none of the recipients get jobs and become Republicans.

Joining them are the social welfare industrial complex of hospitals and health-care professionals beholden to government funding; actual government welfare agencies; and the "Non-Government Organizations" (NGOs), which are nominally nongovernmental and certainly nominally nonprofit, government contractors providing an ever-expanding menu of "social services" with taxpayer funds.

Never absent from this table are the big-city political machines. Elbow to elbow are those who live off government grants in universities and others in the taxpayer-subsidized "nonprofit" world. And in the business community, those businessmen and -women who believe they benefit from government contracts, subsidies, or tariff barriers are comfortable as members of this group.

The Takings Coalition also includes those businesses such as contractors and builders who live or die at the whim of politicians and city bureaucrats who can dispense (sell) or withhold permits to build or operate, without which the businessman is ruined. Some businessmen will tell you they would prefer to be free and left alone. But the regulatory octopus of American cities—the one that requires permits for almost everything—and the uncomfortable truth that the only folks who give contracts to build roads or mass transit systems are tax-supported governments—make them captive members of the Takings Coalition. Still, many of these captives quickly exhibit the Stockholm syndrome, identifying with their captors, and become active, if initially unwilling, members of the Takings Coalition.

The Takings Coalition is always looking for ways to replicate at the state and national levels the petty tyranny it already wields over the business community in cities. They require environmental impact statements and FCC licenses so that businesses and broadcasters will have to come hat in hand to ask "permission" to do business. And they created antitrust laws that make it illegal to charge less (predatory pricing), illegal to charge more (price gouging), and certainly illegal to charge the same (collusion).

The last set of chairs is for the "coercive utopians." These folks want to change the world. They want to change you. And they are willing to wield the blunt instrument of the state to make you, your family, and your life fit their procrustean bed—no matter how much it hurts you or how much it costs you. And they expect to be paid with tax dollars for supervising your moral regeneration.

These are the radical environmentalists, gun control advocates, extreme feminists, safety and health "Nazis," animal-rights extremists, antireligious secularists, and some gay groups that wish to impose their sense of morality on others through the power of the state.

Let's look at the size and strength of these players.

## GOVERNMENT WORKERS

First, it must be said that not all government workers are members of this coalition. We have discussed how those in the armed forces and the police are more open to the Republican Party. They know that in a free society they are part of keeping everyone free. However, this is not true for many employees of federal, state, and local governments. On average, polling data by Scott Rasmussen point out that if you have a government job you are 10 percent more likely to vote Democrat. This does not mean that your child will be ruined by his summer job as a lifeguard at the city pool. But hold that government job until you are fifty to sixty-four years old and it makes you 19.7 percent more likely to be a Democrat. And if you are paid more than $75,000, the tendency to identify as a Democrat jumps to a gap of 33 percent.[1]

Why? In 2004, the average wage-and-benefit package for a private-sector worker was $51,876. The average federal worker earned $100,178 in wages and benefits. (For wages alone, private-sector workers earned $42,635 and federal employees took home $66,589.) Total wages and benefits see federal workers taking in almost twice as much each year.[2]

Let us be clear here. Americans are taxed to pay for federal workers who receive pay and benefits twice as generous as they themselves earn. Every day the federal government plays reverse Robin Hood taking from the relatively poor to enrich a privileged class: modern Mamelukes.

## MODERN MAMELUKES

State and local workers also enjoy higher pay, benefits, and pensions; earlier retirement; more vacation days; and more job security than the taxpayers who foot the bill.

According to the Commerce Department numbers, state employees in 2005 were paid an average of $45,062. The taxpayers who pay for this were paid an average of $43,917. Add in benefits and pensions and the state employees are taking home $58,814 per year, 10 percent more than the taxpayers of the private sector, who take home $53,289.[3]

The benefits of government employment do not only come in higher pay and benefits and a pension often indexed to protect against inflation. Job security is much greater when you work for the government. From your own experience, how many people in the private sector do you know who have been fired? How many times has your job ended? On the other hand, how many government employees do you know who have been forced out of a government job? In fiscal year 2005, the entire federal government fired only 10,655 employees, or less than one-tenth of 1 percent.[4] In the real world, jobs come and go. Workers who don't show up are fired. Incompetence is a reason to fire someone.

I was taught at Harvard Business School that the greatest profit derived from being a monopoly is peace of mind. No fear that anyone is gaining on you. Your job and pension are safe. There is no greater and more permanent monopoly than the government and no greater beneficiaries of peace of mind over job security than government workers.

The late Senator Patrick Moynihan once described India as a Third World nation of eight hundred million within which lives a First World population the size of France's. Sixty million Indians living at First World levels while the vast majority lived at Third World levels. In 2007, the United States was a nation with a workforce of 152.2 million with a relatively free market in labor for most Americans and its own "France" sitting inside.[5] In this case, France is the twenty million Americans with government jobs, many of whom, at the expense of the taxpayers, enjoy "French" vacation days, French length of work-days, French benefits and pensions, France's permanent job security, and too often France's attitude toward the rest of America.

From 1993 to 2006, twenty million net new private-sector jobs were created in America. This one number of net new jobs masks the tremendous dynamism and change in the private sector. During that same period, not 20 million, but 412 million jobs were created and 392 million jobs ended though competition and change. When a job ceases to be productive in the private sector it goes away.

Change is much slower in government work. For years Congress hired staff to man the automatic elevators in the U.S. Capitol. To this day there are government workers in Sacramento still operating the automatic elevators in the California state capitol.

## Labor Unions

Today there are 15.4 million members of labor unions.[6] They pay an average of $500 in union dues each year, giving organized labor a slush fund of $8 billion.[7] This was summed up by prominent labor activist Richard Bensinger of the AFL-CIO, silencing those on the left who whined about the power of Ralph Reed's Christian Coalition: "They have $25 million. We have $11 billion."

Unions bring a great deal to the Democrat table. First, money. Soft and hard. Assume that labor-union bosses can only squeeze out 10 percent of their budgets for political purposes: hiring staff for campaigns, sending mail to members retired and working. Then they are spending some $800 million a year to support Democrat candidates, or $1.6 billion in a two-year election cycle. By contrast the Republican National Committee spent $450 million in the two-year presidential cycle of 2003–2004.[8]

Unions also are allowed under campaign finance law to communicate with their own members—that means retirees as well as present workers—without reporting the expenditure. Unions can and do endorse candidates.

Union political-action committees (PACs) also shower "hard money" subject to FEC limits to the Democrats. To give some sense of the relative power of unions note that of the top ten political-action committees in 2006, six are run by unions directly, three are left-wing, and one is "business," the Realtors' PAC.

## TOP TEN PACS IN 2006 CYCLE
## (THROUGH JUNE 26, 2006)[9]

| SERVICE EMPLOYEES INTERNATIONAL UNION | $ 26.6 MILLION |
|---|---|
| EMILY's List | $ 26.2 million |
| Moveon.org | $ 14.4 million |
| American Federation of Teachers | $ 12.3 million |
| National Assn of Realtors | $ 11.6 million |
| America Coming Together | $ 10.7 million |
| AFSCME | $ 10.4 million |
| Intl Brotherhood of Electrical Workers | $ 9.6 million |
| United Auto Workers | $ 9.3 million |
| Teamsters Union | $ 9.1 million |

Years ago labor unions meant steelworkers and guys in auto plants. In 2006, 47.4 percent of all union members worked for the government. Only 7.4 percent of private-sector workers were unionized, but 36.2 percent of government employees were.[10] The largest union was the National Education Association with 2.7 million members, all government workers.

The overlap of government workers and unions deepens the commitment to the Takings Coalition. AFSCME, the l.4-million-member state and local government workers' union, raised $13,880,683 for its political-action committee in the 2003–2004 election cycle.[11] Every single dollar went to Democrats.

## Big, Blue Cities

Americans are familiar with the concept of big-city political machines. This means less and less the charming if rough-edged "Plun-

*Courtesy of City Journal*[12]

kett of Tammany Hall" and more a pay-to-play archipelago of blue cities where politics is dominated by unionized state and local government workers, social workers (in government employ), those paid with tax money, and those paid with less public scrutiny through not-for-profits foundations

If you take a look at several blue states—Washington, Oregon, New York, Pennsylvania, Michigan, and Illinois—you'll see that they are really red states dominated by blue cities.

The blue islands are getting deeper blue. In 1960, San Francisco County voted 41.8 percent for Richard Nixon. In 2004, Kerry carried San Francisco County with 83.02 percent of the vote. New York County was 62.4 percent Democrat in 1980, 78.2 percent Democrat in 1992, and 79.8 percent Democrat in 2000. Boston went 53.3 percent Democrat in 1980, and 71.7 percent in 2000.[13]

## THE NONPROFIT SECTOR

In 2005, 9,844,115 Americans were working in the nonprofit sector. Those that are privately funded may have little interest in politics and are not likely to be part of the Takings Coalition. Private contributions in 2006, for instance, went 35.8 percent to religious institutions. Conservatively, 10 percent of private money went to groups that could be viewed as having a political interest, say a Heritage Foundation or the Sierra Club. But those "nonprofits" that receive all or the bulk of their funding from the government are almost identical to government workers in their class interests as members of the Takings Coalition.

In Colorado, Jon Caldera, the president of the Independence Institute, ran a campaign to stop Referendum C, an effort by Republican Governor Bill Owens to poke a hole in the state's spending-limitation amendment. Referendum C would increase taxes and spending by at least $3.7 billion over the following five years.[14] The campaign for Referendum C was endorsed by about eight hundred nominally nonprofit groups that are theoretically not political, and only interested in providing services to the good citizens of Colorado. But because many received much or all of their funding from government sources, they weighed in as dues-paying members of the Takings Coalition, ready to fight for higher taxes and spending that would pay their salaries.

The nonprofit sector grew up alongside the government employment sector in the 1960s. Steven Malanga writes in his book *The New New Left* that the explosion of federal spending in the Great Society programs in effect "nationalized" what were once private charitable institutions.[15] Federal spending on social services jumped from $800 million in 1965 to $13 billion in 1980.[16] The Bureau of Labor statistics reported that private social-service employment rose from 500,000 in 1972 to 1.1 million in 1980 and 3.3 million by 2005.[17] These new government-funded, nominally "private" social-service networks are heavily concentrated in cities. In New York City alone social service jobs increased from 52,000 in 1975 to 183,000 in 2000. In Philadelphia and Chicago such social service jobs more than doubled from 1988 to 2000.[18]

Nationally, the nonprofit social-welfare workforce grew from below 1 percent of the total workforce in 1970 to 3 percent of all workers by 2005.[19]

## UNIVERSITIES

University towns are increasingly blue towns. Perhaps because they are increasingly dependent on government funding and even ownership.

In 1955, 44 percent of students attending universities went to private rather than government-run state universities. By 1999, that number had declined to 23.5 percent.[20] And even many private colleges receive much of their funding from government grants and student loans.

Professors know where their bread is buttered.

Professors at elite universities receiving generous grants from the taxpayers are generous themselves with big-spending politicians. Looking at the 2004 election, Harvard University employees gave twenty-five times as much money to Kerry as to Bush. Princeton's ratio was 302 to 1; Yale's, 20 to 1; Georgetown's 15 to 1; MIT's, 43 to 1. Of the top twenty-five elite schools, as ranked by *U.S. News and World Report*, the least-blue-giving patterns were at Washington University and Vanderbilt, which only preferred Kerry over Bush by a ratio of 2 to 1.[21]

Federal and state tax dollars have flowed to colleges and universities, and the cost of education has risen faster than inflation while the productivity of university employees has actually fallen 12.5 percent from 1976 to 2000. Even professors can do the math and figure out that these two trends cannot continue without an ever-expanding flow of your tax dollars.

Not surprisingly, the North American Academic Study Survey of 1999 found 72 percent of professors described themselves as left/liberal and 15 percent right/conservative. In the same year, a Harris poll found that the general public, who pays the taxes for all this, split 18 percent left/liberal and 37 percent right/conservative.

## Trial Lawyers

If labor unions, and increasingly public-sector labor unions, provide infrastructure and personnel for the modern left, trial lawyers—the guys who get rich suing companies because their own stock went down or the coffee is too hot or, surprise, cigarettes aren't good for you—are the financial deep pockets of the Democrat Party.

In state after state, trial lawyers rather than union bosses raise the most political money for Democrats as well as campaigns for cooperative and appreciative judges, and receive billions of dollars in fees in return.

The American Association of Justice, formerly known as the Association of Trial Lawyers of America, has the largest membership of an estimated 56,000 trial lawyers worldwide.[22] Their votes wouldn't elect a city councilman. But they own the Democrat Party in most states. The French aristocracy was a larger percentage of the entire population and wielded less power pre-1789.

Victor Schwartz, once a plaintiffs' lawyer himself and now one of their most trenchant and effective critics, explains that there are two kinds of plaintiffs' trial lawyers. The first group he calls the "yellow pages" lawyers because you find them in the phone book when you have really been harmed in a car accident. They are not rich. These "yellow pages" lawyers are a necessary part of a free economy and this legal friction costs the economy about 1 percent of GDP each year. This is in line with what other nations pay for civil justice.

But America pays two or three times as much as other countries for lawsuits, roughly $290 billion in 2005. That is $3,870.20 per family of four, each and every year. The President's Council of Economic Advisers conservatively estimates that $87 billion of this is wasteful and excessive.[23] An estimate by the Pacific Research Institute adds that lawsuit abuse reduces the value to shareholders of American companies by $685 billion.[24]

When a trial lawyer sues a city because a drunk fell in front of a subway car and the city pays, the taxpayers of the city pay for this. In 2004, New York City was sued thousands of times and paid out $575.6 million in settlements. How hard do you think New York City or any city fights these lawsuits? They pay with "Monopoly money"—aka yours.

The law firms in Mississippi, Florida, and Texas that began the first lawsuits that led to the "Tobacco Master Settlement" will be paid more than $8 billion. The Florida lawyers alone will rake in $3.4 billion, averaging $233 million per lawyer.[25]

The relationship between rich trial lawyers and the Democrat Party is symbiotic. Billionaire trial lawyers have been created and protected by those politicians. They have been given "letters of marque" and operate as privateers despoiling the real economy, killing the jobs, and looting the retirement nest eggs of millions of Americans. They are protected by the Democrat Party's leaders who give them laws that make it easy to sue, and pliant judges, who shower them with other people's money.

How important is trial-lawyer money to the Takings Coalition machine? Consider that the Democrat Party has made itself the uncompromising enemy of the entire business community and most professionals such as doctors because of its opposition to tort reform. It must be a very big payoff.

## COERCIVE UTOPIANS

There has always been a strain of utopianism in American politics that is willing to use the power of the state to "perfect" man at the point of a gun. Voluntary associations for self-help and moral regeneration are wonderful things. This brought us Methodism, Alcoholics Anonymous, and Dale Carnegie's courses on how to win friends and influence people. But the modern left has a menagerie of busybodies looking to perfect the world through state action. Many of these groups are actually front groups for the trial lawyers: the consumer groups, the "health" groups. Just as with unions and government workers and big-city machines, there is a fair amount of overlap.

These are the buttinskies that have made our toilets too small to flush, our cars too small to fit families in and too lightweight to be safe. They would forbid us to wear leather or eat chickens, and they demand that we participate in their weekly religious ceremonies where we separate the brown glass from the green glass for the recycling priests. Remember Jimmy Carter's desire to sic the Boy Scouts on your family, going door to door playing Thermostat Gestapo? They tell you when and where you can smoke cigarettes. They ban pâté de foie gras. They make you wear a helmet while on your motorcycle. They want to tell us what kinds of fast food we and our children can eat. They would take away your right to hunt or to own a gun to protect your family. They use the public schools to promote their secular-left views while insulting the values of faith communities. They raise your taxes to subsidize *Piss Christ* while explaining that your church cannot be used for child care until you cover up all those icky crucifixes. Their secular faith should be taught to your children. Your faith must not be mentioned.

Critics of the "religious right" often insist that social conservatives wish to impose their morality on others. The coercive utopians really do wish to use the power of the state to impose on others how they think we should live. If you are a vegetarian animal lover who simply wishes to be left alone to raise your own food and keep the government from telling you what to do, you can fit comfortably in the conservative movement. If you wish to drive around in tiny cars to save fuel or power your home with solar energy panels or abstain from perfume or only wear makeup that has not been tested on animals, then your personal decisions may be viewed as odd by some but they are not in conflict with a conservative, Leave Us Alone society. There has been an entire book written about "Crunchy Conservatives," suggesting that some folks who think of themselves as Reaganites eat only free-range chicken or no chicken at all.

The Rubicon is crossed from the Leave Us Alone Coalition to the Takings Coalition not by lifestyle choices, but by whether you are willing to use political force to require everyone else to live as you demand. Some folks like to drive small cars and feel virtuous about not using too much gasoline. Fine, up to them. But when the federal government is lobbied by these "virtuecrats" to pass a law called the Corporate Average Fuel Economy (CAFE) law, which requires each car company to build and sell cars that average a certain number of miles per gallon, this forces cars to be made with less steel and more plastic, making them smaller and more vulnerable in car accidents.

The National Academy of Sciences reported that CAFE has probably cost between 1,300 and 2,600 lives in 1993 by forcing automakers to build smaller cars. The Competitive Enterprise Institute estimates that of the 21,000 auto deaths in 1997, an estimated 2,600 to 4,500 fatalities were caused by the CAFE standards forcing folks into smaller, lighter cars.[26] This is not leaving people alone. It is taking things from others—namely, their lives.

One can belittle these moral poseurs and their grand schemes to run everyone else's lives, but when you marry the power and clumsiness of the state with their innumerable enthusiasms, there can be a great deal of blood left on the floor. The several-hundred-year struggle to separate the state from religious enthusiasms, solved only one possible corruption of state power. There are new ones.

Rachel Carson's book *Silent Spring* was the early "bible" of the coercive environmental movement. It led to the banning of DDT sprayed to kill mosquitoes on the theory that even used responsibly it might affect some bird eggs and would harm humans. This turned out to be false. But the ban, which was extended to the Third World, led to a resurgence of mosquito-borne diseases such as malaria.

Today malaria is found throughout the tropical and subtropical regions of the world. Health authorities believe it causes more than three hundred million acute illnesses and at least one million deaths every year.[27]

## THE TAKINGS COALITION: INTERNAL CONFLICTS

The Takings Coalition can hold together as long as there is more money flowing into the state to finance the demands of each constituent group. Higher taxes can give more money to the government workers; keep the big-city political machines financed; send more government grant money to universities and the "nonprofit" sector; and fund the coercive utopians. The Takings Coalition thrives when the government is growing in resources and power. The coalition holds together when the scene looks like the part of the movie after the bank robbery where the robbers meet around a table and the boss divvies up the loot. But when the Leave Us Alone Coalition succeeds in cutting off the flow of tax dollars, when we put our foot on the air hose, when we say "no new taxes" and mean it, then those sitting around the Takings Coalition table see that there is not enough money for everyone in the gang.

At that point the assembled members of the Takings Coalition begin to look like the scene in the lifeboat movie where everyone must decide whom to eat or throw overboard. This is when we clearly see that the left is not made up of friends and allies. They are competing parasites. If we refuse to send them even more of our tax dollars, they will gnaw on each other.

This realization gives the center-right its simple strategy. Stop raising taxes to finance the Takings Coalition. Every tax hike leads to more Democrat precinct workers. Our task is to cut off the flow of taxpayer dollars that fund the left and force them to gnaw on each other so that, come the next election, there are fewer of them and they are shorter.

Unlike the Leave Us Alone Coalition, the Takings Coalition's members have serious conflicts on primary issues. Trial lawyers earn billions of dollars suing companies that then have to pay their unionized workers less or lay them off. The costs imposed by unnecessary environmental regulations demanded by the radical environmental groups have driven the unionized auto and steel industries to downsize dramatically.

The government workers and trial lawyers and environmental extremists have cannibalized the union worker part of the Takings Coalition. They have driven industry, businesses, and jobs (aka the tax base) away from blue cities and out of blue states. To be fair, the steel-and autoworkers' unions' leadership have created some of their own problems by insisting on work rules, high health-care costs, and pensions that have forced unionized industries to downsize. Here the union bosses have deliberately damaged their own workers. All parasites do some damage to their host. But the union bosses, radical environmentalists, and tax-and-spend local governments are close to killing the American auto industry and the coal and mineral mining industries.

We saw the same conflict in the asbestos industry. The industrial labor unions wanted to unionize their workers and extract above-market wages that would then kick back forced union dues to the union leadership. The public-sector unions wanted to raise property taxes on the asbestos businesses. But the trial lawyers came swooping in, suing these companies into bankruptcy, laying off 51,000 workers and ending the property-tax revenues.[28] The trial-lawyer parasites killed the host. There was nothing for the rest.

There is no part of the Takings Coalition that produces wealth. They all spend it. Unionized workers produce wealth, but unions and union bosses only spend it. Tax collectors take. Trial lawyers sue and take. And as soon as there is a limit to the size of the host, all parasites are in conflict over who gets what.

## OUTSIDE THE TWO COALITIONS

Two types of voters do not fit obviously into either the Takings Coalition or the Leave Us Alone Coalition. The first group comprises voters who cast their votes based on residual loyalties of the past—"legacy voters." The second group is those who vote in response to real or imagined exclusion by one of the coalitions, which, for reasons explained later on, are classified in this book as "Gypsies."

## FADING LEGACY VOTERS

Do you ever wonder about those polls that show a small percentage of liberals who voted for Reagan in 1980 or self-described conservatives who voted for George McGovern in 1972? What were they thinking? What moved their vote in what seems to us an irrational direction?

Legacy voters vote for the party they always voted for, or even the party their parents and grandparents always supported. By definition such voters are not responding to modern issues, but are still driven to vote by old attachments or resentments.

Some little old ladies in Georgia agreed with Ronald Reagan on the major issues of the day, but voted for George McGovern and Mike Dukakis because General Sherman was mean to Atlanta recently. And there are older folks in Maine who agree with Howard Dean on economics and foreign policy, but pull the lever for

Republicans because the guy at Little Round Top, General Joshua Lawrence Chamberlain, was fighting for the North and was therefore a Republican.

There are even today Irish-American small-businessmen who vote for tax hiking, regulating, union-boss-serving Democrats because the guy who insulted their great-grandfather when he arrived in Boston from Dublin was a Protestant Republican.

Legacy voters are fading for two reasons. Over time, a voter who latches on to one party over a key issue and stays with the party after the issue fades will die. And each subsequent generation sees a lessening of the intensity of the old attachment. The second reason is that a political party looking for new recruits finds legacy voters to be one of the best targets of opportunity. If they can be forced to focus on a modern issue, they can be detached from their ancient mooring and moved to the other team. This is largely what has happened with Southern whites who had voted Democrat in response to the War Between the States and the Reconstruction (occupation by Northern troops), which was humiliating and embittering. Northern troops left the Southern states in 1877 as a result of a deal to give the Republican Rutherford Hayes the presidency, despite contested electoral votes in Louisiana, South Carolina, and (guess what) Florida. The first modern elected Republican senator from a Confederate state was Texas's John Tower in 1966—one hundred and one years after Appomattox. Republicans did not win a majority of Southern Congressmen until 1994 and only won a majority of the Southern Senate seats in 1980.[29] One can still see the echoes of the Civil War in a swath of congressional seats otherwise inexplicably held by Democrats in southern Illinois, southern Ohio, and Indiana.

Northern big-city ethnic Catholics (once called BCECs) found in the 1960s and 1970s that the increasingly liberal Democrat Party's attachment to abortion and racial preferences was enough to begin to shake loose ethnic and religious ties that had kept them Democrats for a hundred years.

## Too Many Gypsies

On Christmas Day, 1991, the long-suffering people of Romania revolted against the Communist Party and their dictator Nicolae Andruta Ceausescu and his lovely wife, Elena. They held a brief trial and shot them both.

I traveled to Romania with the Krieble Foundation, working to help organize the non-Communist forces for the local elections in 1991. In the small city of Timisoara, in northern Romania just south of Hungary—or in what really should be Hungary to hear some tell it—I met with about fifty non-Communists who were contesting the local elections against the Communists. Standing in front of a blackboard in a schoolhouse I asked the activists to help me make two lists, those likely to vote with us and those likely to vote with the Communists.

On our team I was told we should expect support from the minority of voters who were Protestants. There were four Protestant churches, and one participant would organize someone to visit each one in the four weeks left before the election. The Catholics, also a minority, were also likely to support our candidates and someone would visit their three churches. We could also expect support for the association of former political prisoners who for understandable reasons were not partial to the Communists. Also we could expect support from the returned POWs or those Romanians who had fought against the Soviet Union during World War Two and then were invited to stay as slave laborers for quite some time before some of them were allowed to return to Romania. They, too, were unlikely supporters of the Communists. The self-employed and the young were likely to vote for our team.

On the other side we expected to find the Communist government officials and those in the army and the police. "All the army and police?" I asked. What about conscripts or those who were younger nonofficers and who hadn't necessarily bought into the Communist system? Well, yes, there were nonofficers who might vote with us. The group explained that those who attended the Orthodox churches were more likely to support the Communists since during the dictatorship their leadership had been penetrated. The group identified two other committed groups supporting the Communists: waiters and Gypsies. "Why waiters?" I asked, adding that in the United States waiters work for tips and might welcome a freer economy where they would be rewarded for hard work. It was patiently explained to me that the waiters were all employees of the secret police because they can listen in on conversations.

Understood. Until this situation changes, the waiters and other elements of the police state are likely to stay with their former (and maybe present) employers. They are the hard edge of the Takings Coalition. But why Gypsies? As I understood Gypsies, they live sort of on the fringes of the law and might prefer a soft American-style law with less sharp edges. No. The Communists would buy the Gypsies liquor, and they would vote for the Communists. They estimated that Gypsies were about 10 percent of the voting-age population.

Heck, George Washington would provide rum for his political supporters on Election Day. "Why don't we buy liquor for the Gypsies and get their votes in play?" I asked. The unequivocal response to the foolish American: "The Gypsies are scum. We won't talk to them."

Well then, you won't get their votes, will you?

One goal in politics is to reduce the number of "Gypsies"—voters who will not vote for you because you will not talk to them. These voters oddly get the impression that you don't like them, respect them, or have their best interests at heart. Political philosopher Lorenzo de Medici picked up on this point when he instructed his family: "Those who speak ill of us do not love us."

You would think this was Politics 101. Everyone knows this. Sure, in a dictatorship the white guys in the Nationalist party in the Republic of South Africa could afford to mistreat blacks, because blacks could not vote. But in a real democracy, one would think that no party would deliberately insult a voting bloc and throw away their votes.

Think again.

On October 29, 1884, one week before the general election, Samuel Dickinson Burchard spoke before the Religious Bureau of the Republican National Committee and proclaimed that "we are Republicans, and don't propose to leave our party and identify ourselves with the party whose antecedents have been Rum, Romanism, and Rebellion."[30] Here we have a speech—not in some one-horse town by Pat Robertson's great-grandfather, but a speech before the Republican Party leadership most sensitive to religious feelings—denouncing Roman Catholicism as the equivalent of Alcohol and Treason. The Civil War had ended only twenty years earlier. Feelings were raw. Such comments were not like chatting about the Confederate-flag symbol in 2004.

One can imagine that there were not too many priests or nuns attending the Religious Bureau of the Grand Old Party, the majority party of the country.

It was not until 1994, one hundred and ten years later, that the Republican Party won a majority of the Roman Catholic vote in congressional elections. The Catholic vote would go for Republican presidents in landslides like that for Richard Nixon in 1972, but the vote for the House of Representatives is a better measure of partisan affiliation or antipathy.[31]

The Republican Party wrestles now with its lack of a relationship with the African-American vote. One reason Republicans do poorly is that they too infrequently go and ask for those votes. They don't show up. But the chasm seems to flow from the sense that the Republicans opposed the civil rights movement and the Democrats supported it.

The present challenge for the Republican Party is to avoid treating Hispanic Americans as they did Roman Catholics—driving them away from the Republican Party for one hundred years. And the nonnegotiable goal is to avoid with Hispanics what the Republican Party has achieved with the African-American vote—a wall of separation that seems impenetrable.

The Leave Us Alone Coalition and the Takings Coalition are Cobras and Mongeese. They are not sometimes in mild disagreement;

they are trying to move in opposite directions on all political issues. They are not arguing over the pronunciation of tomato or potato. The issues of size of government, taxation, the power of the individual or the state are primary vote-moving issues for both coalitions—in opposite directions.

When one wins, the other loses. There are no happy "win-win" negotiations to be had. They will remain in the ring until one defeats the other. What follows is a number of demographic and political trends that each gives comfort to one team and heartache and concern to the other.

PART TWO

# THE TRENDS

As the Leave Us Alone Coalition faces off against the Takings Coalition every two years throughout the next American generation, which will emerge stronger? There is no fixed, inevitable answer.

I have identified trends that will affect the balance of power between Republicans and Democrats. Some are to the advantage of the Leave Us Alone Coalition. Others strengthen the Takings Coalition.

Some of these trends are irreversible. Americans born in 2006 will begin voting in 2024. Most Americans born before 1930 will not be voting, for obvious reasons, in 2020. Other trends, such as the growth in the number of Americans who own stock directly and the declining number of hunters in America, can be accelerated or perhaps slowed or even reversed by changes in law.

How will the two coalitions respond to the trends they cannot change and to those they can shape to gain or maintain power in the future? That answer will determine who runs the American government in 2020 and 2050.

## CHAPTER THREE

# THE GROWTH OF THE INVESTOR CLASS

## TAKING STOCK IN POLITICS

The largest demographic change in the past twenty-five years is not the number of Americans whose parents speak Spanish. It is the number of Americans who own stock—directly, in 401(k)s, in individual retirement accounts, or in mutual funds.

When Ronald Reagan was elected in 1980, less than 20 percent of American households owned stock directly. Today 50 percent of households own stock and two-thirds of all voters in the past two elections were shareholders.[1]

Why does this matter? Years ago, when only 10 percent of Americans owned stock directly, a populist politician could give a speech demanding that we tax the big corporations and give everyone in the room a dollar. The small number of stockholders in the room would understand that this was an attack on them, but they also fully recognized that they were few in number and would slouch down, hoping not to be noticed and further hoping not to be hit too hard. Ninety percent of the adults in the room would say, "Hey, this is great. I get a dollar. Let's play this game again." Taxes on business were largely

hidden taxes. Regulations were not seen as a cost imposed on individuals. Politicians could give speeches calling for all sorts of new
spending programs that would be free because "the big corporations
would pay for them." And with new spending and regulatory programs cost free—since someone else would pay—voters understandably agreed to more of them.

Congress voted to create individual retirement accounts in 1974,
allowing individuals without pension plans to save the lesser of 15
percent of income, or $1,500 per year in an IRA account for their re-
tirement.[2] The money invested in an IRA would grow in value and
that increase in stock prices or interest paid on a bond would not be
taxed until retirement. In 1981, part of President Reagan's tax cut expanded the IRA to a $2,000 annual contribution and made it univer-
sal.[3] Millions of Americans began IRAs; 40l(k)s were created by
Congress in 1978. The mutual fund industry dramatically expanded
in the 1970s and in November 2007 held $11.2 trillion of assets.[4] One
great advantage of a mutual fund was that an individual investor no
longer had to "gamble" a large chunk of his savings on a specific company. One could invest $1,000 in a mutual fund that mirrored the
entire market. You didn't have to start with a million dollars. You
didn't have to believe you could outsmart the market or need to spend
a great deal of time watching over your investment. In the past, only
the idle rich had the time and resources to manage stock portfolios of
individually selected stocks.

These new investment tools greatly increased the number of Americans willing and able to own stock and also increased the amount of
money they had in the market. This has accelerated as more and more
companies have moved away from the traditional "defined benefit"
pensions—where you work till sixty-five at the same job and the company or government employer promises at retirement to pay you, say,
half of your salary until you die. What is "defined" is the benefit you
get. Now most new companies use "defined contribution" pensions.
You and/or your employer put money into a portable pension fund
that is owned and controlled by you. If you change jobs it goes with
you. If you get hit by a bus it goes into your estate. With the old, tradi-

tional, defined-benefit pensions, if you changed jobs before "vesting" in the pension, you walked away with little or nothing. With the defined-benefit plans, if you died the day after you retired you would not have an estate to pass on to your heirs, as you didn't "own" the pension but only had a claim on a stream of income promised as long as you and maybe your widow lived.

## DEFINED-CONTRIBUTION PORTABLE PENSIONS

Today, roughly twenty million American workers have traditional defined-benefit pensions and fifty million have portable defined-contribution pensions.[5] Two-thirds of all private-sector retirement dollars are now held in defined-contribution plans. Advocates of the old traditional pensions liked to claim that the alternative defined-contribution plans were "risky," as they were dependent on the value of the broad stock market. But as we have seen painfully with the bankruptcies in the airline industry and the weakening of the steel and auto industries, greater risk lies in betting your entire pension on the health of one industry or the one company you work for. When your pension is controlled and owned by you and invested in a broad stock portfolio that mimics the entire economy, you are betting on the entire economy being strong. You are not relying on the competence or honesty of your labor union or your employer's company's management. You are not relying on your own judgment or attempting to second-guess the future. You are investing in the strength of the entire economy. The real, after-inflation, average rate of return to pension funds invested in the broad stock market for the last seventy years is *7 percent*. This despite wars, recessions, and periods of inflation.

For years, free-market conservatives tried to tell voters that taxes on businesses were ultimately paid by consumers in higher prices and workers in lower wages. They tried to connect the health of the general economy and of corporations to the promised pensions of workers and life insurance that were backed by the value of stocks. But the connection was viewed as too tenuous. Now that more Americans own stock directly they see costs imposed on business through higher taxation or regulations as more directly affecting them. This effect will grow as the size of each stock portfolio increases, and for most Americans, by age fifty, the annual change in the value of one's retirement assets will dwarf the value of any particular annual wage increase.

## SHARE OWNERSHIP CHANGES ONE'S POLITICS

This change in how workers view politics through the lens of share ownership has already begun. A 6,400-person poll done by Scott Rasmussen in 1997 found that owning at least $5,000 in stock made one 18.54 percent more likely to be Republican and less likely to be a Democrat. Almost every single demographic group became more Republican with share ownership. Senior citizens over sixty-five moved 22 percent more Republican. African Americans with no stock were 6 percent Republican. Those with $5,000 or more of stock were 20 percent Republican. This was not a substitute metric for high incomes. All income groups became more Republican with share ownership. In fact, the smallest change took place with those who earned $75,000 or more. Men earning $75,000 or more only became 0.21 percent more Republican and women earning more than $75,000 actually became 4.9 percent less Republican with share ownership. (If you are acquainted with a woman earning more than $75,000 who doesn't have stock, don't give her any as it doesn't do any good. Buy her a gun instead.)[6]

One might think homeownership would have a similar effect as stock ownership in driving people into the Leave Us Alone Coalition. Home ownership does make Americans more "conservative." Home owners don't like property taxes and neighborhood crime. But home ownership can also drive citizens to interfere with their neighbors' property rights through zoning laws or limitations on how others use their property. Home owners can sometimes ally with the Takings Coalition. Stock owners do not have that countervailing temptation.

Pollsters traditionally ask you what color you are, what your income is, your gender and your age. And presto, everything flows from race, income, sex, and age. Now pollsters such as Rasmussen and John Zogby are beginning to ask a new demographic. Are you a shareholder? Are you a member of the new investor class?

This creation of a mass-based investor class—what President Bush called the "ownership society"—is what made Social Security reform a possible subject of discussion in the 2000 and 2004 elections. Bush understood what most others had missed. Times had changed. It used to be quite true that any discussion of Social Security reform was the third rail of American politics and touching it would be politically fatal. That was back when so few Americans owned stock that you could not engage the general public in a discussion of moving Social Security from the present pay-as-you-go Ponzi scheme of defined benefits to one where each citizen would invest his own FICA taxes in his own personal savings account. Americans knew and understood the government Social Security program. They did not then have personal experience with the idea of a personal savings account that they controlled. Imagine an elected official urging Americans in the 1980s, before the Internet and e-mail, to think about reducing their reliance on the U.S. Post Office. And replace it with what?

But by 2000, a majority of Americans owned stock directly. The idea of moving their FICA taxes out of the hands of the politicians and into a mutual fund they owned was attractive, not bewildering and frightening. Before there was widespread share ownership any discussion of allowing Americans to invest their own FICA taxes could be caricatured as "abolishing" Social Security. Now everyone had a 401(k) or IRA or mutual fund, or had a sibling, parent, child, co-worker, or friend who did.

Bush turned a losing issue for Republicans—Social Security—into a winner. In 2000 and 2004, roughly 50–55 percent of Americans supported reforming Social Security to create personal savings accounts.[7] This was a turnaround from 1986 when the Republicans lost eight Senate seats and their Senate majority after discussing "reforming" Social Security by reducing some benefits.

In a Zogby poll done for the American Shareholders Association one week before the 2000 election, noninvestors opposed personal retirement accounts 37 percent to 53 percent. Investors supported personal accounts 55–40, a thirty-point shift in preference. Investors represented 67 percent of the total voting electorate in 2000; thus there was *strong* support for personal retirement accounts.[8] Support for personalizing Social Security to allow all Americans to invest their FICA taxes in their own personal accounts will continue to grow in the future as more Americans own shares of stock.

## ELECTION 2002: THE WEALTH EFFECT

The new politics of the ownership society was also on display in 2002 when the Enron scandal broke and the Dow Jones Index continued to slide from the high of 11,722 in January 2000 to a low of 7,286 just one month before the 2002 elections. The NASDAQ lost three-quarters of its entire market capitalization, dropping from 5048 to 1116. An analysis by the American Shareholders Association concluded that investors lost $9.6 trillion of shareholder wealth, 52 percent, from March 24, 2000, through October 9, 2002, less than one month before the 2002 midterm election.[9] The Democrats hoped they would win the 2002 elections because Americans were angry at the greedy and dishonest businessmen who had cheated Enron investors. The Republicans feared losing the House, where their margin was only 228–210, and losing seats in the Senate, where they were already down 51–49. They responded to the Enron scandal in the traditional way by enacting a vast and expensive regulatory scheme called Sarbanes-Oxley that is still costing business and consumers billions of dollars a year. (This is the usual and unhelpful "preemptive cringe" by Republicans playing defense.) But an interesting thing happened. Voters strengthened the Republican majority in the House and gave the Senate to the Republicans 52–48. Democrats and Republicans misread American anger.

Americans were angry that their stock portfolios had fallen. They wanted their market capitalization, or market cap, the value of their stocks, to go up. Democrats responded with a 1930s rhetoric of "we'll fix this, we'll sic the trial lawyers and the regulators on Enron and finish it off." Americans owning depressed stock portfolios wanted the looters at Enron hanged, but they also wanted stock prices to go up, not down. They were understandably angry at individual incompetents and/or crooks, not at business or corporations in general.

And the one thing they do know about Republicans—having been told this for sixty years by the Democrats and the press—is that Republicans will do anything to get stock-market prices up. They will pollute the earth, pillage the Third World, and kill baby seals. And voters felt *very* bad about the baby seals, but they voted for the party committed to increasing stock prices.

Voters' expectations were rewarded, because Republicans then introduced and passed the 2003 tax cut that reduced the capital gains tax from 20 percent to 15 percent and cut the top tax on dividends paid out to investors from 38.6 percent to 15 percent. This has caused the stock market to increase in value by *$7 trillion* since May 20, 2003. The entire wealth of the nation—stocks, land, houses—increased by $16.7 trillion. Since total wealth in America is $53 trillion, we see that 30 percent of the nation's entire wealth has been created since the 2003 tax cut.[10]

These changes show up on the cultural front. Bill Gates is a hero, not a robber baron. Warren Buffett, who doesn't make anything, just invests money, is an oracle, not a "speculator."

With the widespread ownership of stocks through defined-contribution pensions there are now three measures of the economic health of the country that politicians need to watch. The first measure, unemployment, was the focus of all political discourse from the Great Depression until the 1970s. If unemployment was falling, politicians were in good shape. If unemployment was increasing—as in 1958 for instance—politicians were in trouble. When Richard Nixon delinked the dollar from gold and announced that "We are all Keynesians now," he ushered in the period of the Great Inflation. As a result there was a second key measure for the economy. Candidate Jimmy

Carter invented the "misery index" by adding the unemployment rate to the inflation rate and claimed that this number showed the poor health of the economy in 1976 and urged voters to turn out then-President Gerald Ford. Carter proved the power of his metric when he increased the misery index from 13.5 when he was elected in 1976 to 20.7 on November 1980[11] and lost the presidency to the cowboy.

Now there is a third measure: the value of stock portfolios owned by individual Americans in their portable pension accounts. And it is here that the growing number of investors in America and the growing size of their investments in the stock market are an exponentially growing problem for the modern Democrat Party.

Republicans have a plan to increase the value of your personal account. They want to increase the amount you can put away tax free. They want to reduce taxes and regulations that hurt the companies you own shares in. They want to fight the trial lawyers who loot the companies in your mutual funds. They want worldwide free trade that will reward American companies that are internationally competitive and already source production from around the world.

To date, Democrats, trapped by their labor-union, big-government-taxing, and trial-lawyer-suing constituencies, have not come up with a way even to talk to the new and growing investor class. There is no Democrat proposal that will increase the value of your retirement wealth in your IRA or 40l(k), and they have hundreds of proposals that will tax, regulate, and litigate them downward in value.

The Democrats, facing the growing number of investors, are in the position of King Canute ordering the tide to stay put. Government labor-union leaders have opposed allowing their members to shift to defined-contribution, personally controlled pensions. They have foolishly stated publicly that their members are not smart enough to control their own pensions. They stand athwart history and are yelling stop.

The number and percentage of shareholding Americans will continue to grow without any changes in the law. But the laws are changing to move more Americans from traditional defined benefit plans, where workers don't actually own the wealth of the investments backing the pension, to defined contribution plans where each worker owns his retirement wealth in stocks and bonds directly.

The "Pension Protection Act of 2006" is estimated to increase the number of Americans with defined contribution plans, and therefore stock ownership, by fourteen million individuals.

States have begun to follow the federal government's lead and moved to increase reliance on defined contribution plans once viewed as "add-ons" to the "real" defined benefit pension.

Florida passed a law to allow its government workers to take all their contributions out of the defined benefit plan and move them to a defined contribution plan of their choice. Michigan in 1997 ended their defined benefit plan for new state employees. All new hires have stock ownership in defined contribution plans.[12] Democrat Jon Corzine of New Jersey and Republican Arnold Schwarzenegger have both called for moving all new state employees to a defined contribution plan.[13]

The growth of the investor class, the ownership society, is accelerating.

## CHAPTER FOUR

# THE DECLINE OF LABOR UNIONS

Organized labor is the skeletal frame and muscle of the left. It is the largest source of financial and political strength in the modern Democrat Party. It provides hundreds of millions of dollars from the $8 billion in coerced union dues from 15.4 million members.[1] It has state and local organizations with full-time staff in every state in the nation.

Campaign finance laws permit unlimited amounts to be spent by unions "communicating" with their members and none of it need be reported. (Thank you, John McCain for leaving this gaping loophole in the Feingold-McCain bill.)

And unions concentrate their giving. In 2004, while business went 55 percent Republican and 45 percent Democrat, unions gave 87 percent Democrat and only 12 percent Republican.[2] After the 2004 election the AFL-CIO website reported that unions "fielded 5,000 full-time employees and 225,000 volunteers," distributed 32 million pieces of literature, knocked on 6 million doors, and ran 257 phone banks with 2,322 lines running in 22 battleground states.[3] Ninety percent of union members report that they received political information from their union.

Labor unions benefit from a string of laws that give them special benefits and powers. They are exempt from antitrust laws, and in most states, even though they are a corporation, they are exempt from corporate laws on fiduciary responsibility to their members. They do not have to ask workers to join the union voluntarily in the twenty-eight states that have no right-to-work laws. Union membership is compulsory. Don't join the union. Don't pay your dues. Lose your job. Unions are exempt from federal prosecution under the Hobbs Act for acts of violence if the purpose of the violence is to promote unionism. Yes, you read that correctly. If the union "activists" burn down your business, murder you or nonunion workers, it is not a federal crime. You can, of course, ask the unionized local police in your city to look into it.

Concurrently, union officials often enjoy an array of benefits as a result of provisions they negotiate into collective-bargaining agreements with public and private employers. For example, school-district union presidents often insist the district provide them with 100 percent of their salary and benefits, but release them from any teaching obligations so they can work full time on union business, including politics, at the taxpayers' expense.[4]

Lesser amounts of "release time" are often included in union contracts for rank-and-file members as well. In many union negotiations, a top priority is to get Election Day declared a holiday—as the United Auto Workers have done—so that top union staff and members can be directed to work on political campaigns that day.

Unions are the funding source for many of the other seemingly independent parts of the left's coalition. Many of the organizations that organize in the African-American and Hispanic communities are funded and controlled by organized labor. This funding comes with strings, perhaps chains. When the interests of teachers' unions and black parents conflict on an issue such as parental choice in education—despite the fact that black parents overwhelmingly support parental choice in education—few black "political leaders" buck their labor union masters.[5]

But membership in labor unions is declining in absolute numbers and as a percentage of the total workforce.

## U.S. PRIVATE-SECTOR TRADE-UNION MEMBERSHIP[6]

| YEAR | PRIVATE-SECTOR UNION MEMBERSHIP | PERCENTAGE OF PRIVATE-SECTOR EMPLOYEES | YEAR | PRIVATE-SECTOR UNION MEMBERSHIP | PERCENTAGE OF PRIVATE-SECTOR EMPLOYEES |
|---|---|---|---|---|---|
| 1900 | 917,000 | 6.51% | 1972 | 18,181,000 | 30.00% |
| 1901 | 1,167,000 | 7.70% | 1974 | 18,538,000 | 29.00% |
| 1902 | 1,500,000 | 9.26% | 1976 | 17,882,000 | 28.00% |
| 1903 | 1,908,000 | 11.47% | 1978 | 17,834,000 | 26.00% |
| 1904 | 1,995,000 | 12.19% | 1980 | 15,243,000 | 20.60% |
| 1905 | 1,923,000 | 11.07% | 1983 | 11,933,000 | 16.80% |
| 1910 | 2,109,000 | 10.47% | 1984 | 11,646,000 | 15.50% |
| 1915 | 2,508,000 | 12.23% | 1985 | 11,226,000 | 14.60% |
| 1920 | 4,664,000 | 19.17% | 1986 | 11,051,000 | 14.00% |
| 1925 | 3,495,000 | 13.21% | 1987 | 10,827,000 | 13.40% |
| 1930 | 3,482,000 | 13.30% | 1988 | 10,694,000 | 12.90% |
| 1935 | 3,337,000 | 14.20% | 1989 | 10,541,000 | 12.40% |
| 1940 | 6,848,000 | 24.30% | 1990 | 10,247,000 | 12.10% |
| 1941 | 8,268,000 | 25.90% | 1991 | 9,898,000 | 11.90% |
| 1942 | 9,716,000 | 28.10% | 1992 | 9,703,000 | 11.50% |
| 1943 | 11,182,000 | 30.80% | 1993 | 9,554,000 | 11.20% |
| 1944 | 11,598,000 | 32.40% | 1994 | 9,620,000 | 10.90% |

| YEAR | PRIVATE-SECTOR UNION MEMBER-SHIP | PERCENTAGE OF PRIVATE-SECTOR EMPLOYEES | YEAR | PRIVATE-SECTOR UNION MEMBER-SHIP | PERCENTAGE OF PRIVATE-SECTOR EMPLOYEES |
|------|------|------|------|------|------|
| 1945 | 11,674,000 | 33.90% | 1995 | 9,400,000 | 10.40% |
| 1950 | 13,550,000 | 34.60% | 1996 | 9,385,000 | 10.20% |
| 1955 | 15,341,000 | 35.10% | 1997 | 9,363,000 | 9.80% |
| 1956 | 17,114,000 | 38.00% | 1998 | 9,306,000 | 9.46% |
| 1958 | 16,871,000 | 39.00% | 1999 | 9,419,000 | 9.42% |
| 1960 | 16,907,000 | 37.00% | 2000 | 9,418,000 | 8.99% |
| 1962 | 16,390,000 | 35.00% | 2001 | 9,113,000 | 8.97% |
| 1964 | 16,403,000 | 34.00% | 2002 | 8,800,000 | 8.61% |
| 1966 | 17,409,000 | 33.00% | 2003 | 8,452,000 | 8.23% |
| 1968 | 17,939,000 | 32.00% | 2004 | 8,205,000 | 7.92% |
| 1970 | 18,295,000 | 31.00% | 2005 | 8,255,000 | 7.78% |

## U.S. PRIVATE-SECTOR LABOR-UNION MEMBERSHIP

In 1958, fully 39 percent of the private-sector workers were members of labor unions and paid mandatory dues.[7] Fewer government workers were unionized then. By 1980, only 23 percent of private-sector workers were members of unions. In 2006, 12 percent of all workers were members of unions. And the composition of union membership has changed. In 2007, 36.6 percent of the 16 million state and local government workers were unionized and only 7.4 percent of the 105 million private-sector workers were unionized. Unions increasingly represent government employees, not private-sector workers.[8]

To comprehend how the world has changed imagine for a moment what American politics would look like if there had been no decline in the unionization rate of the private sector since the 1950s. There would in 2006 be about thirty-five million dues-paying members of organized labor in the private sector rather than nine million. Add in the government workers who are paying union dues today and the total number of labor union members would be forty-three million rather than the 15.4 million union members there are today, and the total dues they would pay each year would be $21.5 billion rather than the $8 billion paid today.

The decline in organized labor's strength is felt not just in the lower number of today's workers who pay union dues. Unions wield real power in communication with their retired members who vote more regularly than younger union members and who still view the union as a trusted source of political information.

While union membership is declining as a percentage of the workplace, the number of retired union members and their spouses is declining in absolute numbers. Remember that 35 percent of workers in 1955 were unionized. A union member thirty years old in 1955 is eighty-two in 2007. Every year 2.4 million Americans pass away.[9] For that age cohort, one-third were members of union households.

In 2005, 1,924,000 private-sector jobs were created and only 50,000 were unionized. Of 411,000 government jobs created in 2005, 163,000 involved compulsory union dues. In sum, in 2005, there were 2,335,000 net new jobs created, of which 213,000 were unionized. So, 9 percent of new job entrants were unionized in a year when one-third of deaths were from union households. You can see that every year the number of Americans who know the words to "Solidarity Forever," and remember the union as something other than the institution that takes dues without consent, is declining sharply.

As unions mutate from "representing" private-sector workers to "representing" government employees, they become politically redundant. A government worker who votes for a Democrat cannot vote twice, because he is both a government worker with an appetite for higher taxes and a union member lobbied by his union. One liberal lamented that affirmative action had put more African

Americans into unionized government jobs. "Great. One African-American voting Democrat, one union member voting Democrat and one government employee voting Democrat. All totals to only one vote."

Will the decline in organized labor's membership continue, reverse, or accelerate? For how long can organized labor continue to make up for fewer members by raising dues? Or exercising strength through politicizing the pension funds they often control "on behalf" of their members?

Four factors might accelerate or reverse labor's political fortunes:

1. **Paycheck Protection.** Over time, more states will follow the lead of Utah, which passed legislation prohibiting the use of dues paid by public employees for political purposes altogether. Under the law, public employee unions need to raise their political money separately, and without help from public employers. When this law took effect in Utah in 2001, the portion of teachers' union members who choose voluntarily to contribute to their political war chest fell from 68 percent to 6.8 percent.

   Paycheck protection was placed before California voters in 1998 and again in 2005. The initiatives had strong support and the unions were forced to spend more than $20 million each time to convince voters to turn down the initiatives.

   Internal polling during the 1998 campaign for paycheck protection in California showed that a strong majority of members of the California Teachers Association (an affiliate of the National Education Association) supported the Proposition 226 paycheck-protection initiative. Yet, rather than advocate for the position favored by their members (to support the initiative), union officials instead budgeted an additional $1 million for an "internal campaign" to persuade their members that paycheck protection was somehow not in their interest.

   That internal campaign demonstrated one fact that paycheck protection proponents learned early on: No truthful argument against the reform succeeded with either the general public or union members themselves. Instead, union officials spent their members' dues making false claims back to them that giving them the right to choose how their dues would be spent would mean their pensions would be jeopardized, as would their health benefits, etc.

In Washington State, a similar paycheck-protection measure passed in 1994 and participation in union political funds fell from 80 percent to 11 percent. By 2006, fewer than 7 percent of the teachers voluntarily contributed to the unions' political action committee. What this means is that, given a choice, even a majority of liberal Democrat teachers do not wish to fund the union agenda. However, in most states, their mandatory dues, regardless of their own preferences, are used for the union leaders' radical politics without their consent. In total dollars, contributions to union political funds fell from $624,000 to $83,000. In 2007, the Democrat legislature and Democrat governor Gregoire of Washington State voted to abolish this worker protection law.[10]

But since paycheck-protection measures regularly poll at 70 percent and can only be defeated when unions outspend their opponents by a serious multiple, over time more and more states will pass paycheck protection through the initiative process, and those states with Republican legislatures will follow Utah's example and union dues will only flow from voluntary contributions in more and more states.

And as long as union leaders continue to promote candidates and legislation at odds with the wishes of their members, voluntary dues will mean less cash for the union political machine.

2. **Nonunion Teacher Associations.** A growing threat to the teachers unions is a nonunion alternative teachers professional association that doesn't dabble in the politics of abortion, Iraq, or gay rights, but is actually a professional association. It also offers liability insurance for teachers, which is important because many teachers join teachers unions for the sole purpose

of getting insurance against trial-lawyer suits. (This is a political thing of beauty: Trial lawyers threaten teachers. Teachers pay dues to teachers unions for protection. Teachers union bosses and trial lawyers contribute to candidates who legislate in the interests of the union leaders and trial lawyers and the poor teachers pay for it all unwillingly.) States can also protect teachers from being stampeded into paying union dues to buy protection against trial lawyers by passing laws making such lawsuits very difficult—as Texas has. Or by having taxpayers pay for liability insurance as a teacher benefit (the one benefit the teachers unions actually fight against).

There are well over three hundred thousand teachers in nonunion associations such as the Association of American Educators, which has fourteen state chapters. As each of those teachers is not paying $500 in union dues, they are denying the most left-wing union $150 million each year.[11]

3. **State Right-to-Work Laws.** The number of right-to-work states is likely to grow in the future. The most recent states to enact right-to-work laws have been Louisiana in 1976, Idaho in 1986, and Oklahoma in 2004. Since 1943, twenty-two states have passed right-to-work laws using Section 14B of the Wagner Act, which allows any state to choose to give its workers a choice of whether to join a union or not. Only one state—Indiana in 1965—has ever repeated it.

4. **New Reporting Requirements.** Elaine Chao, the secretary of labor for President Bush, adopted reporting requirements that are just now beginning to require unions to tell their members how their dues are spent. (As recently as last year, the National Education Association reported to the Internal Revenue Service, with a straight face, that they spent no dollars on politics.) But with real requirements for public disclosure of how unions spend their money it will enable journalists and union members to see just how union dues are being spent. This will create more accountability. In 2004, union members voted 61 percent to 38 percent for Kerry over Bush.[12] But union leaders spent

## RIGHT-TO-WORK LAWS AND THEIR DATE
## OF ENACTMENT

| STATE | LAWS ENACTED OR APPROVED | STATE | LAWS ENACTED OR APPROVED |
|---|---|---|---|
| Arkansas | 1944 | Alabama | 1953 |
| Arizona | 1946 | South Carolina | 1954 |
| Nebraska | 1946 | Utah | 1955 |
| Georgia | 1947 | Mississippi | 1960 |
| Iowa | 1947 | Wyoming | 1963 |
| North Carolina | 1947 | Florida | 1944 |
| South Dakota | 1947 | Kansas | 1958 |
| Tennessee | 1947 | Louisiana | 1976 |
| Virginia | 1947 | Idaho | 1985 |
| North Dakota | 1948 | Texas | 1947 |
| Nevada | 1952 | Oklahoma | 2001 |

*Source: Department of Labor*

their members' money 87 percent, $53,858,000 to 12 percent, $7,707,633 contributing to Democrats over Republicans.[13]

A new group, the Center for Union Facts, run by Rick Berman, gathers information on the size, scope, political activities, and criminal activity of the labor movement. It posts a powerful website, Unionfacts.com, which has begun running full-page ads explaining to union members how their dues are being spent. This has gotten under the skin of the union leadership, which has criticized UnionFacts.com, not for being

## HIGH PAY FOR UNION BOSSES

| | | | |
|---|---|---|---|
| John Sweeney | President | AFL-CIO | $279,301 |
| Andrew Stern | Intl President | SEIU | $249,599 |
| James Hoffa | Gen President | Teamsters | $297,772 |
| Ronald Gettelfinger | President | UAW | $156,278 |
| Joseph Hansen | International President | UFCW | $336,776 |
| Kenneth Neumann | National Director-Canada | United Steel Workers | $186,304 |
| Reg Weaver | NEA President | NEA | $438,920 |
| Edward Mcelroy | President | AFT | $373,723 |
| Rogelio Flores | National Vice President | AFGE | $191,520 |
| Gerald Mcentee | Intl President | AFSCME | $584,980 |

Union leaders' pay and other fun facts the union bosses do not want you to know can be found at www.unionfacts.com.

inaccurate, but for blowing the whistle on their spending that has been unexamined by the press for decades.

More transparency of union spending will lead to more attention paid to union corruption and political use of members' dues by both the media and ultimately union members themselves. Already, just by reporting on news stories that appear in the establishment press, Ken Boehm and Peter Flaherty of the

National Legal and Policy Center's watchdog group, the Organized Labor Accountability Project, publish the *Union Corruption Update,* a bimonthly newsletter that includes examples of union corruption and convictions across the nation. The reports can be found at www.nplc.org.

## A Possible Route Back to Power: Card Check

Union leaders are finding fewer and fewer workers willing to vote in elections to create a union at their place of work. They have a plan based on serious study of those who have had a similar problem, Pinochet of Chile, Castro of Cuba, Italy's Mussolini: Don't have elections in the first place.

Unions have written a new law that would replace silly elections that can be lost with a "card check" system where a labor union "organizer" can ask individual workers to sign a card asking for a union. The card can be signed in a bar or in your home (message: we know where you live), with several union organizers standing helpfully nearby. In the past such signed cards have been forged as well as coerced.

Real elections have not been working well for the union bosses. David Denholm of the Public Sector Research Foundation reports that in the past five and a half years, labor unions have tried to organize 14,743 workplaces. They won 8,260 elections and lost 6,483 elections. In the same time span, unionized workers have demanded 2,379 elections to allow them to "decertify" their union, and workers have thrown out their union 66.2 percent of the time.[14]

Union bosses pretend to believe that they are losing all those secret-ballot elections because management is intimidating their workers. Their solution shows they are not serious. They want to abolish a secret ballot that is free from intimidation and allow union bosses to stand over workers while they "make up their minds."

Democrats know that "card check" will lead to intimidation of workers by the unions. In August 2001, sixteen leading liberal Democrats wrote to the Mexican government demanding they "use the secret ballot in all union recognition elections. . . . The secret ballot is absolutely necessary in order to ensure that workers are not intimidated into voting for a union that they might not otherwise choose." Of those sixteen Democrats, eleven were in Congress in 2007, and to a man they voted to deny American voters the right to secret ballot.[15]

It is a sign of the power of who really runs the Democrat Party—and how scared Democrats are to see their enforcer in failing health—that Nancy Pelosi has made the elimination of secret-ballot votes for union elections her top priority in the 110th Congress. This was almost never mentioned by Democrat candidates running in 2006, but as soon as the election was over it was top of Pelosi's wish list in speeches explaining her goals. Every single freshman Democrat elected in 2006 voted for "card check." There are no "blue dog" or "independent" Democrats when the demands of the labor bosses are at stake. "Card check" passed the House on March 1, 2007, 241–185. Republicans have more than the forty votes in the Senate needed to filibuster this union power grab. For now. This is the Takings Coalition's first territorial demand. Should "card check" pass the Senate it would dramatically increase forced union dues to union bosses, who would then recycle much of that money to the Democrat political machine that makes it possible.

Democrats will also continue trying to increase their power over state and local government workers by requiring more of them to pay forced union dues. Senator Ted Kennedy has long championed legislation to require police and firemen to pay union dues. There is a great deal of money at stake here. On average, 37 percent of government workers are members of unions. Imagine how much money unions could get their hands on if they follow the example of New York, which has forced 69 percent of government workers to kick in dues. Not coincidentally, Tony Soprano's home state of New Jersey forces 64 percent of its government workers to "contribute" union dues to the bosses.

If, however, no laws are changed, organized labor will decline as

the number of union members decline as a percentage of the workplace and the number of retired workers with strong historic union
ties falls as an older industrial generation dies out and new companies
grow union free. Today's workers have little interest in labor unions
and less in paying mandatory dues. A Zogby poll in August 2006
asked workers if they would like to be members of a labor union: 74
percent said no, 19.8 percent said yes.[16]

Fifty-four percent of workers think unions already have too much
influence on public policy. Sixty-four percent support the principle of
right to work—that no one should be required to join a union as a
condition of employment.

What union growth will occur will largely be in the government
employment sector. Smaller government means fewer union members. And vice versa. Paycheck protection at the state level could dramatically slash the unions' political funds—and this is increasingly
likely in the ten or so states with a Republican state legislature and
governors and in the twenty-three states with the initiative process.

One last observation:

Barbara Kopple's documentary *Harlan County, U.S.A.*, covers the
1973 strike at the Brookside Mine in Harlan County, Kentucky. The
film was a powerful and effective propaganda movie for unionization. After a violent thirteen-month strike, the union won the ability
to force all the workers into the union. When the DVD of the film was
released in 2006 *The Nation* magazine reported that not a single mine
in Harlan County was unionized.[17]

## CHAPTER FIVE

# VOTERS COME AND VOTERS GO: ENTRY AND EXIT

We often think about the American electorate without noticing that the electorate is constantly changing. Between the 2000 and 2008 elections some thirty million Americans will have turned eighteen and joined the voting-age population. In the same eight years almost twenty million Americans, most of voting age, will have passed away.

Just as you cannot put your foot into the same river twice, you never hold elections with the same America.

Morton Blackwell, who grew up in Louisiana when there were few Republicans in the state, quoted a wise and patient Republican Party leader who said the two friends of the postwar Republican Party in Louisiana were the obstetrician and the mortician.

The Leave Us Alone Coalition benefits for the foreseeable future at both ends of this process: entry and exit.

# Rabbit Is a Republican. Maybe Rich. Certainly Not at Rest

"My seven children will outvote your one child."
—*Arizona Republican activist Len Munsil "debating" a liberal friend*

A recent study by Arthur C. Brooks, of the Maxwell School of Citizenship and Public Affairs at Syracuse University, looking at General Social Survey data, found that if in 1974 you chose 100 randomly selected and unrelated self-described liberals they would report that collectively they had 188 children. Thirty years later, in 2004, 100 unrelated liberals would report they had 147 children among them. In thirty years, there was a drop from 188 to 147—41 fewer children, or 21 percent, for the same number of liberals.

Same question passed to 100 conservatives in 1974 found they had 231 children. Thirty years later, 100 conservatives reported 208 children.

In 1974, 100 conservatives had 43 more children than the 100 liberals.

In 2004, 100 conservatives had 61 more children than the 100 liberals.[1]

The decline in the overall fertility rates that has been well reported by the establishment press obscures the question of "whose" fertility. The fertility gap to the advantage of future conservatives over future liberals rose from 22.9 percent in 1974 to 41.5 percent in 2004, an increase of 0.6 percent each year.

And as 80 percent of voting Democrats in 1992's American National Election Survey report a Democrat father, and 79.7 percent of Republican voters in the same year reported a Republican father, we can posit that there is a strong likelihood that more fecund conservatives will breed more conservatives than their reproductively challenged liberal brethren, who evidently watch *Sex and the City* in lieu of raising rugrats.[2]

Thirty years of birthing more conservatives than liberals has an impact on today's voting. Children born in 1974 could begin voting in 1992. The wider gap in 2004 will show up in 2022's reapportionment election. For the next twenty-five years this fertility gap will tend to advantage Republicans. It may accelerate.

Just for fun we looked at the handbook for the 109th Congress (2005–2007) and found that the 232 Republican congressmen and women have 637 children and the 203 Democrat congressmen and women have 422 children for an average of 2.75 children per Republican and 2.08 children per Democrat. In the Senate, Republicans average 3.18 children and the Senate Democrat caucus (including the hermaphrodite James Jeffords with two children) average 2.26 children.

The Michigan Legislature has 2.3 children per Republican state legislator and 1.74 children per Democrat. In Minnesota, Republican state legislators average 2.77 children and Democrats average 2.26 children. In Alaska, they are going to run out of Democrats in a generation or two. Alaska Republican state legislators have 100 kids total, or 2.6 per legislator, 72 grandkids, and 5 great-grandkids. Alaska Democrat state legislators have 22 kids, or 1.4 per legislator, 0 grandkids, and 0 great-grandkids.

Two studies suggest the trend is real and will deepen.

## GOP Baby Boom

In the thirty-one states carried by Bush in 2004, the census estimates in 2005 that there are 38,355,472 Americans under eighteen years of age. That is 3.2 million more than the 35,114,512 children under eighteen in the nineteen states plus the District of Columbia carried by Kerry.

One of the most widely noted factoids of the 2004 election was that George Bush won ninety-seven of the hundred fastest-growing counties in the United States.

The Democratic Leadership Council, run by Al Frum, published a study in July 2006, entitled "Expand the Base!: To build a majority coalition, Democrats must appeal to more voters outside cities," that looks beyond that startling number.[3] Perhaps winning ninety-seven of the fastest-growing one hundred counties means little or nothing. Maybe all those rapidly growing counties were small in population. There are 3,070 counties and parishes in the United States.

The DLC study divided counties into two groups, those with more than fifty thousand in their voting-age population, which represented 82 percent of the total national vote, and small counties with fewer than fifty thousand, which cast 18 percent of the national vote.[4]

Large and small counties were then divided into three groups. Counties where the John Kerry presidential vote was below 45 percent, between 45 percent and 55 percent, and above 55 percent were labeled Republican trending, marginal, and Democrat trending.

In the nation as a whole, looking at the large counties with voting-age populations over fifty thousand, the population of Republican-trending counties grew 9.18 percent, marginal counties grew 6 percent, and Democrat-trending counties grew 2.2 percent.

Nationally, small counties that trended Republican grew 4.9 percent, marginal counties grew 3.7 percent, and Democrat-trending counties grew 2 percent.

Republican-trending counties, both large and small, are growing faster in population than Democrat-trending counties. This study picks up both natural increase—children coming of age—and migration.

But perhaps blue states are just getting a little less blue and red states are getting redder. This would not change presidential electoral votes. To test this the DLC then focused on swing states.

Looking just at states that the DLC designates the "seventeen battleground states," the larger counties between 2000 and 2004 saw their voting-age population grow 9.5 percent in Republican-trending counties, 6.3 percent in marginal counties, and 1.7 percent in Democrat counties. Smaller counties from 2000 to 2004 saw their voting-age population grow by 5.4 percent in Republican-trending counties, 4.9 percent in marginal counties, and 3.7 percent in Democrat-trending counties.[5]

## MARRIED TO THE PARTY

Steve Sailer, a writer for the *American Conservative*, was looking for which factors correlated most highly with red or blue status for states in the 2004 election. His first stab found that "Bush's share of the vote by state closely correlated with the number of babies that the white women in the state are expected to give birth to over their lifetimes." He focused on the white vote, which makes up 75 percent of the total vote, and Bush carried the white vote 58–41. He found that Bush carried the nineteen states with the highest white fertility rate in 2000 and 2004, and in 2004 he carried twenty-five out of the top twenty-six states, Michigan being the lone fecund Kerry state. Total white fertility—the number of children the average white woman will bear in her lifetime—had a .85 correlation with the Bush vote in 2000 and .86 in 2004.[6]

Sailer then looked further and found that the factor that correlates most highly with red state status is "being married." "The more years of their young adulthoods that the people in a state spend in wedlock on average, the more Republican the state is overall. This is especially true for non-Hispanic whites, but for the total population, the correlation is quite strong, as well. Overall Bush carried the top 25 states ranked by years married for white women. When ranked on years married for women of all races, Bush carried 22 of the top 25," Sailer reported.

Sailer points out, "I calculated that in 2002's House of Representatives elections, 56 percent of married women voted for the GOP (similar to their husbands' 58 percent) compared to 39 percent of unmarried women (and 44 percent of unmarried men). There's an exceptionally large partisan difference between married women with children (58 percent Republican) and unmarried women with children (32 percent.) These figures are for all races."[7]

To summarize the above, red states have more children already. Red counties, both large and small, are growing faster than blue counties. This is true in "battleground" states that will decide the presidential elections in 2008 and 2012. And red states and blue states are most completely explained by how long women are married and how many children they have.

Steve Sailer argues that the correlation between being married, having children, and red states results from young singles living in blue cities, and when they marry and have children, they are fleeing the high cost of housing, government schools run to please the Democrat Party's key constituency of government workers rather than parents, and they are moving to areas where they can afford larger houses with backyards. When couples have such a house with a backyard and enjoy the lower cost of living and lower taxes outside blue cities, they can afford to have more children, and they do.

This is a challenge for Democrats as they look to future elections.

Sailer does point out that this nexus between the economics of having a family and the decision to have a family explains the compatibility of red-state economic conservatism and a respect for traditional values. Parents want lower taxes and less regulation, which gives you lower housing costs, and they want to protect their children from what the secular left dishes out. They are not frightened by social conservatives who overreact to threats to their children. They may or may not completely share those concerns, but they feel more threatened by the libertine left than by those conservatives who confront them. Now married and raising children in the suburbs or exurbs, they may continue to support legalized abortion or "gay rights" as they did in their single city-living youth, but it is no longer a strong contender to be a primary vote-moving issue.

Republicans will strengthen their advantage if they can reduce the cost of housing and make it easier to live in suburbs, exurbs, and rural areas. Democrats have wisely countered with their attacks on urban sprawl—aka young married couples escaping high-tax, high-crime blue cities and moving into newly built homes on what used to be farmland. Every young couple that makes this move takes their tax payments with them and the big-city machine loses cash. Worse, outside the city walls they will breed little Republicans who will vote for governors and state legislators unwilling to spend state tax dollars funding the political machine and associated nonfunctioning "school system." This is not just "white flight." Hispanics, Asians, African Americans, and European ethnics who leave the big cities also flee the ethnic enclaves that can keep them voting on legacy issues. Much of what the Democrats believe to be votes they win from "minorities" are actually votes cast by members of minority groups living in cities. One cannot pander to racial or ethnic divisions when speaking to families in a suburb, exurb, or rural area. In suburbs, there is no Armenian vote, or Italian vote, or fill-in-the-blank ethnic vote as exists in Chinatown or Little Italy in the emptying city.

Of course, the Democrats have to cloak their concerns as environmentalism. Otherwise, in discussing "their" citizens fleeing to the suburbs, they sound too much like the East German border guard who missed. Much of the left's energy has gone into increasing the costs of new housing outside cities, not building roads to allow easy entry and egress from cities, and diverting gas-tax dollars to mass transit that only transports people from one highly populated (blue) area to another. Zoning laws that require new homes to have many acres used to be known as "snob zoning" and were viewed as racist ploys to keep black people out of suburbs. Now the liberals want the same laws used to keep Asians, Hispanics, and African Americans, in fact, arrivistes of any color, trapped inside cities. The snob-zoning laws have been dyed green and this soothes the liberal conscience, but fools no one else.

## DYING DEMOCRATS

"You cannot count on people to change. You can, however, count on them to die."

—*Joel Garreau, Edge City*

The most partisan Democrat age cohort is, for understandable reasons, the group that turned twenty-one and became voters between 1932 and 1952. The elders in this group grew up with FDR and Truman as their presidents for the first twenty years of their adult lives. They only knew a Republican Congress for four of the sixty-four years between 1930 and 1994. This age cohort saw the draft imposed in peacetime and continued for twenty-five years after the end of World War Two, universal and compulsory national pensions through Social Security, and labor union legislation that treated workers as a proletariat expected to stay in one job until retirement. They lived through and mostly tolerated wage and price controls and government rationing of milk, butter, rubber tires, and gasoline. Government spending ran at 42 percent of GDP during the height of the Second World War. It is the most statist generation in American history. To be clear, all these one-size-fits-all government rules, programs, and mandates were imposed on them by the previous generation that had absorbed statist views from the progressives at home and the socialists of all parties abroad. Those who grew up under FDR were accustomed to and became comfortable with more government and more government control than any generation before or after.

They are more likely to be registered as Democrats than those both older and younger than they are. A series of Gallup polls showed that those Americans who turned eighteen between 1935 and 1938 had a Democrat-over-Republican gap of 21 percent; those who turned eighteen between 1939 and 1942 had a ten-point Democrat advantage; 1943–1946 and 1947–1950: 13 and 11 percent advantages in favor of the Democrats.[8]

A conservative estimate is that Democrats outnumber the Republicans by 10 percent in this seventy-five to ninety-five age cohort. Therefore, when 2.4 million Americans die each year there is a net loss of 240,000 Democrats. From 2000 to 2008, that is a net loss of 1.9 million Democrats. One can make all the jokes one wishes about dead people voting in Chicago, but this is a serious challenge for Democrats. Those legacy voters that were voting Democrat because of the Civil War, or because they were immigrants and befriended by Tammany Hall, are passing from the scene.

Those Americans who turned twenty-one during the twenty years of the Democrat dominance of FDR and Truman are in 2006 now

## THE ANES GUIDE TO PUBLIC OPINION AND ELECTORAL BEHAVIOR

## AGE COHORT OF RESPONDENT 1948–2004

| YEAR | BORN BEFORE 1895 | BORN 1895 TO 1910 | BORN 1911 TO 1926 | BORN 1927 TO 1942 | BORN 1943 TO 1958 | BORN 1959 TO 1974 | BORN 1975 OR LATER | TOTAL SAMPLE SIZE |
|---|---|---|---|---|---|---|---|---|
| 1948 | 24 | 46 | 22 | 9 | - | - | - | 654 |
| 1952 | 22 | 30 | 39 | 8 | - | - | - | 1,773 |
| 1954 | 13 | 33 | 48 | 7 | - | - | - | 1,132 |
| 1956 | 15 | 26 | 41 | 18 | - | - | - | 1,742 |
| 1958 | 15 | 26 | 39 | 21 | - | - | - | 1,822 |
| 1960 | 14 | 27 | 38 | 21 | - | - | - | 1,950 |
| 1962 | 13 | 25 | 34 | 28 | - | - | - | 1,290 |
| 1964 | 9 | 22 | 34 | 33 | 2 | - | - | 1,566 |
| 1966 | 8 | 22 | 32 | 31 | 7 | - | - | 1,280 |
| 1968 | 6 | 21 | 31 | 32 | 10 | - | - | 1,552 |

| YEAR | BORN BEFORE 1895 | BORN 1895 TO 1910 | BORN 1911 TO 1926 | BORN 1927 TO 1942 | BORN 1943 TO 1958 | BORN 1959 TO 1974 | BORN 1975 OR LATER | TOTAL SAMPLE SIZE |
|---|---|---|---|---|---|---|---|---|
| 1970 | 5 | 21 | 27 | 31 | 17 | - | - | 1,476 |
| 1972 | 4 | 16 | 25 | 27 | 28 | - | - | 2,688 |
| 1974 | 3 | 16 | 24 | 23 | 34 | - | - | 2,487 |
| 1976 | 2 | 15 | 24 | 23 | 36 | - | - | 2,850 |
| 1978 | 1 | 10 | 21 | 25 | 39 | 3 | - | 2,294 |
| 1980 | 1 | 11 | 22 | 23 | 37 | 7 | - | 1,612 |
| 1982 | 1 | 8 | 24 | 21 | 37 | 10 | - | 1,416 |
| 1984 | - | 8 | 19 | 21 | 37 | 16 | - | 2,232 |
| 1986 | - | 5 | 17 | 20 | 38 | 19 | - | 2,173 |
| 1988 | - | 6 | 16 | 20 | 36 | 122 | - | 2,037 |
| 1990 | - | 3 | 16 | 19 | 32 | 30 | - | 1,980 |

| Year | | | | | | | |
|---|---|---|---|---|---|---|---|
| 1992 | – | 3 | 15 | 19 | 32 | 30 | 1 | 2,488 |
| 1994 | – | 1 | 12 | 18 | 31 | 33 | 5 | 1,795 |
| 1996 | – | 1 | 11 | 18 | 30 | 34 | 6 | 1,708 |
| 1998 | – | 1 | 10 | 17 | 30 | 31 | 12 | 1,267 |
| 2000 | – | 1 | 8 | 17 | 29 | 32 | 14 | 1,800 |
| 2002 | – | 0 | 6 | 13 | 27 | 36 | 17 | 1,503 |
| 2004 | – | 0 | 5 | 16 | 28 | 30 | 21 | 1,212 |

This chart shows how each generation is represented in each election year in percent, by time period.[9]

seventy-five to ninety-five years old. There is yet another decade of disappearing Democrats.

The Republicans need to watch younger voters. In 2000, Bush received 46 percent of voters eighteen to twenty-nine years of age compared to 48 percent of all voters. In 2004, Bush's share of the youth vote was 45 percent, six points below Bush's 51-percent share of all voters. In 2006, that trend continued as youth voters supported Democrats with 60 percent of their votes.[10] If this was a temporary reaction to the war, it can be fixed when Iraq is behind us. Or it could be an age cohort that moves through the years, troubling Republicans just as the Reagan-era voter cohort helps Republicans.

The Grim Reaper is nonpartisan. It was the Republicans with the fuzzy end of the lollipop from 1960 to 1980 as those who were dying had been born between 1880 and 1900 and had become of age from 1900 to 1920 during a period of Republican dominance outside the still-seething Democrat South. Republicans noticed that they could no longer count on retirement communities and wondered why the older voters were turning on them. In fact we were just getting new older voters as newly retired Democrats were replacing older Republicans who passed on.

A changing electorate changes more than just the relative strength of the parties. New ideas and new taboos often enter the popular imagination, not through teaching old dogs new tricks, but teaching young dogs new tricks and waiting for the old dogs to die. Some have suggested that the civil rights movement largely erased racism from the public sphere in America, not by convincing sixty-year-old racists to abandon personal bigotry, but by teaching teenagers that racism was wrong and waiting for those new teenagers to eventually displace, demographically, their bigoted elders.

Not all political views lock in at twenty-one and remain unfazed by life's twists and turns. I once watched a highly rated "Republican" pollster explain that the country would soon become pro-abortion through the same mechanism. "See, older Americans are more pro-life, younger Americans are more pro-choice on abortion. Over time the pro-lifers die, the young pro-choicers age and the whole country will support *Roe v. Wade.*" I asked if she had tested the idea that people may tend to being pro-choice before they marry and have kids and then more pro-life later. If marriage and children changed someone's views on abortion, then the political cohort would not be marching unchanged through the years. This had not occurred to the pollster.

How the nation views "gay rights" might change if one's views are set at an earlier age—as with the rejection of racism—or they might not if they are a response to perceived cultural threats to one's own children. Sympathy with the gay community might be easier for younger, single, and urban citizens than married-with-children suburbanites.

## Today's Missing Voters

Since the Supreme Court decision *Roe v. Wade* legalized abortions in the fifty states, there have been forty million abortions in America. By definition, for every abortion there is a voter who does not enter the voting-age population eighteen years later. That voter misses an election every second year for the next sixty or seventy years. Larry Eastland wrote a provocative essay for the *American Spectator* in June 2004 entitled "The Empty Cradle Will Rock," pointing out that in the 2000 election there were 205,815,000 Americans of voting age—and 12,274,368 missing voters who were aborted between 1973 and 1982. In the 2008 election there will be 24,408,960 missing voters who were aborted between 1973 and 1990 that would otherwise have been between the ages of eighteen and thirty-seven years old.[11]

Eastland looks at polling done by Wirthlin Worldwide and examines the partisan effect of the fact that 4.48 percent of all voters were absent from the 2000 election due to previous abortions. Eastland finds that in 2000, there were 19,748,000 missing Democrats and 13,900,000 missing Republicans, or 5,848,000 net missing Democrats. Wirthlin's numbers reflect what a neutral observer might expect: Liberal Democrats are more likely to have abortions than conservative Republicans.

Planned Parenthood founder and bigot Margaret Sanger is getting exactly what she wanted, but she perhaps had not thought through the politics of her eugenicist movement.

This trend will continue with two amendments. Already, red states are more willing today to pass restrictions on abortion. Parental notification laws and restrictions on partial-birth abortions have largely passed in red states. These have caused small reductions in the abortion rates in those red states.

Looking ahead, should *Roe v. Wade* be overturned by a future Supreme Court decision, then the legality of abortion will be determined by each state. New York, California, Massachusetts, and other blue states will most likely retain extremely liberal abortion laws. It is the red states that will discourage, limit, or even criminalize abortions. While women can travel from red states to blue states to get abortions—reducing pressure to change restrictive laws in the red states—there will be a tendency to see more abortions in blue states than red states. This can be extrapolated from the experience of Mississippi, which simply required parental notification in 1993 and saw a decrease in abortions among minors of 3 percent.

## CHAPTER SIX

# THE
# POLITICAL TRAINING
# OF THE YOUNG

Politics is not wholly driven by demographics. Adding people to the voting-age population doesn't accomplish anything if they do not register to vote and then actually vote. Also, some voters are more equal than others. A voter who also contributes money, time, and activism multiplies his or her impact on an election. Morton Blackwell, a former Reagan White House staffer, now president of the Leadership Institute, correctly stresses that "a political contest is determined by the intensity and talent of the committed activists on each side."

To date, the Republican Party has been more committed to and successful at training young activists in preparation for a lifetime of political action. Because the current trend by definition extends the GOP brand into the future, it is enormously important.

## COLLEGE REPUBLICANS

Today, there are more than 200,000 members of the College Republican National Committee (CRNC) in 1,800 campus chapters. College Republicans have their own offices separate from the Republican National

Committee and raise all their own funding. In 2006, the CRNC had a national staff of over fifty and a budget of $2.3 million. College Democrats have a cubicle in the DNC offices and refer questions on their membership and number of chapters to the senior party.[1]

As of March 2007, Facebook had nineteen million college students placing their photos and short bios on their university-based websites. They report that the most frequently listed identifier is "lifeguard," and third is "College Republican." ("College Democrat" is not second.)

James Francis Burke organized the first National Convention of College Republicans in 1892 with one thousand students at the University of Michigan, where he had previously organized the nation's first College Republican chapter.[2] The keynote speaker was the governor from neighboring Ohio, William McKinley. In 1900, the College Republicans organized a get-out-the-vote drive that included sending students home to vote. They successfully targeted Democrat presidential candidate William Jennings Bryan's home precinct in Lincoln, Nebraska. (That was just mean.)[3]

In the modern era, Republicans have had significant advantages in organizing on college campuses, going back at least to the 1970s. Morton Blackwell, who was the youngest delegate for Barry Goldwater in 1964 at the age of twenty-four, served on and off as the executive director of the College Republicans from 1965 to 1970. In 1968, Blackwell held his first training program with 210 graduates. They included a young man named Mitch McConnell, who would go on to lead the effort to bring Kentucky from a Democrat Party state to a consistently Republican state and become its senior senator. Terry Branstead was a youth organizer who later served four terms as governor of Iowa. Warren Williams of Utah sent a promising nineteen-year-old to a March 1970 training program in Illinois. His name was Karl Rove.

## CRNC: Leadership History

Rove was elected chairman of the College Republican National Committee in 1973, defeating Terry Dolan, who went on to create NCPAC, the National Conservative PAC that is credited with helping swing Senate elections in 1978 and 1980. Rove was reelected unopposed in 1975. (N.b.: Karl Rove led the "liberal" wing of the Republican student movement.) Harvard student, Rove ally, and fellow Texan John Brady was elected chairman in 1977. Brady created one of the first computer programs to help run congressional races—an early political dot-commer. In 1979, Frank Lavin, who lost in a last-minute upset to Pennsylvania's Steve Gibble, went on to serve as U.S. ambassador to Singapore. In 1981, Jack Abramoff became the first Orthodox Jew elected chair of the CRNC and was reelected in 1983. Now-Congressman Phil English of Pennsylvania was the vice-chairman of the CRNC in from 1977 to 1981. Ralph Reed, later to create the Christian Coalition, was executive director in 1982. James Higgins, who now co-chairs the center-right coalition meeting in New York City, was elected co-chairman in 2003 and became chairman in 2004.

In 1980, the Reagan campaign inspired many students to create or strengthen College Republican chapters. In 1981, newly elected CR chairman Abramoff launched a national organizing campaign that sent twenty field organizers to five hundred campuses, and the number of organized campus chapters rose to one thousand and held through 1985.

Elected in 1999, Chairman Scott Stewart brought the total number of organized colleges to 1,248 clubs with 120,000 members by December 2002.[4]

In 2004, newly elected chair Eric Hoplin brought the CNRC budget to $2.4 million and built the organization up to 1,500 chapters; 150,000 members, and 56 field representatives who went campus to campus. Hoplin went on to become the deputy Republican Party chairman in Minnesota at age twenty-seven.

Paul Gourley was elected chair in 2005 and by 2006 had organized chapters on 1,820 of the 2,557 four-year colleges in America. In the fall of 2006, sixty field reps fanned out to organize campuses for the November election.

While Morton Blackwell has served as the *éminence grise* for the College Republican National Committee, he also created his own nonpartisan, conservative student-training organization, the Leadership Institute, in 1979. Just as war is too important to be left to the generals, Morton Blackwell has long understood that organizing college students is too important to the future of the conservative movement to be left to college students alone.

Over the years, the Leadership Institute has trained 51,500 students and the number of students trained each year has grown exponentially. In its first five years, 1981–1985, LI trained 1,256 students. From 2001 to 2005, it trained 20,011.[5]

The Institute began training students how to run a youth campaign parallel to and in support of congressional or gubernatorial campaigns. It now runs thirty-six different schools, everything from "How to pass the Foreign Service exam" to "How to run your life to be a candidate in ten or twenty years" to "How to start and run a conservative student newspaper," and even "How to look good on camera."

The Leadership Institute has also begun organizing independent conservative clubs on campuses. By the fall of 2006, when LI deployed sixty-four student field organizers, it had organized 1,059 such conservative groups, including 153 conservative student newspapers.

The Intercollegiate Studies Institute, captained by Ken Cribb, who served in the Reagan White House as Ed Meese's chief of staff, provides intellectual kindling to fifty thousand members, twenty thousand of whom are college and university faculty. ISI runs training programs, distributes conservative magazines and books, and sponsors more than ninety-five conservative student newspapers.

Why are the conservatives better at organizing future leaders for the Republican Party on college campuses than the Democrats? And what does this mean for the future?

Morton Blackwell offers one explanation. He points out that the Goldwater movement in 1963–1964 and the Reagan campaigns in 1976 and 1980 attracted many active conservatives to work within the Republican Party. Young, energetic, rebellious, anti-establishmentarian (i.e., anti-Rockefeller and anti-Ford and anti–Bush 41) college students found an attractive and comfortable home in the College Republicans and from there easy entry to the national party. They could rebel against their professors and the Nixon wing of the Republican Party and be safely inside the Reagan coalition.

On the left, however, the most motivated activists were of the hard left: red diaper babies and other radicals who hated LBJ first and foremost. (LBJ had the college Democrats expelled from the DNC headquarters when they passed an anti–Vietnam War resolution.) Should some establishment liberal students begin a chapter of the college Democrats it would often find itself taken over by hard-left students whose pronouncements were an embarrassment to the national Democrat Party and its candidates. National candidates and state parties found those who took over their student groups a net negative. More danger and downside than opportunity.

A stronger College Republican presence on campus in 1980, 1990, and 2000 will be felt in elections as far away as 2050. Will all the two hundred thousand College Republicans organized in 2006 remain active in Republican Party politics? No. But there are 1,800 chairmen of college chapters who have tasted political leadership and been credentialed. Eighteen hundred this year. Another 1,800 next year. Eighteen thousand campus chapter leaders over ten years. They know they don't have to ask permission to become involved in politics in years to come. They have already been elected to something. It is in their blood.

Not only are the colleges turning out more skilled Republican activists, they are graduating tougher, smarter, abler activists. Why do the deep blue zones of campus liberalism create conservative leaders? My theory is the "Boy Named Sue" phenomenon.

In Johnny Cash's song, the young man was named "Sue" by his father, who, knowing he was abandoning his family, gave his son a name that would require him to be tough as he grew to manhood. Young conservatives on any campus find themselves challenged by professors. It is easy to be a liberal and mouth politically correct platitudes. No professor asks a follow-up question in response to liberal pabulum. But suggest that property rights are important and you get twenty questions. "What if you own a plane, can you tell all the passengers at twenty thousand feet, 'Okay, you are all trespassing, get out'? Or 'What if one person owns all the water on an island?'"

I remember one night at Harvard when a leftist announced that the death marches in Phnom Penh, Cambodia, were actually the Khmer Rouge moving people to "rural hospitals." Every liberal in the room nodded and no one questioned the assertion. The editors of the *Dartmouth Review* had to go *mano a mano*, not with eighteen-year-old debate partners, but with the sixty-year-old faculty and administrators and adult journalists out to upend them. Conservative greats such as Dinesh D'Souza, Laura Ingraham, and Peter Robinson (the Reagan speechwriter who wrote the famous "Mr. Gorbachev, take down this wall" speech) were forged in this kiln.

A decade earlier the New Left inspired conservatives to organize Young Americans for Freedom (YAF), which began in the home of William F. Buckley, on September 9–11, 1960. At the founding meeting that created the iconic "Sharon statement" were Howard Phillips, Alan Mackay, David Franke, and Carol Dawson.

In 1967, R. Emmett Tyrell founded *The Alternative* magazine at the University of Indiana that in 1977 became the *American Spectator.*

Thinking they were stomping down the right, the left-wing professors and administrators have inadvertently created a liberal-resistant strain of young conservatives. They should not be surprised by the generation of Ann Coulters they toughened up. They honed those sharp edges.

And if College Republican leaders pouring out of universities will plague Democrat state legislators and congressmen for decades to come, the Federalist Society, a group of libertarian and conservative law-school students founded in 1982, is already keeping serious leftists awake at night. The Federalist Society is now organized in all of the 194 accredited law schools. By 2006, there were six thousand student members. There are also sixty Federalist Society lawyer groups that bring twenty thousand law-school graduates together in sixty cities for regularly scheduled lunches and dinners.

The Federalist Society was brought into being by founders David

McIntosh, Professor Steven Calabresi, Lee Liberman Otis, and E. Spencer Abraham. Their first executive director, now president, was Eugene Meyer, the son of famed fusionist leader Frank Meyer.

Here is the conservative and libertarian legal community whence come federal and state judges for the next century. They know one another. They have known one another since law school. They are the quality-control committee for future judges. They are unlikely to let a future Harriet Miers slip past them.

## CHAPTER SEVEN

# BAMBI IS GETTING SAFER; MUGGERS, LESS SO

> "Political power grows out of the barrel of a gun."
>
> —*Mao Tse-tung*

## THE POWER OF THE GUN

Bill Clinton blamed the National Rifle Association for winning the House of Representatives for the Republicans in 1994. Six years later he credited the gun issue with carrying Tennessee, Arkansas, and West Virginia for George W. Bush in 2000. Thus, one of the smarter Democrats credits the gun issue for winning both the House and presidency for the GOP.[1]

The electoral power of the gun issue was first recognized in the surprise defeat of Senator Joseph Tydings in Maryland after the passage of the Gun Control Act of 1968.

For years, it was less a partisan issue than a rural/urban clash. Republican president (we had lower standards back then) Gerald Ford endorsed a complete ban on inexpensive handguns known as "Saturday Night Specials." Many Democrats who represented districts with large numbers of hunters, such as John Dingell of Michigan, opposed gun control. But when Bill Clinton pushed the so-called Brady bill though Congress the vote in the House was 238–187 and in the Senate 63–36.[2] Only seventy House Democrats voted against the Brady bill and only fifty-six Republicans supported it. In the Senate, fifteen Republicans were in support and eight Democrats opposed.[3] Clinton also pushed through the so-called assault-weapons ban, a ten-year ban on rifles with certain attachments, such as a bayonet lug, that made them look cool. Opponents of the ban referred to this as the "ugly gun ban," as reportedly Senator Metzenbaum of Ohio went through a catalog and picked out the "scary"-looking ones to ban. (For the record, this was not a ban on machine guns; those are already heavily regulated.)

Of the 182 House Democrats who voted for Brady, 24 lost in 1994. Of the forty-eight Democrat Senators who voted for Brady, seven lost in 1994. Of the fifty-six Republican House members and fifteen Republican senators who voted for Brady, there were only *twenty-five House members and four senators* still in office in 2006.[4]

The number of members of the National Rifle Association moves up and down as the perceived threat to gun ownership waxes and wanes. Membership reached a peak of 4.5 million during the 2000 election. Polling data shows that 20 percent of Americans claim to be members—not just supporters, but members—of the NRA. Thirty-two percent of union members told Zogby polling that the NRA speaks for them all or most of the time.[5]

My father used to tell me about a college roommate who would drink too much on Friday night and spend Saturday and Sunday swearing off demon rum forever . . . until the next Friday when the cycle repeated itself. For some reason, Democrats are condemned like Prometheus crossed with Bill Murray in *Groundhog Day* to revisit the gun issue—and at the wrong end of the barrel. There is no sign that they have learned from being burned by the hot stove again and again.

One reason the gun issue fools Democrats over and over and over is that there has often been a split between preference and intensity. Polling data in 1988 showed that 80 percent of Americans said they were for the Brady bill, which would require a three-day waiting period to buy a gun. Eighty percent said they supported legislation to ban "assault" rifles. On Election Day the only folks who even remember how a congressman voted on gun control are those gun owners who hate gun control.

When the new Democrat majority in Congress wanted to give representation in the House of Representatives to the District of Columbia (completely unconstitutional, but whatever), the Republicans offered an amendment to abolish the District's ban on handgun ownership. Democrats once again voted lockstep against gun rights and scuttled the D.C. voting-rights bill. (Reminding the largely African-American district of their place in the Democrat pecking order—way below the suicidal losing issue of gun control.)

As 1994 and 2000 highlight, a small number of voters—2 or 3 or 4 percent of the electorate—that will switch on the gun issue alone creates a powerful group.

## Three Trends

Powerful today, will the gun vote be more powerful in the future or will it fade? There are three major trends.

First, the National Rifle Association, the nation's oldest and largest civil rights organization founded in 1871, has become increasingly competent and tough, and it is still growing. No brag, just fact. The NRA total budget has grown from $33 million in 1980 to $86.9 million in 1990, $231.8 million in 2000, and $196.8 million in 2006.

To vote for the board of directors an NRA member must be either a life member, which is a one-time $750 contribution, or be a dues-paying member for five years in a row. Those eligible to vote in the board elections were 48,091 in 1963; 110,063 in 1970; 270,113 in 1980; 1,377,276 in 1990; 1,299,360 in 2000; and 1,547,277 in 2006.[6]

There is no voluntary political organization in America with this level of commitment in its membership.

## FEWER HUNTERS

A second trend bodes poorly for the gun movement: the declining number of Americans who hunt.

The Fund for Animals is an ambitious antihunting organization that published a report in 2004 on "The State of Hunting in America" cheerfully subtitled "A Dying Sport." The fund cites a study by Decker, Enck, and Brown of Cornell University arguing that the percentage of the American population twelve years of age or older that hunts held steady at between 9 percent and 11 percent for the twenty-five years between 1955 and 1980 and then fell to 9.9 percent in 1975, 9.1 percent in 1980, and 7.5 percent in 1991. The Cornell study concludes, "The future of hunting looks bleak given prevailing social values coupled with recent and projected trends in American demographics." The study cites U.S. Fish and Wildlife Service numbers reporting that there were 16.7 million hunters age sixteen or older in the U.S. in 1985, 14 million in 1991, and 13 million by 2001.

The Fund speaks to "the long-term decline in the number of hunters, which promises an end to hunting by mid-century (2050)." Families Afield, a coalition supportive of hunting, confirms that downward trend in their study "An Initiative for the Future of Hunting." They report that "they calculate that only 69 percent of hunters over 16 are being replaced by younger hunters under sixteen."[7]

Trends continue until they don't.

Various animal-rights groups are hoping to make the decline permanent and take it to zero. "If we could shut down all sport hunting in a moment, we would," said Wayne Pacelle, current president of the Humane Society of the United States. And Cleveland Amory of The Fund for Animals explains that "hunting is an antiquated expression of macho self-aggrandizement, with no place in a civilized society."

The National Rifle Association and other prohunting groups see just this danger and are moving legislation to reverse the antihunting trend.

Kayne Robinson, president of the National Rifle Association in 2003 and 2004, pointed out that in both Britain and Australia the antihunting and antigun forces ran a determined effort to make it more difficult and more expensive to hunt and keep guns. Every hunter who dropped out became one less voice for hunting and gun rights. With fewer Brits and Aussies who cared about gun rights, a school shooting tragedy led to a total handgun ban in 1997 for the Brits. Australia banned all semiautomatic center-fire rifles, and many semiauto and pump-action shotguns, in 1996.

Robinson sees the same strategy being employed here by animal-rights activists and gun-control advocates. Hunting permits are becoming more expensive. More land is being put off limits to hunting. It is difficult for fathers to bring their sons and daughters with them hunting, and hunting permits require long training periods that stop you from being able to invite a nonhunting friend along on short notice to introduce him or her to a new sport.

Legislation supported by the NRA and enacted in four states requires that any change in state law or regulations that limits or prohibits hunting on an acre of state land must open up a compensating acre of state land for hunting. (This mirrors the very successful "No net loss of wetlands" campaign led by the environmentalists in the 1980s.)

Forty-six states have passed laws protecting rifle ranges from abusive lawsuits trying to shut them down because of "noise pollution."

The NRA is working to change the laws to allow hunters under sixteen to accompany hunting parents. This is forbidden in twenty states and limited in others.

And the NRA is working to simplify the requirements for a hunter license. When I got my Virginia hunter-safety license it required sixteen hours of course time. Two four-hour evening classes and a third eight-hour full-day class, little of which necessary for hunting-safety instruction. The movies of charging Cape buffalo were cool, but I have encountered few in Virginia during turkey season.

The NRA has campaigned successfully to enact laws in fifty states that criminalize efforts by the animal-rights crowd to interfere with hunting parties.

While the battle to decide whether the decline in hunting acceler-
ates or is reversed continues, there is another trend affecting gun
ownership: the growing number of Americans who can and do legally
carry a weapon for self-defense.

## CONCEALED-CARRY LAWS

In 1987, Florida gained national attention by passing "shall issue"
concealed-carry legislation that instructed state and local officials to
grant a permit to carry a concealed weapon to any citizen who was
twenty-one years old, not crazy or a criminal, and had passed a safety
course.

As of December 2006, thirty-six states had passed "shall issue"
concealed-carry laws giving their citizens the right to carry a gun
concealed on their person or in a vehicle.

Alabama, Connecticut, and Iowa have concealed-carry permits
that are granted under "fairly administered" rules, but still at the dis-
cretion of the government. Only two states, Illinois and Wisconsin,
prohibit all concealed carry. In other states like Massachusetts and
New York, the law is "may issue," meaning the decision to grant a
concealed-carry permit is up to the local law-enforcement officers, a
sheriff, or police chief. So in Boston and New York City, the mayors'
friends get guns. In Republican suburbs and rural areas, the local
police chief is more likely to grant permit requests. The liberals who
set this up have disarmed the Democrat cities and armed the Republican suburbs and exurbs. Interesting strategic thinking on their part.

Alaska and Vermont allow their citizens to carry a gun without any
permit other than that granted by the Constitution. One can get a
government-issued permit if one wishes, so that it can receive reci-
procity from other states, but none is required for citizens within
Vermont or Alaska.

Since Florida's law was liberalized in 1987, fully 1.1 million permits
have been issued there. (Some citizens move or allow their permit to
lapse over time.) Permit holders are extremely responsible. Just 158

or .01 percent of all permits have been revoked for any type of firearms violation. Even this low number exaggerates the risks, as almost
all of these were for nonthreatening incidents such as accidentally
carrying a gun into a restricted area such as an airport.[8]

Texas has 247,345 active concealed-carry licenses; North Carolina,
59,597, or 1 percent of adults; Virginia, 296,728, representing 2.3 percent of the adult population.[9] There are today 412,825 valid concealed-
carry permits in Florida. This is 2.9 percent of the adult population.[10]
A relatively lazy mugger working to union rules who only mugs one
Floridian a day would find himself (or perhaps herself) at the wrong
end of a pistol once every thirty-seven days.[11] This higher risk of retirement through gunshot has been a measurable disincentive to robbers, rapists, and murderers. John Lott's famous study encompassing
every county in the United States has found that those states that
passed concealed-carry laws have had 5 percent fewer rapes, 8.5 percent fewer murders, and 7 percent fewer assaults than would have
happened without the concealed-carry laws.[12]

Making it easier for citizens to lawfully carry firearms to defend
themselves has reduced crime. Crime can be further reduced by passing concealed carry in more states and making the permits good for
life, recognized nationwide, just like a state marriage license or driver's license, and lowering the cost of the license.

Seventeen states have now passed "Castle Doctrine" laws that legally protect citizens who use deadly force in protecting themselves
from attack. Courts have ruled in the past that you were required to
retreat, even in your own home, in the face of an attacker and could
only shoot a robber, rapist, or would-be murderer if you were cor-
nered. Now in states that enact the "Castle Doctrine," the moment an
attacker threatens you or your children, you have the legal right to use
deadly force—your shotgun, handgun, a baseball bat—to protect
yourself and your family.[13] With clearer legal protection Americans
will feel safer buying a gun to protect their families.

The left came close to crippling the gun-manufacturing industry
in America during the Clinton administration when Andrew
Cuomo, the secretary of HUD, and a collection of Democrat mayors

# Right to Carry Laws 2006

**Right to Carry States (40)**
Shall Issue (36 Incl. AK)
Discretionary-Reasonable Issue (3)
No Permit Required (2 VT & AK)

**Non-Right to Carry States (10)**
Right Restricted-Very Limited Issue (8)
Right Infringed / Non Issue (2)

Alaska does not require a permit but
has a shall-issue permit system.

*National Rifle Association Institute for Legislative Action. Used with
permission.*

sued gun manufacturers, arguing that Smith and Wesson should be
held responsible for the criminal misuse of handguns. The tobacco
lawsuits had made Democrat trial lawyers rich. The gun lawsuits
hoped to enact policy that the left could never win through the legislative process.

In response to this legal assault, the NRA worked successfully to
have thirty-five state legislatures pass laws forbidding such lawsuits.
Three states had already passed similar laws in the mid-1980s. Congress passed a nationwide ban in October of 2005. This required a
sixty-vote supermajority in the Senate to defeat the Democrat filibuster. (So much for the idea that Democrats have finally learned to
avoid the gun-control issue.) In comparison, the effort to reform Social Security or abolish the death tax or drill for more oil in ANWR in
Alaska, which had active support from the president, could not win

## Castle Doctrine: Protecting Our Right to Self-Defense

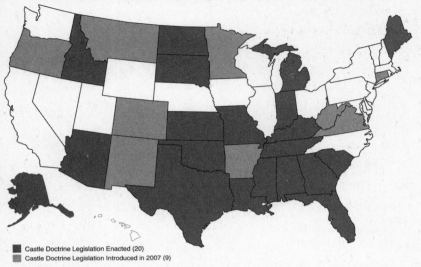

■ Castle Doctrine Legislation Enacted (20)
■ Castle Doctrine Legislation Introduced in 2007 (9)

*National Rifle Association Institute for Legislative Action. Used with permission.*

sixty votes. From time to time the nice folks at the Chamber of Commerce belittle the social issues and suggest that corporate lobbyists are the real powers in the corridors of Washington, D.C. Compare for a moment how little success the entire business community has had fighting the trial lawyers, who have looted business of tens of billions of dollars, with the Second Amendment community's defeat of the trial lawyers.

Who wields power in America?

The Clinton administration wanted to reduce the number of gun voters and aggressively used its control over the bureaucracy to reduce the number of those legally allowed to sell guns. There were 281,000 Federal Firearms Licensees in 1993. This was dropped to 89,000 by 1996 as a result of a deliberate campaign of harassment. The cost of the FFLs was increased by fiat from $90 to $200, and the Clinton BATF sent threatening letters to FFLs and to city authorities suggesting that the licensees were violating zoning laws by running a business out of their home.[14]

Under the Bush administration that harassment has reduced somewhat, but surprisingly has not ended. The number of FFLs had continued falling to 66,651 by September 2005.[15] Overall, the effect has been dramatic. Kmart no longer sells guns, Wal-Mart just recently stopped selling guns at a third of its stores, and tens of thousands of other gun shops have gone out of business.

One attack by the antigunners shows great political insight, but lacked the political muscle to win. John McCain was bitter that the NRA opposed the Feingold-campaign finance-reform legislation that McCain had attached his name to in an attempt to put his participation in the Keating Five scandal behind him. In retribution, McCain wanted to punish gun owners. He led the fight to "close the gun show loophole." The "loophole" was that the law that required an instant check when you buy a gun from a gun store does not apply to citizens who sell their own personal guns to a neighbor, friend, or acquaintance, or someone at a gun show. The frequent delays in getting an answer from the "instant" check would make it impossible for most gun shows to have citizens display and sell their own firearms. The states with these regulations have seen up to a 25 percent reduction in the number of gun shows relative to other states without the rules.[16]

But damaging gun shows was a bigger prize for McCain and the antigun forces than simply screwing a few gun owners who could not sell their own property. Gun shows are the mega-churches of the gun culture. McCain was targeting the ability of gun owners to meet, organize, and discuss the antigun positions of politicians such as, say, Senator John McCain.

Europeans looking to explain America's support for the Second Amendment often point out that Americans own more than 250 million guns, or that nearly half of households have guns, or that millions of Americans hunt.[17]

But the relevant number today and twenty-five years from now is the number of Americans who will cast their vote in defense of their Second Amendment rights. For that purpose the growing number of Americans with a concealed-carry permit suggests growing strength for the "progun community." A hunter may take out his

shotgun or rifle once each year for his or her favorite hunting season. But someone used to the security of carrying a firearm in his or
her car or purse is unlikely ever to give that up. The intensity of the
gun vote will likely increase with the number of states with concealed carry and the growing number of citizens availing themselves
of that right.

## CHAPTER EIGHT

# BACK TO EUROPE OR FORWARD TO AMERICA

## THE DEPENDENCY TRAP

The goal of the modern Democrat Party is to maximize the number of Americans who believe they are totally dependent on politics for some key zone in life: their retirement income, their children's education, their health care, or their parents' health care, housing, food stamps, or even their employment. The greater the number of dependent Americans, the stronger the left. The goal of the Republican Party is to reduce the number of Americans who need such aid and see the government as their parent.

Here the two parties are, once again, completely at odds. They are not trying to do the same thing in different ways. They have opposite, and conflicting, goals.

That is what the fight over Bill and Hillary's effort to nationalize health care in 1993 and 1994 was all about. The Clintons wanted to take over the half of health-care spending not already run by government. The Clintons' goal was not to reduce the cost of health care or make it more widely available. That could have been easily done in a bipartisan effort. Republicans have argued for years that we should pass medical malpractice reform to stop trial lawyers from driving up the cost of health care. Conservatives have advocated for reducing the cost of health insurance by repealing state laws that force consumers to buy "gold plated" coverage that includes many mandatory "services" such as drug rehab or sex changes, which citizens might be willing to take a pass on in return for lower insurance rates. Republicans have long supported tax credits for the poor to pay for their own health care and for health savings accounts. No deal.

No, the Democrats did not want to reduce the cost of health insurance with free-market responses that would make every American more independent, more in control of his or her health care and its costs. They wanted to make more Americans dependent on the government for their health care. They wanted government control over health care and then they would ration it.

Their model was and is the European welfare state, where the government is responsible for your health care, your education, your pension, and, for much of the workforce, your job. Would you want to stand up against that government? This is why there are no free-market political parties in Europe. Conservative parties, yes. American-style, Reagan conservative parties, no. If a European was to fight for limited government the politicians would quietly explain, "If you don't give us more money and control over your life we can and will take away your job, or your mother's health care, or your dad's pension or maybe your housing subsidy or your children's education. Do you really want to wait even longer for a CAT scan?" Who can stand up to that? They don't in Europe. There has not been a major governing party in a European nation dedicated to reducing the size and scope of government and empowering citizens to take care of themselves since Margaret Thatcher left Number 10 Downing Street in 1990. "Conservative" parties in Europe have been reduced to arguing that they can run the present bureaucracy more efficiently. Or they have turned themselves into nationalist parties arguing to keep the swarthy-looking foreigners out of their wonderful welfare state. That's it. Our welfare state would work flawlessly if everyone in our country was blond.

The future envisioned by the American left can be glimpsed in Europe today. Near-guaranteed job security and unemployment payments almost as high as the after-tax pay for work. This in return for a lower standard of living: only 74 percent of America's per-capita GDP. More security and less innovation. Everyone will be more equal. Poorer all, but more equally poor. Little chance to create tremendous wealth, but also little chance that your neighbor will make you feel bad by creating the next Microsoft while you were in the pub.

We do not have to guess at the costs of trading liberty for security. Moving from an opportunity society to a welfare state. In 1960, the fifteen members of the European Union had government spending at 26 percent of GDP. The United States was spending 25 percent—including shouldering Europe's defense as well as our own. As Europe built its welfare states, and reduced defense spending, the EU-15 average level of government spending went to 45 percent while the United States' rose to 33 percent.[1]

Bigger government and a cushier welfare state slowed the growth of the EU-15 compared to America. From 1994 to 2004 America grew at a average annual rate of 3.3 percent, the EU-15 at 2.2 percent. Over time the slower growth brought per-capita GDP for the EU-15 to $28,700. The American average of $39,700 is 40 percent more. Unemployment in the EU was 8 percent in August 2006, while it was 4.7 percent in America. And of those without jobs, in America only 12.7 percent of the unemployed had been without work for twelve months. In Europe it was 42.6 percent. This is fodder for creating an underclass that votes rather than works for a living.[2]

Given present trends, if there were no economic growth in the United States it would still take Europe eighteen years to catch up to American income levels, fourteen years to reach American productivity levels, and twenty-six years to reach U.S. employment levels.[3] But of course, America is not standing still. We will continue to put distance between us and Europe. Unless. Unless the Takings Coalition can grab power and put us on Europe's path to dependency and stagnation. The European model is the Takings Coalition's goal. A dependent, static society that votes to keep in power the dispensers of government favors. A sad warning from the "Ghost of Christmas Future" comes from Canada, where a poll showed that 45 percent of Canadians who were waiting for health care described themselves as being "in pain."[4] The government takes over health care, rations it, and its subjects—no longer citizens—beg for their rations. Do we wish to replace the American dream with the Canadian dream of shorter waiting periods to get health care?

One need not fly to Europe to see the liberal welfare state future. A citizen in a European welfare state lives life as an American would if he never left high school. Groundhog Day as junior year in high school. Graduation never comes. Teachers and school administrators demand little of you. Mom and Dad feed and house you. You have lots of activities to keep you busy. Motion without any forward movement. They do seem to take attendance a lot and have a bunch of silly rules. Pride in individual achievement is replaced with a false pride of school spirit. Our team is better than their team. One never grows up and leaves the nest. But the nest is warm and comfortable and not demanding. And it looks so scary out there. As Dan Aykroyd in *Ghostbusters* warns of life in the private sector: "They demand results."

Europe revels in the sorts of freedoms that are to be found in a well-run high school. Sex without consequences. Naughty words can be used without censure. One can converse at length of one's outlandish hopes and desires without anyone ever asking, "So what are you doing to achieve that?" Criticism of others is seen as cleverness. Whining replaces work.

So will America become more dependent on welfare or less? More Democrat or more Republican? Before 1996, many Republicans believed we were in a permanent slide toward more dependency. The Democrats were changing America, changing the electorate by making them more dependent on government.

The left has a good head start in trying to make a functioning majority of Americans see themselves as dependent on the government. The construction of this Venus flytrap for once-independent men and women, this enticing lazychair covered with superglue, this Faustian bargain where one trades one's independence for security and barters with the state for one's vote rather than competing in the market with one's work and talents, has taken a great deal of time and effort.

The number of Americans receiving welfare payments through the old AFDC program grew from 3 million in 1960 to 8.5 million in 1970 and 10.5 million in 1980 and 11.5 million in 1990.[5] Medicaid, begun in 1965, was at first providing taxpayer-subsidized health care to five hundred thousand low-income Americans. This jumped to 17.3 million by 1970; 21.6 million in 1980; 36.3 million in 1995; 44.5 million in 2000; and 54.6 million in 2004.[6] Food stamps began in 1939, subsidizing 4.3 million Americans in 1970; 21 million in 1980; 20 million in 1990; 17.2 million in 2000; and 25.5 million in 2006.[7]

A 2007 study by economist Gary Schilling found that 52.6 percent of Americans receive "significant" income from government programs. Including dependents as beneficiaries, Schilling reports 20 percent of Americans work for their government, 20 percent live off government pensions, nineteen million get food stamps, two million receive subsidized housing, and five million receive education grants. The percentage of Americans "dependent on government" went from 23.8 percent in 1950 to 55 percent in 1980, then down to 52.6 percent in 2006.[8]

Some libertarians count the number of Americans getting government checks and project that they are all lost to the statist team. But Americans who worked all their lives and receive a Social Security check each month do not believe that the government is giving them anything. True, the money they are getting is not directly related to the taxes they paid and they are indirectly looting their children and grandchildren every month. But they have been told all their lives that the government was saving their Social Security taxes for them and they do not see themselves as getting something for nothing. Ditto, Medicare. This is why Democrats are frustrated with Medicare and Social Security recipients. They are insufficiently appreciative. They don't think they are being given things by the politicians. They were told their Medicare and Social Security FICA taxes were covering the costs of their retirement and health care in old age. Hence the Democrat call in the Clinton years to "cut and invest." Cut the benefits to Social Security and Medicare beneficiaries who ungratefully do not vote as if they were on welfare and "invest" those now-available dollars in more productive government programs that will command votes in return. Welfare, food stamps, housing subsidies, and Medicaid are not "earned" or "paid for" by taxpayers. They are given by politicians in return for expected political support.

Jack Kemp explains that the compassion of a society is not measured by how many people are on welfare, but by how few people need welfare.[9] It is also a good measure of how successful the Republican Party will be in winning votes.

A man with a job, better yet, a self-employed man or woman, who created his own job, does not need the government's "help." He stands up straight and independent. Any politician who said, vote for me or you will be poor, you won't eat, and you won't have a house would be spat upon.

Welfare reform as passed in 1996 shows that we can reform welfare programs and turn back the level of dependence. How did we do it? Ronald Reagan called for welfare reform in 1970 and was alone among the fifty governors in supporting such reform. It took twenty-six years for his ideas, first pushed in California by his welfare director, Robert B. Carleson, to become law.

Michael Barone, author and political analyst, told this author that one of the reasons the Democrats hated Newt Gingrich even before he took away their House majority was that he "refused to grant them moral superiority." The old Republican model began the conversation conceding that "the Democrats are trying to help poor people, but this welfare spending is very expensive and we Republicans would suggest that we spend less and help poor people less." The Democrats responded by thanking the Republicans for recognizing the Democrats' moral superiority. They would then greatly increase welfare, but not as much as they first suggested so that they could explain to the welfare recipients, "You are getting this money over the objections of the Republicans and courtesy of us. Remember this on Election Day."

Newt Gingrich broke the rules, armed with the accumulation of serious studies of the effects of welfare by scholars such as Charles

Murray, author of *Losing Ground*. Gingrich pointed out that the welfare programs were damaging the individuals and families they were supposed to help. Professor Walter Williams exposed that taxpayers were spending significant amounts of money on poor people in America and little of that was actually getting to poor folks. It was actually used to finance "overhead," meaning great numbers of Democrat precinct workers and contributors whose job was to manage welfare. The real welfare queens were not on welfare, they ran it—and also ran the lives of millions into the ground.

The new argument was: "Year after year you Democrats are enriching your unionized government employees while damaging the families of the poor, locking them into welfare dependency generation after generation. We are going to stop you from hurting more people." Now the Democrats were not expensive philanthropists. They were bad people, knowingly and contemptuously doing bad things to poor folks with other people's money.

Gingrich dramatized this in his speeches with a thought experiment. Imagine two Korean cousins arriving in Los Angeles. One is met by a government welfare worker who explains all the wonderful benefits that exist for this new American—housing subsidies, job training, food stamps. The second cousin is met by a relative who explains that he cannot pay him minimum wage, he can sleep in the back of the store, and will need to hold down two jobs.

Fast-forward twenty-five years. Which brother, the one helped by the government welfare system or the one who avoided all government help, owns his own home? Which one has a child in college? Which one is wealthier? Healthier? And why are we as taxpayers funding a set of government programs that we know makes people worse off?

The 1996 welfare reform was passed twice and was twice vetoed by Bill Clinton before his adviser Dick Morris suggested that Paris was worth a mass and Clinton signed the measure the third time it passed on August 22, 1996.

The number of families on Aid to Familes with Dependent Children (AFDC), renamed Temporary Assistance for Needy Families

(TANF), fell from 4.3 million to 1.89 million.[10] The littering of the streets with the bodies of the starving poor promised by "moderates" who spoke and voted against welfare reform never came to pass.

One of the great failures of the Bush administration, both policy and political, was the failure for five years to extend the welfare reform when its five-year authorization lapsed in 2001. If the 2002 or 2004 election had been held in the light of a knock-down, drag-out fight over Welfare Reform Two, there would be more Republicans in the House and Senate and a much more popular president. A national debate on welfare reform would have moved votes more than Bush's impersonation of the mayor of Baghdad. Eventually, without a public fight, welfare reform was strengthened and extended for another five years beginning in January 2006. Few read about it. Fewer noticed.

The use of dependency as a political tool is not lost on the Democrats. In 2005, a College Republican attended a College Democrat convention. There he was lectured that the best way to register Democrats to vote was to go to the grocery stores the days immediately after welfare checks arrive in certain neighborhoods and register potential voters.

Senator John McCain offered an amendment in 1993 to the Motor Voter Act to forbid anyone from registering to vote at a place where they receive government money to eliminate the idea that one was being paid to vote. This was voted down by a wise Democrat Senate majority, unanimously.

If nothing is changed, the various welfare programs will simply grow, creating more dependency and Democrats.

But the welfare-reform model can be applied to all such means-tested welfare programs. The free-market economist Peter Ferrara, who led in promoting such ideas as enterprise zones, health savings accounts, and the privatization of Social Security, has pointed out that the next wave for Republican reformers is to reform all welfare programs using the reform of 1996 as a model.

There are dozens of means-tested federal programs. Medicaid, food stamps, and housing subsidies are simply the largest. If they were block-granted to the states with a commitment to increase the block grant at the rate of inflation, then they would not grow as a percentage of the economy. States would be allowed to experiment just as they did with welfare reform. Block-granting and limiting the growth of these programs to the inflation rate would save more than a trillion dollars over ten years. Democrats lost their ability to claim the world would end with such a reform. They shot their wad in welfare reform—now recognized as the most successful federal government initiative since . . . well, there haven't been many.

## CHAPTER NINE

# "HE WAS HOMESCHOOLED"

## THE GROWTH OF HOMESCHOOLING

Michael Farris founded the Home School Legal Defense Association in 1983 and served as its president through 2000. He chairs the group today. He built up the HSLDA to an association of eighty thousand sets of parents. He estimates that there are six hundred thousand sets of parents homeschooling two million students, or 4 percent of school-age children, in the United States.[1]

"If this trend were to continue at a modest 7 percent annual growth rate," said Brian D. Ray, president of the National Home Education Research Institution in Salem, Oregon, "about 3 million students would be home-educated during the fall of 2010."

Farris is the founder and current chancellor of Patrick Henry College, which provides a college education focused on the graduates of homeschooling households. The college began with 92 students in its first year and had 260 in its 2006 entering class.

Farris points out that in the 1950s homeschooling was frequently pursued by countercultural parents on the left who found the flag-saluting, public-praying government schools offensive. Today it is mostly religious parents, predominantly Protestant but also Roman Catholic, Jewish, and Muslim parents, who opt to homeschool. These are generally two-parent families where one parent makes the sacrifice to stay home and educate the children, a task that the government has offered to do for "free." One can begin to understand the level of personal and political commitment that can be found in the homeschooling ranks when it is pointed out that in all fifty states the homeschooling movement had first to take on and defeat the teachers unions, which view homeschooling as a threat to their union dues.[2]

In 1979, the largest teachers union, the National Education Association, wanted a national department of education. The AFL-CIO was aligned with the smaller American Federation of Teachers and opposed the new department. The NEA defeated the AFL-CIO, foreshadowing the coming dominance of government-worker unions over traditional industrial unions.

Homeschoolers beat the guys who beat the AFL-CIO.

Fast-forward to 1993 and the homeschool movement flexed its muscle in self-defense, responding to a perceived threat of government regulation. When a homeschooler brought to Congressman Dick Armey's attention that a proposed bill might—just might—open the door to federal regulation of homeschooling, it kicked off the largest firestorm in modern congressional history. This was before e-mail and faxes had replaced snail mail as the preferred method for communication with organized constituents. Faxes went out to the homeschool network on Monday, and the next day the phone lines in the capital were jammed to the point that offices sent runners with written messages to other offices. Within three days the Congress voted unanimously to strike the potentially offending passage. This is political power.

Every year there will be more homeschoolers. And they are smarter, harder-working, and more serious than the products of government schools.

The children of homeschooling have not been socialized to believe in the sanctity of government education. They begin life as skeptics of the competence and necessity of government. Their parents have said no to the offer no one is supposed to refuse "We will educate, at least baby-sit, your children for 'free' for twelve years."

As government schools spend an average of $9,000 per student in 2005, the two million children schooled at home each save taxpayers $108,000 between kindergarten and twelfth grade.[3] Two million students and six hundred thousand sets of parents growing at an estimated 7 percent a year is a political force that greatly strengthens the Leave Us Alone Coalition.[4] It is difficult to see how the Democrats can outlaw homeschooling. The movement is too large to crush. And there is nothing the left can offer families willing to make such sacrifices in order to avoid being "helped" by the state.

Years ago, conservative activist Morton Blackwell told this writer that he should meet with a young activist, but Morton warned, "He was homeschooled." This was to alert me to the idea that he might not be completely "socialized." That concern has been a roadblock to faster growth in homeschooling.

One might wonder where we got the idea that having a bunch of five-, ten-, or fifteen-year-olds hanging out together where they vastly outnumber adults would provide positive socialization. Maybe people don't read *Lord of the Flies* anymore in the government schools. Nowhere else in life are we organized by age cohort. How is such segregation useful in public schools? What does it prepare one for?

Parents who worry about too little socialization are quick to fear "peer pressure," which is Latin for socialization by one's age group.

But the data are in. Brian Ray's study of young adults who were homeschooled demonstrates that homeschooled citizens are more civically active and engaged. Fourteen percent of homeschoolers between ages eighteen and twenty-four have worked for a political candidate, compared with 1 percent of those not homeschooled. As you can easily see, this 14:1 ratio is good news for the Leave Us Alone Coalition. Seventy-six percent of young men and women who were homeschooled vote in elections compared to only 29 percent of others. Think of homeschooling as a very long-term get-out-the-vote campaign. Ten percent of homeschoolers now eighteen to twenty-four have contributed to a candidate or party, compared to only 3 percent of others.[5]

Perhaps surprisingly, given the social conservative background of many of today's homeschoolers, when asked, "Should a person be allowed to make a speech against church and religion?" some 91.5 percent of homeschoolers say yes, compared to only 88 percent of others.[6]

And homeschooling families have an average of 3.9 children—twice the national average.[7]

## CHAPTER TEN

# TAKING THE KING'S SHILLING: FRIENDS OF GOVERNMENT

The number of government workers has been growing, and the advantages in pay and benefits that government workers have over private-sector workers is increasing.

This is good news for the Takings Coalition.

The good news for the Leave Us Alone Coalition is that it is unlikely that the taxpayers will allow this to continue.

In 2004, the average federal employee earned $100,178 in wages and benefits. That year, the average worker in the private sector earned $51,876 in wages and benefits.[1] Federal government compensation per employee grew 115 percent from 1990 to 2004 while compensation in the private sector grew only 69 percent. This explains the August 30, 2006, headline in the *Washington Post*, D.C. SUBURBS TOP LIST OF RICHEST COUNTIES.

Oversized government is an international phenomenon. Former Israeli prime minister Benjamin Netanyahu tells the now-famous "story of the fat man and the thin man." There is an exercise in Israeli boot camp where each soldier is required to take the soldier to his right onto his back and run a hundred yards. In the story, the soldier who had a smaller-built Yemeni to carry won the race. The soldier who was standing next to the fat man and tried to carry that load could not finish the race.

Netanyahu's point was that the Israeli government had become a fat man and that the private-sector economy could no longer carry and still run the race. In the United States, we have two obesity challenges. Our children eat too many Doritos and our government employees are way out of our financial weight class.

State and local government workers increased in number from 13.9 million in 1994 to 15,788,000 in 2004.[2] In 2005, those paid with tax dollars earned $36 per hour in wages and benefits. In that same hour, those paying the taxes in the private sector earned $24.

Back in 1950, the average taxpayer earned $222 more in total compensation than the average state and local employee. By 1960, the private-sector worker was $350 ahead. In 1969, the advantage flipped to state and local government workers by $50. By 1981, the government employer's annual advantage was $153; by 1983, it was $1,032; and by 2002, it was $3,924.[3]

Government pensions are usually indexed to inflation. Federal workers have an "involuntary separation" rate—layoffs—that is one-quarter of the private sector's.

An Alabama Policy Institute study by Wendell Cox compared public and private compensation and found that full-time state employees spent 10 percent fewer hours on their job for their pay than private employees. They used twice as many sick days. Private-sector workers in Alabama who pay the taxes for the state workers were working on average a month per year more than the state workers they subsidized. Over a career, an Alabama state employee receives an estimated $350,000 more in wages and benefits than the equally educated and skilled employee working the same number of hours in the private sector.[4]

How much time and effort would the rational state employee put into politics to maintain this advantage over the serfs who keep him in the style to which he has become accustomed? How hard did the French aristocracy fight to keep their privileged existence?

The "excess cost" of state-employee compensation costs taxpayers in Alabama between $295 and $360 million each year.[5]

Much of the growth in pay and benefits for government workers has been hidden in promised pensions and health-care benefits. State and local governments have more than $700 billion in unfunded pension liabilities and $1.4 trillion in unfunded health-care liabilities for retired government workers.[6] New accounting rules coming into full effect in 2007 require state and local governments to make these costly and heretofore secret political promises transparent.

The goal for taxpayers is to reduce this disparity in pay and pensions to zero. Fairness demands that the government not be used to transfer wealth from taxpayers to a protected class of government workers who are paid more, work less, and retire with unheard-of benefits and pensions paid for by taxpayers.

This sheer cost of each government employee both in wages and benefits today and in pension and health-care spending in retirement has begun to price new hires out of the market. When the United Auto Workers priced their workers out of the market, people stopped buying American cars and the number of autoworkers dropped.

State and local governments are monopolies. This has protected them for decades. But there are limits to that monopoly power. Some states have smaller burdens than others. Who will stay forever in Louisiana, where 14.6 percent of the workforce works for the state and local government, when New Hampshire will only make you pay for 9.8 percent government workers? Taxpayers can and do leave New York State with a 13.4 percent government worker burden or the District of Columbia with a 16.2 percent of all the workforce on the taxpayer nickel.

Government workers' gold-plated contracts also find competition from the private sector. Cities, states, and the federal government are increasingly outsourcing various jobs to the private sector. Why should the fellow who picks up your trash or cuts the grass at City Hall or serves food at the school cafeteria be a government worker who cannot be fired, is paid more than his neighbor for similar work, and carries the price tag of a gold-plated packet of benefits and an endlessly growing pension?

There is also an opportunity to painlessly downsize government as there is a bulge of highly paid government workers becoming eligible for retirement. The Office of Personnel Management (OPM) estimates that three hundred thousand federal employees, 16.2 percent of the federal workforce, are projected to retire by 2010.[7] In the 1980s, the Fortune 500 slashed middle management, laying off a great number of white-collar fifty-year-olds who expected lifetime employment in their company. It was painful, but it made American companies competitive worldwide. We have the opportunity to similarly reform government middle management simply by replacing only every second or third retiree. No layoffs would be necessary. Governor Tim Pawlenty of Minnesota has worked to make his state government more effective by simply replacing only every second retiree.

Of course, Hillary Clinton sees this trend as reducing the number of Democrat precinct workers on the taxpayer gravy train and she is pushing in the opposite direction. Campaigning for president in early 2007, she demanded that five hundred thousand jobs that the federal government had contracted out to the private sector—saving taxpayers billions of dollars—be brought back into the cocoon of government pay, government pensions, government benefits, and home to the Takings Coalition.

## STATE AND LOCAL GOVERNMENT
## EMPLOYMENT IN 1994 AND 2004[8]

|  | 1994 | 2004 | CHANGE |
|---|---|---|---|
| **U.S. Total** | 13,912,227 | 15,788,184 | 13 percent |
| **Education** | 7,098,807 | 8,538,180 | 20 percent |
| K-12 schools | 5,310,339 | 6,473,425 | 22 percent |
| Higher education | 1,586,663 | 1,848,997 | 17 percent |

|  | 1994 | 2004 | CHANGE |
|---|---|---|---|
| Other | 201,805 | 215,758 | 7 percent |
| **Safety** | 1,925,986 | 2,323,323 | 21 percent |
| Police | 749,308 | 892,426 | 19 percent |
| Corrections | 584,387 | 701,905 | 20 percent |
| Judicial and legal | 321,168 | 409,944 | 28 percent |
| Fire | 271,123 | 319,048 | 18 percent |
| **Welfare** | 2,123,500 | 2,038,584 | −4 percent |
| Hospitals | 1,053,356 | 912,496 | −13 percent |
| Public welfare | 492,387 | 498,092 | 1 percent |
| Health | 360,694 | 424,158 | 18 percent |
| Housing & development | 123,173 | 114,281 | −7 percent |
| Social insurance admin. | 93,890 | 89,557 | −5 percent |
| **Services** | 1,701,548 | 1,766,101 | 4 percent |
| Highways | 544,233 | 542,642 | 0 percent |
| Parks and recreation | 239,605 | 262,815 | 10 percent |
| Transit | 205,994 | 231,897 | 13 percent |
| Natural resources | 187,432 | 186,006 | −1 percent |
| Water supply | 153,143 | 162,251 | 6 percent |
| Sewerage | 121,594 | 126,136 | 4 percent |

| | 1994 | 2004 | CHANGE |
|---|---|---|---|
| Solid waste | 110,156 | 108,882 | −1 percent |
| Other | 139,156 | 145,472 | 5 percent |
| | | | |
| **Other** | 1,062,386 | 1,122,596 | 6 percent |

## CHAPTER ELEVEN

# FINDING MORE VOTERS: INCREASING TURNOUT, VOTING THE PRISONS, AND VOTER FRAUD

In 2000, there were 209,128,094 Americans over the age of eighteen and therefore eligible to vote.[1] Of those only 159,076,685 registered to vote and only 106,913,005 voted. In 2002, 70 percent of eligible voters registered and 37 percent voted. In 2004, 77 percent of eligible voters registered and 122,286,610, or 72 percent, of registered voters actually voted.

The establishment media wrote a great deal about how 2002 and 2004 were "base" elections where Republicans and Democrats were concentrating not on motivating independent or middle-of-the-road voters but focused on bringing their ideological brethren, who had failed to vote in the past, kicking and screaming or, preferably cheerful and highly motivated, to the polls on Election Day.

In 2000, the Bush campaign looked at the late polls and believed they had a five-point lead and that Florida was safe for Bush. On Election Day, the Democrats did a better job of GOTV (Getting Out the Vote), and Gore won the popular vote by 543,816, and instead of losing Florida by five points he lost it by 537 votes.

In 2002, determined that they would not be outhustled again, Karl Rove, Ken Mehlman, and the national Republican Party transferred resources and focus to the "72 Hour" program that focused on identifying potential Republican voters, getting them registered, and to the polls.

In 2004, both parties pushed hard to increase turnout. Republicans thought they had been outworked in 2000. Democrats knew the Republicans' reaction to 2000 had helped their turnout enough in 2002 to gain Republican seats in the House and Senate in an off-year election when tradition would have suggested losses. In 2004, the total Bush vote increased by 22.96 percent (from 50,460,110 in 2000 to 62,040,610 in 2004). The Kerry vote was 15.74 percent higher than Al Gore's "winning" 2000 vote total (59,028,444 votes over Gore's 51,003,926).[2]

The *New York Times Magazine* commissioned a long article profiling the key Get Out the Vote leader for the Kerry campaign. Writing for a magazine rather than a newspaper, they avoided a DEWEY DEFEATS TRUMAN headline, but the fact that the *NYT* focused on Steve Bouchard rather than his Republican counterpart suggests that the writer assumed the Democrats' higher turnout would win Ohio and thus the presidency. He was not alone. On Election Day, when reports came in to Kerry headquarters that Ohio Democrats were hitting their targeted Get Out the Vote numbers in the cities of Cincinnati and Cleveland, they assumed the election was won.

But Republican turnout in Ohio jumped from 2,351,209 in 2000 to 2,859,768 in 2004, defeating the Democrats who turned out 2,186,190 votes in 2000 and 2,741,167 in 2004.[3]

In other key states, Florida Republicans increased turnout by 36 percent (from 2,912,790 to 3,964,522), and Florida Democrats by 23 percent (from 2,912,253 to 3,583,544). West Virginia Republican turnout was up 26 percent (from 336,475 to 423,778) and Democrat turnout was up 10.5 percent (from 295,497 to 326,541).[4]

Two *Los Angeles Times* political reporters, Tom Hamburger and Peter Wallsten, have written a solid book, *One Party Country*, arguing that the Republicans have a strong lead in voter identification and therefore GOTV efforts in the foreseeable future. They dedicate an entire chapter to the Republican "voter vault."[5]

A May 2006 study by the Democrat Leadership Council reached the same conclusion. Authored by Ed Kilgore, the study examined two theories of how the Democrat Party can recover its status as the governing majority party. The first argument is that the growing number of Hispanics combined with "the assumption that Republican politics will continue to keep minority voters, unmarried women, and socially moderate professionals disproportionately in the Democrat column" will be enough for Democrats to win in the future. The second theory is that "perfecting state-of-the-art voter mobilization techniques and making heavy investment in the infrastructure for maximizing 'base' turnout" can boost the Democrat vote sufficiently to create a national majority." "This theory," Kilgore points out, "is typically associated with the belief that Republican victories in 2002 and 2004 were primarily attributable to superior GOP mobilization efforts."[6]

The DLC would prefer that Democrats reach out to "increase their geographical and demographic reach" beyond the black vote, unions, feminists, and the present left. But in arguing for door number three, their study does actually raise questions about whether Democrats can substitute greater turnout efforts for changes in actual policies.

In 2004, large Democrat-leaning counties nationwide saw their total voting-age population increase by 1.3 million over 2000. The numbers voting in those Democrat-leaning counties grew by 4.1 million and the Democrats increased their margin in their large Dem-trending counties by 890,000. Not bad.

The Republicans countered in their large Republican counties nationwide where the voting-age population had grown by 5.6 million and the total vote increased by 5.7 million. The Republican margin in their large GOP-leaning counties increased by 2.9 million.

Turning to the seventeen battleground states: The large Democrat-majority counties grew their voting-age population by 316,000, but by boosting turnout, the Democrats increased the total vote by 1.6 million and the Democrat margin of victory by 570,000.

Republican-majority counties in the seventeen battleground states saw their voting-age population increase by 1.6 million, total votes cast increased by 2 million, and the Republican margin of victory increased by 846,000. And 846,000 is a bigger number than 570,000.[7]

In both large and small Democrat-majority counties, the Democrat turnout was three times greater than the increase in the voting-age population. In other words, the Democrats are squeezing a higher percentage of their available votes. Republicans had voter turnout increase no faster than the growth of the voting-age population in large Republican counties and only 150 percent higher in small counties. Republicans have more "room" to increase their vote totals by increasing turnout.

The DLC study concludes, "It is clear that Republican margins owed relatively more to population growth, while Democrat margins owed relatively more to turnout."

Driving the point home, the DLC study suggests, "A glance at large cities around the county, and especially in battleground states, shows the pattern of heroic Democratic turnout efforts in 2004 even more dramatically."

Cuyahoga County, aka Cleveland, Ohio, lost 22,000 in voting-age population, from 2000 to 2004. But Democrats increased the total vote by 105,000 and the Democrat margin by 55,000.[8]

Denver County, Colorado, lost 11,000 in voting-age population, but the Kerry campaign increased the vote by 43,000 and the Democrat margin by nearly 32,000.

Philadelphia, Pennsylvania, lost 36,000 in voting-age population. Total votes cast grew by 116,000 and the Democrat margin rose by 61,000.

Detroit, Michigan, lost 26,000 in voting-age population. Total votes cast increased by 96,000 and the Democrat margin grew by 32,000.

Looking ahead, how much more blood can be squeezed out of this turnip? Have Democrats hit a wall in increasing turnout? And even if they can keep increasing turnout, will it be offset by growing populations in those states in Republican-trending areas?

Let's examine four examples from 2004.

Targeted Ohio saw Cuyahoga County increase its Democrat margin by 55,000. Columbus pushed out an additional 41,000 net Democrat votes while the voting-age population only grew by 13,000. But while these two cities increased the Democrat margin by 100,000, they were more than offset by an increase of 137,000 in Republican margins in GOP-tilting counties that saw their voting-age population grow by 190,000.

Targeted Pennsylvania saw Philadelphia and Pittsburgh produce an additional margin of 61,000 for the Democrats, despite those cities losing 53,000 in voting-age population. Elsewhere in Pennsylvania, Republican-leaning counties had a 151,000 increase in voting-age population and an increase of 127,000 in GOP margins. While Kerry won the state, his margin of victory fell by 86,000 votes from Gore's four years earlier. And this with a Republican governor auditioning for a cabinet spot in 2000 and a Democrat governor auditioning for the vice presidency in 2004.[9]

Minneapolis, Minnesota (Hennepin County), increased its Democrat margin by 37,000, while the total voting-age population grew less than 9,000. Republican counties grew 116,000 in the same period and contributed a net increase of 44,000 GOP votes.

In Colorado, the two large Democrat-leaning counties lost 20,000 in voting-age population, but the 2004 Kerry campaign squeezed out a 63,000 increase in their Democrat margin. In the three fastest-growing Republican counties, the GOP increased its population by 81,000 and offset 42,000 of the Democrat margin gain.

The DLC study summarizes, "Democrats may be nearing the point where they can no longer wring ever-higher margins out of declining (populations) in reliably Democratic cities and counties, despite even the best base-voter mobilization efforts."

The converse of this study is that Republicans have a great deal of running room in catching up to the Democrats in turning out a larger percentage of their growing number of voters. If the Hamburger and Wallsten and DLC studies are correct, Republicans are beginning to increase their turnout strength and they have relatively larger and relatively faster-growing virgin territory to exploit.[10]

*And Then There's the Felon Vote.* If the Democrats cannot squeeze out enough additional voters through further increasing the relative turnout from their present voter base, some smart Democrats see an opportunity to increase the size of that base. It does not require someone to start having more kids, which always has a time lag on election results, or entail voting dead or moved constituents, which, at least on paper, risks prison terms for precinct workers. It doesn't even require convincing taxpayers that they enjoy taxes.

The voter vault targeted by Democrat activists is a true pot of gold—as many as seven million voters—although getting to them may open up a political Pandora's box.

The Bureau of Justice Statistics reports that in 2004 there were 1,421,911 Americans in prison, 713,990 in jail, 765,355 on parole, and 4,151,125 on probation for an estimated total—given some double counting—of 6,996,500 Americans in the "correctional population." Many of them, but not all, are prohibited from voting. In forty-eight states Americans imprisoned for a felony conviction cannot vote while in prison. Two states, Maine and Vermont, allow inmates convicted of felonies to vote. Massachusetts and Utah until recently allowed inmates to vote.[11]

But during the 1988 presidential campaign, some focus was brought to bear on Dukakis's corrections philosophy, which was that no one was to die in prison, and everyone, even those specifically sentenced to life without parole, was to be released.

In preparation for their release, prisoners were allowed "furloughs" over a series of weekends. One murderer, William Horton, who brutally killed Joey Fournier, a teenager who was working at a gas station, was sentenced to life without possibility of parole. Dukakis let him out on furlough in 1987 and he went to Maryland and robbed a home and raped a woman. He was caught, arrested, and convicted in Maryland. Massachusetts kept asking Maryland to return Horton, but would not explain why a convicted murderer supposedly in prison in Massachusetts was in Maryland raping and robbing its citizens. When the judge sentenced William Horton to a real life sentence in Maryland, he told him to let the folks in Massachusetts know he wasn't going back.

The William Horton furlough story was treated as a Republican campaign trick by the establishment media, but there was a small problem with this effort to cover for the Democrats. The first candidate to highlight the Horton murder/furlough issue was Senator Al Gore of Tennessee. Secondly, the issue was not brought to public attention through the machinations of (before Rove there was) Lee Atwater, but through a series of newspaper articles by the *Eagle-Tribune* newspaper, which had won the Pulitzer Prize for investigative journalism in 1988. While the *Boston Globe* and the *New York Times* and the *Washington Post* pretended not to be aware of the story, *Readers' Digest* helpfully summarized the Horton murder/rape crime spree, and Mike Dukakis and his Massachusetts attitude toward crime and punishment were shown to be severely at odds with that of "fly-over country." The Bush campaign cheerfully printed and distributed millions of copies of the July *Readers' Digest* article written by Robert Bidinotto.

As the issue of crime and punishment mushroomed in 1988 it was pointed out that William Horton was able to vote while in the Massachusetts prison. Indeed, there was a Lifers PAC that organized prisoners sentenced to life in prison to vote, and politicians solicited their support.

The lingering bad publicity for Massachusetts led to a constitutional amendment, passed by vote of the people in 2000, to strip persons actually in prison for a felony conviction from voting.

Someone in Utah noticed that they had the same law, and in 1998, voters approved an amendment banning imprisoned felons from voting.

In addition to the forty-eight states that do not allow felons to vote while in prison, thirty-six states prohibit felons from voting while they are on parole, and thirty-one states exclude felons from voting while on probation. Three states, Virginia, Iowa, and Kentucky, join the federal government in refusing criminals the right to vote for the rest of their lives.[12]

One trend to watch is the effort by the left to liberalize voting rules for criminals. They have been losing the effort to allow felons actually in prison to vote (witness backsliding in Massachusetts and Utah). But George Soros's Open Society Institute published a study by Manza, Uggen, and Brittan entitled, *The Truly Disfranchised: Felon Voting Rights and American Politics*. They released the unfinished study on January 3, 2001, as a bright flare to Democrat legislators of the opportunities presented by bringing more criminals into the voting place.[13]

Their study argues that if felons were allowed to vote, Al Gore would have won in Florida and been elected in 2000. The authors write: "Our results suggest that felon disfranchisement played a decisive role in several US Senate elections, contributing to the Republican Senate majority in the early 1980s and mid-1990s." To further inflame Democrat passions, the study claims that Richard Nixon, his very self, would have won the 1960 election if present rules for felons had been in effect.

Democrats have had some success in recent years. Ambitious Democrat, Iowa governor Tom Vilsack, who had his staff recommend him as a potential Democrat presidential candidate every few months, issued an executive order giving all criminals the right to vote once they are finished with probation and/or parole. The Iowa law states that there is a lifetime ban on criminals voting, but it shows how someone auditioning for national leadership in the Democrat party understands the importance of this issue even if the niceties of the rule of law must be skirted.[14]

Maryland delegate Jill P. Carter, a Democrat, frankly explained in 2006 that Democrats were moving legislation to allow an estimated 150,000 felons to vote in Maryland in order to defeat Republican governor Robert L. Ehrlich.[15]

In 2002, a baby step forward for felon voting in Maryland was the repeal of its lifetime voting ban on two-time felons (unless both felonies were violent).

The Soros study reminds Democrats of the juicy target. They claim that while McGovern would have won 71.6 percent of the felon vote, Bill Clinton would have won 85.9 percent in 1992 and 92.8 percent in 1996. They further estimate that one-third of felons would vote if allowed. The Sentencing Project, a left-of-center group, estimates that 5.3 million Americans are without voting rights by virtue of being criminals. They estimate that four million African-American men, or 13 percent of black men, are thus disenfranchised, a rate seven times the national average. And 676,730 women are similarly ineligible due to felonies.[16]

A national high-profile campaign to make it easier for criminals to vote might bring back the bad old days for Democrats when being soft on crime was an electoral death sentence. But Democrats have made progress. Republicans may be further mau-maued if Democrats conflate the felon-voting issue with legitimate civil rights/race issues. This evidently happened to Governor George W. Bush when as governor he signed legislation in 1997 that eliminated the two-year waiting period after completion of sentence before convicted criminals could vote again. And in 2007, newly elected Republican governor Crist signed legislation removing the lifetime ban on felon voting.

Soros has funded efforts to promote felon voting and perhaps not coincidentally he has been active in opposing drug prohibition. Should Soros win the argument that America should end the "war on drugs" as we ended the "war on liquor" in 1933, it would significantly affect the voting population over time. Drug offenses produced 55 percent of federal inmates in 2003 and, in 2002, represented 21.4 percent of all adults serving time in state prisons.[17]

"*Elections are not determined by those who vote, but by those who count the votes.*"

—*Joseph Stalin*

## VOTER FRAUD

Voter fraud is an increasingly important part of the Takings Coalition. While the number of union members is declining, the number of invented votes is increasing. Republicans remember the voter fraud in Illinois and Texas that may well have stolen the 1960 presidential election. More recently John Thune narrowly lost the 2002 Senate race to Senator Tim Johnson only when additional votes appeared in one of the few polling places that was not policed. Senate races in Louisiana have regularly been won by the margin of expected fraud. A U.S. Senate investigation found in the 1996 Louisiana Senate race that there were more than 1,500 cases where two voters used the same Social Security number.[18]

Liberalizing and expanding absentee voting and voting by mail and the ease of registration without real proof of identification opens more opportunities for voter fraud in the future.

The 2004 gubernatorial race that was "won" by Democrat Christine Gregoire in Washington State is instructive of the dangers of voter fraud in America today. Gregoire was credited with 133 more votes than her Republican opponent, Dino Rossi. This out of a total of 2.8 million votes. Rossi was initially reported the winner with 261 more votes than Gregoire. A mandatory recount reduced Rossi's winning margin to 42 votes. Then left-wingers, including Moveon.org and Senator John Kerry, raised the money for yet another recount. This time Gregoire won with a margin of 133 votes. The long period of press coverage of the close election gave Washington State citizens a window on how voter fraud happens, not in Chicago or New Jersey, but in their own "clean" state.

Bob Williams, president of the Evergreen Freedom Foundation, a Washington State think tank, produced a study of election irregularities in King County,[19] the Democrat-dominated urban center, that included the following:

- On at least ten occasions after Election Day, King County officials "found" new, unsecured ballots, and on nine of those occasions, the votes were counted in violation of state law.
- 348 provisional ballots were inserted directly into the vote-counting machine in violation of state law.
- There were at least 875 more absentee ballots counted than people credited with voting absentee.
- An estimated 1,500 duplicate absentee ballots were mailed to voters. After the error was discovered, King County officials advised the voters to vote one ballot and to please discard the other.
- According to the GOP, 754 felons voted illegally. The Democrats later identified an additional 647 felons who voted.
- At least 47 dead people voted in King County, Washington.

In other counties it was discovered that there were organized voter-registration drives in at least one state mental institution and at extended-care facilities where Alzheimer's patients are treated. When the secretary of state certified the manual recount in December, there were at least 8,500 more votes cast in five counties than the number of registered voters who officially voted. (That number is forty-three times greater than the "margin of victory" of 133.) Of those, fully 875 ballots were officially counted in excess of the number of people who voted. That 875 is six times as large as the "margin of victory" of 133.[20]

Years after this fiasco, polls show that a majority of voters believe that Dino Rossi really won the election and that Christine Gregoire was fraudulently elected.

Washington is not alone in facing voter-fraud problems. The United States Election Assistance Commission was required by the Help America Vote Act of 2002 (HAVA) to study "voter fraud" and "voter intimidation" and reported in December 2006 that "there had never been a comprehensive, nationwide study of these topics."[21]

The two political parties have very different views on voter fraud. John Fund, the *Wall Street Journal* editor whose book *Stealing Elections: How Voter Fraud Threatens Our Democracy* pointed out that the National Voter Registration Act, known as the "Motor Voter Law," was the very first law signed by entering President Bill Clinton in 1993 after being passed by partisan Democrat majorities in the House and Senate. Motor Voter "imposed fraud-friendly rules on the states by requiring driver's license bureaus to register anyone applying for licenses, to offer mail-in registration with no identification needed, and to forbid government workers to challenge new registrants, while making it difficult to purge 'deadwood' voters (those who have died or moved away)." As a result, in 2001, the voter rolls in many American cities included more names than the U.S. Census listed as the total number of residents over age eighteen.[22]

The Democrats deliberately defeated all efforts to require voter identification, such as a driver's license, or to make it easier to remove dead people from the voting rolls.

Liberal Democrat professor Larry Sabato co-authored *Dirty Little Secrets*, a book highlighting the sad history of voter fraud. He agreed with John Fund's findings that voter fraud was today primarily a tool of the Democrat Party. Sabato noted that the Republican base is more solidly middle class and unlikely to participate in such fraud, but "the pool of people who appear to be available and more vulnerable to an invitation to participate in vote fraud tend to lean Democratic."[23] In addition, Paul Hernson, the director of the Center for American Politics at the University of Maryland, explains the Democrat Party's natural advantage in voter fraud, noting that "most incidents of wide-scale voter fraud reportedly occur in inner cities, which are largely populated by minority groups."

## In Missouri

In Missouri, recent federal indictments against the liberal group Association of Community Organizations for Reform Now (ACORN) accused them of submitting twenty thousand phony voter-registration forms in an effort to get names onto the voting rolls. One person registered seven times. Other "voters" were "Jive Turkey" and "Dick Tracy." A Missouri newspaper found ten thousand dead people on the voter rolls. Many had voted. The point of putting and keeping nonexistent or dead people on the voting rolls is to be able to have someone vote that "person" later on. It is the necessary preparation for voter fraud.[24]

## FIVE REFORMS TO STOP VOTER FRAUD

Bob Williams, who witnessed the voter fraud in Washington State, calls for five reforms to minimize voter fraud:

First, voter fraud needs to be treated as a serious crime and prosecuted. Too few people go to jail for stealing votes.

Second, voter rolls need to be cleaned up to remove dead people, noncitizens, and those who have moved.

Third, a photo ID and signature should be required of all voters. By the end of 2006, five legislatures passed requirements for voter ID. In Georgia and Indiana the Republican governors signed the legislation. In New Jersey, Arizona, and Wisconsin the Democrat governors vetoed the bills.

While Democrat politicians often oppose photo ID, claiming that African Americans somehow don't have driver's licenses, they are speaking for their own interests in facilitating voter fraud, not speaking for any minorities. Eighty percent of Hispanics, 67 percent of African Americans, 83 percent of whites, 89 percent of Republicans, 72 percent of Democrats, and 81 percent of independents favor requiring a photo ID for voting, according to an NBC/*Wall Street Journal* poll.[25]

Fourth, voting by mail should be limited. One can make it easier for voters to vote early, as in Texas where voters can show up in person at actual voting booths for one month before the "election day." That way travelers or those who will be away on Election Day do not need an absentee ballot that is easy to steal, lose, or request on behalf of nonexistent voters.

Fifth, military absentee ballots should be sent out in a timely manner. And counted.

Those benefiting from voter fraud will continue to fight against voter ID and for extensive use of vote by mail. If your state moves toward voter ID, expect less voter fraud and, where elections are close, fewer Democrats. If your state expands vote by mail, expect more fraud and, where elections are close, more Democrats elected.

Voter fraud is only worthwhile where votes are close. But in those cases lie control of the House, the Senate, many governorships, and from time to time, the presidency.

## CHAPTER TWELVE

# THE ECUMENICAL RIGHT

Not everyone in the Leave Us Alone Coalition identifies as a member of a religious faith. And those who do are as diverse in their religious beliefs as the rest of the population. But if, as is true for an increasing number of Americans, your faith as it intersects with politics becomes a vote-moving issue, you are a likely member of the Leave Us Alone Coalition. And those growing numbers can be identified in several trends that bode well for the GOP.

## THE GROWTH OF THE LDS CHURCH

There are 5.7 million Mormons, aka members of the Church of Jesus Christ of Latter-Day Saints, in the United States today, just under 2 percent of the population. Interestingly, VNS polled Mormons in Utah and Idaho and found they voted 75–20 and 86–13 for Bush over Gore in 2000. They are the most Republican religious voting bloc. There are eleven Mormon members of the House of Representatives and five Mormons in the Senate. They are the fastest-growing religion in the United States, up 19.3 percent between 1990 and 2000, and up 9.3 percent from 2000 to 2005. A *Time* magazine story in August 1997 reported the church's annual growth rate was 4.7 percent. Should that continue, by 2050 there would be 50 million Mormons, or 9 percent of 450 million projected Americans.[1] (If things don't work out for Mitt Romney in 2008 he might run in 2052.)

And they no longer just live in Utah.

There are 1.483 million Mormons in Utah. Most of these votes are wasted as Utah has voted 71.54 percent for Bush in 2004, 66.83 percent in 2000, and 54.37 percent for Bob Dole as he lost to Clinton in 1996.[2]

California has 529,000 Mormons, and Idaho 311,000. Nice large numbers but unlikely to rescue California, and overkill in safely Republican Idaho.

But let's take a look at some swing states. Bush lost Oregon in 2004 by five thousand votes. There are 104,312 Mormons in Oregon. Washington State was carried by Kerry by ten thousand votes in 2004, where there are 178,000 Mormons. Florida—won by a whisper in 2000—has 75,620 Mormons.[3]

Mormons are overcoming an interesting partisan legacy. Before Utah became a state in 1896, there was a concern (okay, fear) that Utah would have only one party: the Mormon People's Party. Therefore Congress insisted that in addition to abandoning the practice of polygamy that they establish two political parties.

The president of the church had a vision that made polygamy a practice of the past. (Modern polygamists operate outside church sanction.) Members of the church were encouraged to join the Republican and Democrat parties in roughly equal numbers. While the state has sorted itself out moving more toward the Republican Party, there are still families following in the footsteps of great-grandparents who were instructed to become Democrats.

Every young male Mormon is urged to spend two years proselytizing, inviting other folks to become Mormons. Mormons also have higher marriage rates and an average of 2.5 children. And while a ban on caffeine may be an annoyance, the prohibition on cigarettes and alcohol in the Mormon faith helps keep Mormons healthy and voting longer than dissolute liberals.

## THE JEWISH VOTE

Jews are on the other end of the partisan divide from Mormons. In 2004, Jews voted 75–25 for Kerry and, in 2000, went 80–20 for Gore.[4] The Jewish vote went 78 percent for Clinton in 1996 and 80 percent for Clinton in 1992.

In 2006, the Jewish vote went 87 percent Democrat for Congress and only 12 percent for Republicans.[5]

This has been a perennial frustration for Republicans. Jews, it is said, "earn like Episcopalians and vote like Puerto Ricans." But this is the flip side of Democrat strategists' anger that some union members vote Republican on the gun issue rather than their "obvious" class interests as part of the lumpen proletariat. Not everyone votes on economics, and Michael Barone and Grant Ujifusa have suggested that Jews in America are "still voting against the czar" and fear the prominence of the Christian right in the Republican Party. Jews have also tended to live in Democrat-controlled cities.

Both parties have competed to be supportive of the State of Israel. Republicans hoped that their strength on national defense would win Jewish votes. The Republican Party has won support from individual Jewish intellectuals, but has not gained from a significant shift in voting patterns. (An August 16, 2004, Greenberg Quinlan Rosner Research poll found Jewish voters preferring Kerry on the Israel issue: 66 percent for Kerry versus 34 percent for Bush, with only 24 percent of Jews saying they were closer to Bush on Israel than Kerry.)[6] Democrats can and do argue that whatever Bush does in support of Israel, a Democrat president would have matched. Republican hopes of luring significant numbers of Jewish voters away on the issue of Israel's security have not come to pass.

Yet two trends trouble Democrats. First, the overall Jewish population is not growing and it is possibly shrinking. The National Jewish Population Survey piggybacks on the American Religious Identity Survey (ARIS) that interviews fifty thousand adult Americans every ten years. Respondents to the ARIS survey who "said they were Jewish or have a Jewish background" were asked another twenty questions designed to mirror those asked in the 1990 National Jewish Population Study.[7] The results of the 2000 survey were summarized in the *New York Jewish Week* of November 2, 2001. The "total number of Americans who say they are Jewish either by religion or upbringing has remained stable at 5.5 million for more than a decade." Of that 5.5 million, "1.4 million Jews say they are Jewish by dint of parentage or ethnicity but align themselves with another faith community. In 1990, 625,000 Jews identified themselves that way. An additional 1.4 million Jews—another quarter of the population—say they are secular or have no religion at all, leaving just 51 percent of American Jews to say they are Jewish by religion."

The 2000 and 1990 studies found that the Jewish population is older than the rest of the American population, it marries later, has fewer children, and for the half that intermarry about one-third of the next generation is raised Jewish.

In 1997, the leader of a national Jewish organization said in a private briefing on demographics that there were 5.5 million Jewish Americans and that this would decline to 4 million by 2012. This was not predicted through conversion or intermarriage, but due to an older population with deaths outnumbering births.

Others have predicted an even greater decline in total population. In 1977, Elihu Bergman, the then-assistant director of the Harvard Center for Population Studies, wrote in *Midstream* in 1977 that "when the United States celebrates its Tri-centennial in 2076 . . . the American Jewish Community is likely to number no more than 944,000 persons." In that year the total American population would be 500 million.[8]

For Democrats it is precisely this older Jewish population that provides its most consistent voters and financial supporters. The *Forward* newspaper estimated that the national Democrat candidates raise half of their campaign contributions from Jewish Americans.[9]

The second piece of bad news for Democrats is the growth of the

Orthodox Jewish population. The NJPS study found that half of all Jews are nonaffiliated with any synagogue, and of those who are affiliated, 50 percent belong to Reform congregations, 30 percent to Conservative, and 20 percent to Orthodox.[10]

But members of the Orthodox Jewish communities marry earlier, average more than four children, and have intermarriage rates of only 3 percent. An essay, originally published in 1996 in the *Jewish Spectator* by Antony Gordon and Richard Horowitz entitled, "Will Your Grandchildren be Jewish?" projects the relative growth in the Orthodox, Conservative, Reform, and secular populations (it can now be found on the website www.simpletoremember.com). Looking at that analysis, Jeff Ballabon, the president of the Coalition for Jewish Values, points out that in 2000 fewer than 15 percent of America's Jews were Orthodox, but that percentage grows to 45 percent by 2025, 80 percent by 2050, and 95 percent by 2075.[11]

It is precisely the Orthodox community, with serious social conservative views that make Jerry Falwell look a little pink around the edges, that is most open to the Republican Party. And because Orthodox Jews, like the Amish, feel that they can best pass on their faith to their children by avoiding the assimilation of public schools, they are the strongest advocates of tuition tax credits, vouchers, and/or home-schooling.

How can the Republican Party win the Jewish vote?

First, they need to be talking to the leaders of the various Orthodox communities. This is an entirely different set of leaders from many of the well-known secular organizations that have traditionally been on the left. Second, they need to recognize that as a community of faith they have the same concerns as conservative Catholics, Mormons, Muslims, and evangelical Protestants. They worry about an aggressively secular left, the coarseness of the present culture, parental control in general.

In twenty-five years the Republican Party will begin to carry the Jewish vote with regularity.

## The Conservatization of Catholics

Roman Catholics were 1 percent of the population of the United States in 1790. This grew to 2 percent by 1820 and 5 percent in 1840. Immigration increased the number of Catholics to 12 percent of the population at the beginning of the Civil War in 1861, 14 percent by 1880, 19 percent in 1900, and up to 21 percent in 1920. With the 1921 legal restrictions on immigration, the Catholic population dropped to 15.1 percent in 1950, but rose to 21.9 percent by 1990.[12]

The number of Catholic voters in the United States should continue to grow as Hispanics become citizens, begin to vote, and younger Hispanics get old enough to vote regularly. The official 2002 Catholic Directory found 65.3 million Catholics in America, making up 23 percent of the population.

George J. Marlin, in his book *The American Catholic Voter: 200 Years of Political Impact*, has an introduction by Michael Barone which argues that "the years from 1896 to 1930 were years of Republican majorities in most elections. One reason was that the Democrats of that period had little appeal to Catholic voters. Predominantly urban, they distrusted the agrarian politics and Protestant piety of William Jennings Bryan and went over in large numbers to William McKinley, Theodore Roosevelt, and William Howard Taft. Irish Catholics disliked Woodrow Wilson's partiality toward Britain and many German Catholics opposed his decision to go to war with Germany." Even while voting Republican for president, Marlin points out, Catholics "were also the mainstays of the Democratic political organizations—machines—that grew up in almost every large northern city and were usually headed by and largely manned by Irish Catholics." Al Smith lost to Herbert Hoover in 1928. And although he "rejected the New Deal and opposed Roosevelt in 1936 and 1940 (they reconciled before Smith's death in 1944) Smith had established part of what would become Roosevelt's New Deal Coalition: The Catholic masses in the big cities."[13]

In 1960, John F. Kennedy, the first Roman Catholic to win the presidency, won 83 percent of the Catholic vote. Forty-four years later, John Forbes Kerry, also a Massachusetts senator and also a Roman Catholic, won only 47 percent of the Catholic vote in 2004, losing 52 percent of the 26 percent of all voters who were Catholic to the Methodist from Texas. Four years earlier, Bush had lost the Catholic vote 47 percent to 50 percent to Tennessee's Protestant Al Gore.[14]

Deal Hudson, the editor of *Crisis* magazine, in 1996 commissioned a study on the American Catholic vote by Steve Wagner of QEV Analytics that was much studied by Karl Rove and the Bush team in preparation for the 2000 presidential election. The study's major observation was that "the Catholic vote is not monolithic. Active Catholics constitute a coherent political constituency. Inactive Catholics do not." Active Catholics were defined as Catholics who attended mass weekly.[15]

The National Elections study in 1996 found 29 percent of voters self-identified as Catholic; the study put those 15 percent active and 14 percent inactive. That would make the 15 percent of Americans who are active Catholics roughly analogous in size and behavior to the white, born-again, evangelical Protestant cohort of 18 percent of the electorate.

The *Crisis* study found that Catholics as a whole were becoming less Democrat and more "conservative" from 1960 to 1996. Sixty-four percent of Catholics said they were Democrats in 1960, 42 percent by 1980, and 41 percent in 1996. In 1972, only 35 percent of Catholics described themselves as "conservative" and by 1996 this increased to 51 percent.[16]

The Catholic vote fell only 4 percent, from 83 percent in 1960 to 79 percent for Lyndon Johnson in 1964. In 1968, Hubert Humphrey won 58 percent of active Catholics and 52 percent of inactives. In 1972, George McGovern won 39 percent of all Catholics, with no difference between actives and inactives. This was the first year that Catholics did not vote more Democrat than the rest of the nation.[17]

In 1980, active Catholics voted 54 percent for Reagan and inactive Catholics voted 44 percent for Reagan. In 1984, Reagan won 59 percent of the active and inactive Catholic vote and 60 percent of the nation's vote.

These numbers are brought to life in Samuel G. Freedman's 1996 book *The Inheritance: How Three Families and the American Political Majority Moved from Left to Right* chronicling three Catholic families' metamorphosis from union Democrats to politically active Republicans in three generations. The Irish Catholic family, the Careys, moved right because of the Democrat Party's move away from anti-communism during the Vietnam War. The Polish Catholic family, the Maeby/Obryckis, reacted to the Democrat Party's support for affirmative action and the politics of envy and class antagonisms. The Italian Catholic family, the Trottas, was repulsed by the Democrats' social libertinism and moral relativism.[18]

The Democrat Party, which only three generations ago could take the immigrant Catholic vote largely for granted, now works overtime to treat orthodox Catholics like Gypsies. William A. Donohue, president of the Catholic League for Religious and Civil Rights, watches for anti-Catholic bigotry and was amazed to see the Democrat National Committee deliberately antagonize Catholics. In 2002, Mark Shields nominated as his "outrage of the week" on the CNN show *The Capital Gang* the fact that Democrat party chairman Terry McAuliffe placed "Catholics for a Free Choice" on its website as the only link under the heading "Catholic." Donohue pointed out in letters and eventually press releases aimed at McAuliffe that Frances Kissling's Catholics for a Free Choice is a pro-abortion group that attacks the Vatican for its pro-life positions.[19] Kissling's group led efforts to have the Vatican expelled from its observer status at the United Nations, and she has been quoted saying her goal is to "overthrow" the Catholic Church. "Bob Jones," William Donohue said, "is small potatoes next to Kissling's hate group." The DNC refused to remove the link, and later unveiled a new website on April 8, 2004, that removed Catholics for a Free Choice from the "links" section only to have it reappear under its "Religious Affiliated" section.

The left's growing antipathy for Roman Catholicism, the priesthood, the pope, and active believers has driven active Protestant and Catholic believers into a partnership unimagined only decades ago. Pat Robertson's Christian Coalition regularly hosted Roman Catholics

Phyllis Schlafly and Bill Bennett at their national conventions. Kansas Senator Sam Brownback, a convert from Protestantism to Roman Catholicism, heads the "Values Action Team," which organizes the social conservative agenda in the Senate. Neither Brownback's Catholicism nor his conversion has been considered problematic in his leadership role or in his campaign for the Republican nomination for the presidency in 2008.

The modern Democrat Party has placed taxpayer-subsidized abortion at the head of its nonnegotiable demands. The Reverend Jesse Jackson, who had viewed abortion as "black genocide," was compelled to change his position 180 degrees to taxpayer-funded abortion on demand in order to be considered a possible Democrat nominee in 1984.[20]

One challenge for the American Catholic community is the demographic challenges to its leadership. In 1920, there were 21,019 total priests in the United States. This number grew each year to 53,796 in 1960. This dropped to 45,000 in 2002. By 2020, there will be about 31,000 priests and only 15,000 will be younger than seventy. In 1920, there were 8,904 seminarians training for the priesthood. This grew to 39,896 in 1960. This dropped from 49,000 in 1965 to 4,700 in 2002. In 1945, there were 138,079 nuns and 180,000 in 1965. In 2002, this dropped to 75,000 sisters: average age sixty-eight. In 2020, the number of sisters will be 40,000 with just 21,000 below the age of seventy.[21]

Damaging to both the active Catholic community and the private-school movement is that the number of diocesan high schools fell from 1,566 to 786 between 1965 and 2002 while the number of high school students fell from 700,000 to 386,000. Parochial grade schools fell from 10,503 schools in 1965 to 6,623 in 2002. The student population fell from 4.5 million to 1.9 million. In 1960, 12 percent of American students were attending Roman Catholic parochial schools. By 2006, this fell to 6 percent.[22]

The overall Catholic vote is becoming less distinctive. A Pew Research Center poll published on June 27, 2006, found that "Catholics and all Americans voted within a scant five percent of each other on

15 of 19 issues."[23] But dividing Roman Catholics into active and inactive voting blocs shows the active-bloc trending increasingly conservative, Republican, and looking in profile like Ralph Reed's Christian Coalition voters.

## EVANGELICALS VS. MAINSTREAM PROTESTANTS

By numbers America is still a Protestant-majority nation, but only narrowly. Immigration over the past two hundred years has brought the Roman Catholic population to about 24 percent. Jews, Muslims, and Hindus have all entered American life, and secularism now claims the 10 percent who list their religion as none.[24]

America has shifted in both numbers and attitude since Franklin Delano Roosevelt told Leo Crowley, "Leo, you know this is a Protestant country, and the Catholics and the Jews are here on sufferance. It is up to both of you [Crowley and Henry Morgenthau, a Jew and secretary of the Treasury] to go along with anything that I want at this time."[25]

In the 2004 election, 54 percent of votes cast were from Protestants. And they voted 59 percent for Bush and 40 percent for Kerry. But as with the division between active Catholics and inactive Catholics and secular versus Orthodox Jews, religious differences within Protestantism show up in partisan politics and ideological views.

Protestants who attend church weekly (16 percent of the population) voted 70 percent for Bush. Those Protestants who attended less often (15 percent of the population) voted 56 percent for Bush. White, evangelical, born-again voters (23 percent of the population) went 78 percent for Bush.[26]

And just as Orthodox Jews are becoming both more Republican and a larger percentage of the Jewish population, there is a shift within Protestantism to more evangelical sects.

*Christianity Today* reports that in 1960 the seven leading mainline Protestant denominations—United Methodist, Presbyterian,

American Baptist, Disciples of Christ, Lutheran, Episcopal, and United Church of Christ—had a combined membership of twenty-nine million. This dropped to twenty-two million by 2000, a decline of 24 percent, while total Protestant church membership was increasing by 33 percent.[27]

Between 1965 and 2005, the number of Methodists declined from eleven million to just above eight million. Presbyterian Church membership fell from 3.2 million to 2.4 million. The Episcopal Church membership fell from 3.6 million to 2.3 million.

In the same period, more conservative Protestant churches have grown. Southern Baptists increased from 8.7 million in 1960 to 16.4 million in 2003. The Assemblies of God increased from 508,000 in 1960 to 2.7 million in 2003.

While evangelical Protestant churches have become more explicitly conservative in the politics of their parishioners, the "mainstream" churches have become more liberal, at least at the level of their elites.

The growth of the evangelical and conservative churches in membership and the relative decline of traditional/liberal Protestant denominations is a trend that favors the Leave Us Alone Coalition.

Evangelical Protestants have developed a network of hundreds of independent radio and television stations. Americans are familiar with the Christian Broadcasting Network (CBN), run by Pat Robertson. Salem Communications, a radio network that owns or operates 105 stations while reaching two thousand affiliate stations, boasts such talk-show big names as Hugh Hewitt, Bill Bennett, Michael Medved, and Michael Gallagher.

Religious television and radio reach an estimated twenty million Americans. The Christian Booksellers Association, the trade association for Christian retail, has nearly 2,300 member stores selling $4.2 billion worth of products in 2002, up from $4 billion in 2000.[28]

One does not find "mainstream" Protestants on religious TV or radio.

And last, the growing numbers of evangelical churches and members when not drawn to the Leave Us Alone Coalition are pushed away from the Takings Coalition as the establishment left treats them as Gypsies. They are mocked and derided in conversations public and private. Sophisticated leftists talk about evangelical Protestants—and conservative Catholics—with a hostility that is difficult to believe coming from folks who think of themselves as devoid of prejudice. They do not see George Wallace or Sheriff Bull Connor in the mirror, but they sound like them.

## CHAPTER THIRTEEN

# THE NEW MEDIA: CUTTING OUT THE MIDDLEMEN

Conservative-radio talk-show host G. Gordon Liddy begins his daily three-hour radio broadcast with a crackling introduction that sounds as if his broadcast is being jammed. Producer Franklin Raff's mixture of shortwave broadcasts from Russia, China, and France are followed by the words "Warning, Warning. You are about to enter the American Sector." Liddy then announces that his is "Radio Free America" breaking through the establishment media. A tad hyperbolic, granted, but technology and laws have changed since the 1980s, and this has given alternative media voices a greater listening audience than Voice of America or Radio Free Europe won in Eastern Europe.

Before the Internet, before C-Span, before political talk radio, there were the three networks, ABC, CBS, and NBC. The talking heads on the three networks read the *New York Times* and lived in New York and Washington, D.C. The "Fairness Doctrine" was a government regulation that required "equal time" for opposing points of view. This kept most ideas outside the establishment's sense of consensus off the air or chaperoned with an immediate rebuttal.

On a given night in 1980 the three networks were watched by 52.1 million viewers in an America with only 222 million citizens. As the nation grew to 300 million in population by 2006, nightly viewership for the Big Three fell to 42 million by 1988; 40.7 million by 1992; 31.9 million by 2000; and 28.8 million in 2004.[1]

Of those watching TV news, ABC's audience fell from 20 percent in 1993 to 12 percent in 2005, CBS's fell from 18 percent to 11 percent, and NBC's fell from 19 percent to 14 percent.[2]

Let's take a look at what happened.

## Conservatives Rising: A Media Timeline

1972:  Deregulation allows cable TV to enter a period of explosive growth.

---

1979:  C-Span is created.

---

1987:  President Reagan's FCC eliminates the "Fairness Doctrine," which required equal time for opposing points of view. Now a radio talk-show host can express opinions outside the establishment consensus without government restrictions.

---

1988:  Rush Limbaugh is syndicated nationally.

---

1992:  G. Gordon Liddy goes on the air.

---

1994:  The Internet goes public.

---

1995:  Salon.com goes online.

---

1996:  *National Review* Online and Slate.com go live. Congress passes the Telecommunications Act, lifting ownership restrictions on radio stations.

---

1997:  Matthew Drudge creates the Drudge Report online. The

Drudge Report originated around 1994 as a weekly subscriber-based e-mail dispatch.

---

1998:  The Monica Lewinsky Affair is investigated but not reported by *Newsweek*. The *Drudge Report* breaks the story.

---

2003:  After the script of *The Reagans* is leaked on the Internet, CBS is forced to move the comically bitter anti-Reagan movie to its Showtime cable network and delete some of the completely invented scenes.

---

2004:  This is the first election where the Internet plays a major role. The blogosphere embarrasses the mainstream repeatedly. First, on CBS, there were efforts to pass off obviously forged national-guard memos, which eventually leads to the collapse of old-media icon Dan Rather. Kerry's campaign claims that during the Vietnam War he entered Cambodia on Christmas were not challenged by the establishment press, but by the Internet media. Swiftboat Veterans for Truth, ignored by the establishment press, break through on the Internet and eventually paid media.

---

Before the abolition of the "Fairness Doctrine," there were two hundred radio talk shows. Now there are more than two thousand talk-radio stations. Before the Internet there were a few "beyond the mainstream," self-appointed journalists who wrote newsletters that were sent out by snail mail to small numbers of readers. The costs of printing and mailing even a small newsletter made the "cost of entry" high.

When Walter Cronkite and Dan Rather and others talked to American households in a one-way conversation, Americans had little way of knowing that many of their fellow Americans rejected the assumptions and assertions of the establishment left.

In unfree European societies, the government monitored the nation's conversations by tapping phone lines. In America, with the invention of national television and radio networks, the establishment went so far as to *have* the conversation on our behalf. America was thinking what Walter Cronkite and Dan Rather and Roger Mudd told us we were thinking. A voice like William F. Buckley's *Firing Line* was a lonely conservative voice on the left-of-center, and infrequently watched, public television. (Allowing Buckley on national television, if only for half an hour each week, was a mistake bred of hubris by the establishment left. It was a crack in the wall that was not insignificant over time.)

It is difficult to overstate the power of the monolithic American oligopoly in television news in the 1950s, 1960s, and even into the 1980s. What passed for conservatives in the Nixon administration recognized that this was a tremendous handicap to those opposed to the liberal consensus. Vice President Spiro Agnew gave a series of speeches on this, and the media did respond by labeling their editorials on television as distinct from the "news." When at the local level a conservative voice did appear it was so unsettling to the liberals and in some cases such a welcome respite for voters that it elected a conservative like Jesse Helms to the United States Senate from his North Carolina local-television perch.

Candidates like Ronald Reagan could only get their messages out by bouncing them off a hostile national press. Reagan said he wanted to cut taxes, reduce spending, limit the government, and confront Soviet imperialism. Few heard this until the establishment press shouted it out, thinking they were damaging his campaign. "This guy Reagan wants to cut taxes, reduce spending, and confront the Soviets." Voters heard, and approved.

Technology changed and the law changed. Cable television gave viewers more options, like Ted Turner's CNN. C-Span removed the filter of the establishment press for any American willing to see for him- or herself what Congress was really doing, right now. Pennsylvania congressman Robert Walker became one of the best-known congressmen by speaking regularly through the unfiltered and unedited medium of C-Span.

Add the fax machine to C-Span, and talk-radio hosts no longer sat around and invited comments on that morning's *New York Times* stories. They could talk about what Congress was doing now.

The 1986 abolition of the "Fairness Doctrine" allowed talk radio to have hosts outside the liberal establishment thinking. This was revolutionary. Now talk radio could have a point of view. Rush Limbaugh was legalized.

## THE "FAIRNESS DOCTRINE" ENDS

Now Rush Limbaugh could *be* "equal time." The law no longer favored the liberal establishment. Liberals were free to run their own radio talk shows, if there was a market for them. It says a great deal about the relative size of the center-right and the left in America that conservatives now dominate the participatory media of talk radio.

The following chart shows that of the top fifteen political talk-radio hosts, twelve are conservative, two are moderate, and one is liberal. The twelve top conservative hosts have a total minimum weekly audience of over 68 million. The lone liberal is in a tie at tenth place with an audience of 3.25 million.[3]

| HOST | CUMULATIVE AUDIENCE (WEEKLY MINIMUM, IN MILLIONS) | POLITICAL VIEWPOINT |
| --- | --- | --- |
| Rush Limbaugh | 13.5 | Conservative |
| Sean Hannity | 12.5 | Conservative |
| Michael Savage | 8.0 | Conservative |
| Glenn Beck | 5.0 | Conservative |
| Laura Ingraham | 5.0 | Conservative |
| Neal Boortz | 4.0 | Conservative |

| HOST | CUMULATIVE AUDIENCE (WEEKLY MINIMUM, IN MILLIONS) | POLITICAL VIEWPOINT |
| --- | --- | --- |
| Mark Levin | 4.0 | Conservative |
| Mike Gallagher | 3.75 | Conservative |
| Michael Medved | 3.75 | Conservative |
| Jim Bohannon | 3.25 | Moderate |
| Bill O'Reilly | 3.25 | Conservative |
| Ed Schultz | 3.25 | Liberal |
| Doug Stephan | 3.25 | Moderate |
| Bill Bennett | 3.0 | Conservative |
| Jerry Doyle | 3.0 | Conservative |

Source TALKERS magazine[4]

TALKERS magazine polled listeners to talk radio and found that 74 percent say they voted in 2004 and 38 percent identify themselves as conservative or ultraconservative. Fourteen percent identify themselves as liberal or ultraliberal.

The Internet also better reflects a more conservative America. NewsMax.com has roughly 500,000 unique visitors each week, while National Review Online has roughly 312,500 unique visitors each week. Little Green Footballs, Instapundit, and RedState are all center-right bloggers with 139,603; 112,617; and 23,125 visitors per day. Some of the more recognized liberal blogs are the Daily Kos at 499,153; America Blog with 73,237; and MyDD.com with 34,682 per day.[5]

There are so many different blogs and so many different websites spanning from left to right that it ends the ability of the liberal establishment to monopolize the national conversation, in a way that Walter Cronkite once did.

Communication has changed in political campaigns. The Bush 2004 campaign compiled 7.5 million e-mail addresses, up from 1 million in 2000. Kerry's campaign had more than 2.7 million.[6]

The leftward bias of the broadcast media also is found in the newspaper business. And just as the establishment liberal broadcasters have been losing market share to cable and the Internet, there has been a similar decline in large-city paid newspaper readership as younger Americans get their news from local free papers, the Internet, and cable TV. Daily newspaper readership in the United States has been declining on a straight-line track since the 1970s. The Newspaper Association of America reports that the number of people employed in the newspaper industry fell by 18 percent between 1990 and 2004.[7] The New York Times Company saw its share price fall from $47.67 as of April 24, 2002, to $23.77 on April 24, 2007.[8]

*USA Today*, with a nationwide circulation of 2.8 million, does allow a conservative response to be printed alongside its more liberal editorials. The *New York Times*, with a circulation of 1,120,420, does not offer such balance. And the *Wall Street Journal*, with a liberal news staff and a conservative editorial and op-ed page, has a circulation of 2,062,312.[9] A new challenger in the field is the *Examiner*, now a free newspaper in Washington, D.C., Baltimore, and San Francisco, but with plans to expand its 600,000 circulation per city to another twenty cities. With conservative writers such as Mark Tapscott, Bill Sammon, and Quin Hillyer, the *Examiner* expects to be a national conservative answer to *USA Today*.[10]

Two studies show the liberal bias in the establishment press. One that "broke" the story in 1981 and another in 1995, demonstrating that this bias continues. The progress for conservatives is not that this bias has been ended, it has not, but that competing sources of news and information have reduced the damage this bias does to center-right issues and candidates.

In 1981, S. Robert Lichter, then with George Washington University, and Stanley Rothman, of Smith College, released a groundbreaking survey of 240 journalists at the most influential national media outlets—including the *New York Times*, *Washington Post*, *Wall Street*

*Journal, Time, Newsweek, U.S. News & World Report,* ABC, CBS, NBC, and PBS—on their political attitudes and voting patterns. The data demonstrated that journalists and broadcasters hold liberal positions on a wide range of social and political issues. This study, which was more elaborately presented in Lichter and Rothman's subsequent book, *The Media Elite,* became the most widely quoted media study of the 1980s and remains a landmark today.[11]

The survey found that elite journalists voted more than 80 percent for the Democrat candidate for president from 1964 to 1976. Fifty-four percent of the elite journalists described themselves as "left of center" while 19 percent said they were "right of center." Describing their co-workers, 56 percent said they were "mostly on the left" and only 8 percent said "mostly on the right."[13]

The Soviet Union has collapsed. Leisure suits are gone. But the leftward bias of the media establishment has remained. A May 2005 study of three hundred TV and print journalists found that they voted 68 percent for Kerry in 2004 and 25 percent for Bush. (Five percent either didn't vote or said they did not know for whom they voted.)

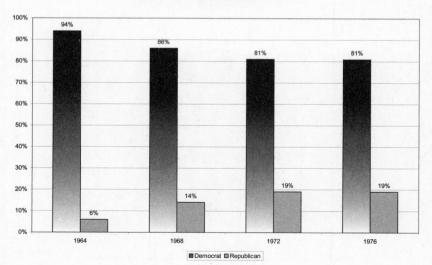

**The Media Presidential Vote[14]**

This study also found that 33 percent considered themselves Democrats and 10 percent Republicans. Eighteen percent said they were liberals and 10 percent considered themselves conservative. Ninety-six percent thought "freedom of religion was essential," 95 percent thought that of "free speech."[15]

Shrinking giants are still giants. Like organized labor, whose decline in numbers has been unrelenting from 1953 to the present, the political power of the three networks is no longer overwhelming; it is declining, but very much with us. Those who like to brag of the power of Fox should remember that at any given time 9.5 million Americans are watching CBS News and Fox News's best-watched show has 2.1 million viewers.[16]

The McCain-Feingold "campaign finance reform" legislation made it a crime for you or me to buy an ad on television criticizing or praising a candidate by name within thirty days of an election. There are no restrictions on the three networks. They can give as much free positive publicity to any candidate of their choice at any time of their choice. And they do.

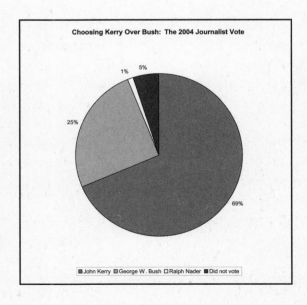

Choosing Kerry Over Bush: The 2004 Journalist Vote

McCain chose well in crafting his bill. He was repaid with millions of dollars in campaign contributions from a grateful and fawning industry—the exempted television networks. In 2000, a minute of advertising on ABC's *Good Morning America* cost $80,000. The network gave McCain many "free" minutes to talk about campaign finance reform. A quarter-page ad on the op-ed page of the *New York Times* cost $28,170. Under present campaign law it is illegal for any individual to contribute more than $2,300 to a campaign or more than $50,000 to all political parties or campaigns in total. One *Times* editorial is worth more than any one individual can give in a year. Ann Coulter calculated that McCain's positive press in the editorial pages of the *Times* was worth $2.2 million in 1999.[17]

That year, McCain appeared on *Face the Nation* five times, *Meet the Press* six times, and *This Week* six times. A one-minute ad on *Meet the Press* costs $220,000. Average ten minutes per show, and NBC gave McCain $13.2 million in free advertising. Every minute of pro-campaign finance reform puff pieces on *NBC News* is worth $170,000.[18]

McCain is largely alone as a Republican receiving such campaign contributions (which would be illegal for General Motors to give). Democrats still benefit from a supportive and comforting establishment press including the three networks. But that world is rudely and repeatedly rocked by competing sources of information—the Internet, talk radio, C-Span, and cable competitors.

The move from a monolithic media that pumped out an establishment-left smog into the public debate for decades to a much more competitive marketplace for ideas has been traumatic for the left. They were accustomed to a world that reinforced their biases and never challenged them. Today, the rhetoric of Moveon.org and David Brock's Mediamatters.org sounds like the rights' Pat Buchanan and Spiro Agnew in the 1970s. They see the blades of grass breaking through the concrete and believe they are living in a jungle.[19] The average audience for Fox News in prime time was 1.4 million in 2006. That is more than triple the viewership of MSNBC (378,000) and more than triple that of CNN (379,000). More than half (55 percent) of all viewers watching prime-time cable news in 2006 were watching Fox News. The evening newscasts of the dying dinosaurs (CBS, ABC, and NBC), meanwhile, have a combined audience of over 25 million.[20]

The great freeing of the national dialogue from the constraints of the left-dominated mainstream media is excellent news for the Leave Us Alone Coalition.

The left has noticed the power of talk radio and is pushing to re-store the "Fairness Doctrine" either by passing a law through Congress, or if they win the presidency, by a simple vote of the Federal Communications Commission (FCC). A Democrat president would have the ability to appoint three of the five commissioners and, barring a law stopping them, they could and would impose the "Fairness Doctrine" that would ban Rush Limbaugh from speaking for three hours each day unless the station gave similar time to a liberal. Since there is not a market for such a liberal, the stations are unlikely to take the loss of having to use six hours of station time to get three hours of Rush's ability to sell advertisements. Many of the talk-radio stations would move to music or sports. There is a reason this effort has been called the "Hush Rush" initiative.

As long as this threat hangs over the heads of several hundred conservative talk-show hosts with audiences of tens of millions, the new media will have a stake in electing congressmen, senators, and presidents that side with the Leave Us Alone Coalition.

# PART THREE

# THE BATTLEGROUND

The political struggles of the next fifty years will take place on a chessboard or battlefield—choose your visual—that is created by the current and future realities in America's divisions by race and religion, by the power of the media and the business community, and by the Rule Book, the U.S. Constitution, which sets the powers of and limitations on the U.S. House of Representatives, the Senate, the presidency, and the fifty states.

## CHAPTER FOURTEEN

# THE BUSINESS OF BUSINESS: WHAT IS GOOD FOR GENERAL MOTORS

Another foundation of the mythology of the left is that the Republican Party and conservative movement are run by and for big corporations. At the turn of the twentieth century, in 1896 and 1900, corporate America weighed in strongly for McKinley and the Republicans because they feared the inflationary monetary policies of the Democrat William Jennings Bryan. This created a lasting impression that long ago outlived reality.

Business leaders can and should be the engines for political campaigns for free trade, limited government, low taxes, a free labor market, and property rights. But this has not happened. Much of the business community contributes financially to candidates who actively oppose their interests. Why has this happened? Will it continue? And why has the business community spent so little on politics given how significant the cost of government is to them directly? In short, why does the business community not act in its obvious self-interest when it comes to politics?

The retail industry, for instance, sold $2.6 trillion worth of goods in 2006. They suffer losses due to shoplifting and employee theft of

$41.6 billion, or 1.6 percent of sales. They respond to such losses by spending $10 billion to combat theft.

The retail industry, like most industries, takes theft seriously. They spend a great deal of money to minimize the loss of income and wealth to their shareholders, consumers, and employees. But how to react when the guy walking out of the store with their money is the government? The federal government takes 35 percent of their profits in federal corporate income taxes. Right off the top. The same government requires every business to fork over 6.2 percent of every employee's salary to pay the costs of Social Security. (That is on top of the 6.2 percent they take directly from the employee.) The state government wets its beak with a state corporate income tax and a state sales tax. Local governments hit them with property taxes.

And yet retailers and other businesses spend much less time and money fighting "slippage" caused by the costs of government than they do shoplifters. The shoplifters walk away with less. And when shoplifters walk out of a store they cease to annoy the shareholders of the business. On the other hand, politicians take their money and then enact protectionist tariffs and regulations that raise the cost of everything retailers sell. Every business in America, with the possible exception of trial lawyers and casinos, is investing too little in politics compared to the costs of government imposed on them. (And for casinos and trial lawyers, they are usually not spending to stop being looted but to maintain regional monopolies and for trial lawyers, the ability to violate others' freedom of contract.)

The nice folks at Harvard Business School or on Wall Street will tell you that there is a return on investment (ROI) test you should run before a company makes an investment. Businesses generally want a return on an investment of 20 percent or more. That means that they will invest one million dollars in a new machine if it promises to return a profit of $200,000 each year.

One might invest to gain income or to reduce losses.

If a business was losing one million dollars a year in theft from an unfenced area, it would willingly pay to spend five million dollars to build a fence to stop the loss of one million a year. That would also be a return of 20 percent.

When Congress, state lawmakers, or a city threatens to raise annual taxes on a business by one million dollars the rational level to invest to stop that tax increase is five million dollars. Few if any companies or industries have ever spent that much money. They spend too little and are surprised when they lose. Every two years there are actual votes on statewide ballots to raise taxes. The business community has never invested enough to stop the higher tax to the point where their ROI would be 20 percent. They try and win lower taxes on the cheap and often fail.

Name any unreasonable permanent cost imposed on American businesses. In every case, if they had spent five times as much in political activity to stop the threat, they would have won. I would bet that, in fact, even if the business community insisted on a 100 percent rate of return, they would have won every single political fight. A 100 percent rate of return means that a company or industry would spend one dollar to stop the imposition of a one-dollar-per-year cost.

The first tax hike passed by the U.S. House of Representatives in thirteen years was passed on February 17, 2007. It was an $8 billion tax increase on the domestic production of oil over a ten-year period. If passed by the Senate and signed by the president, it would have meant an $800 million tax each and every year on the industry.

Had the oil industry spent five times that annual cost to stop the tax hike it would have meant investing $4 billion in TV ads, public education, mail, e-mail, and radio spots. If that amount had been invested simply to defeat ten congressmen it would have ensured that that was the last tax hike threatened.

Here is the greatest possible change in the future that would affect the political equation. If the business community increased its political activism to the point where it simply invested in politics rationally—as it invests in normal business activity—it would dwarf all other political spending and sweep all political opponents before it.

There is a second revolution that could and would radically alter the balance of power in America. Businesses might, just might, decide to factor in their own rational self-interest when they invest in politics. That would be a great change from how they now behave.

In 2006, the Fortune 500 spent tens of millions of dollars supporting left-wing environmental groups that have over time imposed annual costs of billions on the American economy. The Capital Research Center study of the giving patterns of the Fortune 100 in 2004 found $58,928,303 in contributions to left-wing causes and only $4,049,405 in contributions to foundations or groups that could be considered conservative.[1] If there were conservative trial lawyers they could rightly sue those corporate managers for misuse of their shareholders' wealth.

The business community contributed millions of dollars to Democrat candidates for Congress in 2006. These Democrat congressmen will try to raise the companies' taxes and work to force their workers to pay union dues, stop the expansion of free trade, dramatically expand the costs of regulation, and empower trial lawyers.

In 1980, when Ronald Reagan, the man who would go on to cut taxes and oversee the deregulation of oil and gas prices, railroads, airlines, trucks, and much of the media, ran for president, almost every Fortune 500 CEO supported someone else.

What is the history that brought the business community to its present state where it underinvests in politics and often invests against its own stated goals?

For almost all of the nineteenth century and the first half of the twentieth century much of the business community believed it benefited from protectionism, high tariffs that kept out British and European manufactured goods. Manufacturing was largely in the North and tariffs forced the agricultural and exporting South (and later the conquered South) to buy higher-priced goods from New England rather than Old England. When businessmen saw government as kneecapping their overseas competitors and under the progressive Republicans and later FDR, cartelizing the economy and using wage and price controls to stifle domestic competitors, they were unlikely allies for the limited-government, pro-freedom movement. The pre-Reagan Republican Party of Teddy Roosevelt and Herbert Hoover was thoroughly statist.

The Great Depression was used by Franklin Roosevelt and the left to demonize the business community and drive business leaders from the public arena. Before this, men such as Henry Ford, Andrew Carnegie, and Thomas Edison had been admired household names. Americans looked up to industrial titans, and their views on public policy were welcomed.

In the wake of the Great Depression and business bashing of the FDR Democrats, the business community and business leaders withdrew from public life and sent lobbyists to Washington to represent them rather than speak directly to the needs of their firms, industries, and workforce.

## THREE POSSIBLE STRATEGIES

A business leader has three approaches to choose from. First, he or she can push for general public policies that benefit the entire economy and through that benefit the businessman's firm, employees, and shareholders. Low taxes for all consumers; low taxes for all businesses, property rights, rule of law. This is the approach taken by Charles Erwin Wilson when Eisenhower nominated him to be the secretary of defense. During his confirmation hearings in the Senate he was challenged as to how as former president of General Motors he could be trusted with government powers, and was asked whether he could make a decision that would run counter to the interests of General Motors. Wilson answered in the affirmative, but added that he could not really conceive of a situation of this kind because "for years I thought what was good for the country was good for General Motors and vice versa."[2] Here he articulated a truth that should motivate all businessmen who engage politically. Most Americans remember this quotation as misquoted by the left claiming that he said, "What is good for General Motors is good for America."

A business community following this approach of general good government is the natural and comfortable ally of the Reagan Republican party.

Imagine what could be accomplished if the business community spent tens of millions of dollars each year explaining the benefits of free trade to all Americans. NAFTA and CAFTA were hard sells. Imagine how different future trade battles would be if businesses spent just 1 percent of the benefits America would win from freer trade actually promoting the benefits of free trade.

Every few years Congress votes to increase the minimum wage costing businesses and consumers billions of dollars but, more damaging, this kills just those entry-level jobs for the least-trained young men and women trying to enter the workforce. If businessmen spent a fraction of the money minimum wage laws cost them to maintain a regular conversation on the real-life economics, they could win these votes in Congress. But congressmen will not vote for good economics if it is lousy politics, and without a regular advertising effort, a vote against increasing the minimum wage is assumed to be a loser.

But there are two other business models.


## RENT SEEKERS

Rent seekers are businesses that use the power of the state to enrich themselves at the expense of others. Economic rents are those dollars "earned" as a result of government barriers to competition. High tariffs or quotas on imported sugar, for instance, increase the price of sugar made in America. They also increase the price of alternatives to sugar, such as corn syrup.

These businesses may also benefit from government contracts that pay above-market rates. If you sell the government something for the same price you could sell it to Wal-Mart, there is no economic rent and the government is not a preferred buyer. There is then no point— no profit—in spending money to lobby the government to buy your stuff. But as a business professor once said, there are two ways to get rich in America. One is to buy something from the government and the other is to sell something to the government. Money paid to receive monopoly profits resulting from government action—tariffs, regulations on entry to the industry, or government purchases of goods and services—are simply bribes.

Many Americans believe that all business lobbying is this form of bribery. That is why the general public supports strong restrictions on lobbying. They assume they are stopping bribery. But the best way to stop the government from giving out goodies is not to put fences around elected officials. It is to cut government spending and government power so that they cannot give anything away. If a congressman had no power to hand out earmarks or pork-barrel spending, there would be no need for a law forbidding taking him out for a three-martini lunch or flying him to Tahiti. No one outside his immediate family would buy him lunch. There would be no point.

Honest businessmen who simply wish to promote honest and limited government—here I repeat myself, because this is important—should fight to stop earmarks and pork-barrel spending and regulatory and tariff barriers that attract thieves masquerading as businesspeople.

## PAYING PROTECTION

Last, there is the model of paying protection money. In the gangster movies a tough guy in black shirt and white tie visits the shopkeeper and suggests that he pay the mob each week so that his windows are not broken. Many of the contributions lobbyists pay to Democrat politicians fall into this category.

If you don't contribute to the chairman of the Ways and Means Committee and his friends, perhaps they will raise your taxes. Or the other chairmen of committees might add regulatory burdens to your company.

In California's legislature certain bills that threaten to harm a particular industry are known as "juice bills" because they are introduced to induce contributions. Enough political contributions and the "juice bill" is withdrawn. A window on this world was opened with Brooks Jackson's book *Honest Graft*, which followed Congressman Tony Coelho's systematic harvesting of campaign contributions extracted from businesses that simply wanted lower taxes and tort reform to politicians who want higher taxes and no tort reform. These businesses were not being asked to contribute to support policies or politicians that would benefit all Americans or even their specific firms. They were contributing because it would be a shame if something bad were to happen to them.[3]

Some honest businessmen are forced into paying protection money. They need the entire business community to invest in good government and the rule of law to stop those rent seekers who would pay bribes to get advantage and to stop themselves from being shaken down.

## BUYING ACCESS

Business lobbyists often speak about "buying access." This can be access used to gain monopoly rents or grants or contracts from the government. Pay to Play. Or the access can be defensive. The ability to come and plead with congressmen not to hurt them. Payment can come in campaign contributions or in hiring the family and staff of congressmen to work for said company or trade association.

It is a huge mistake to measure the political spending of Fortune 500 companies or trade associations by looking at the collection of $2,000 individual and $5,000 PAC checks they and their staffs write. That is chump change compared to the resources that trade associations or companies contribute to one team or the other through their hiring practices.

You will often find conservative, free-market leaders of trade associations who hire former Democrat staffers or the wives and children of Democrat congressmen and senators. By this act they are contributing not a few hundred or thousand dollars to the left but a $200,000 annual salary. Bush gave out pins for "Rangers," those Republicans who raised $200,000 one time for his presidential campaign. A free-market businessman who hires a Democrat as a lobbyist is becoming a "Ranger" for the Democrat left. And not one, but every year the salary is paid. More money flows from business to the Democrat left that supports the efforts of the trial lawyers, labor unions, and tax collectors to damage that business and its shareholders than exists in all the PAC contributions the watchdog groups examine. Democrats hired by the business community not only earn lucrative salaries, they then often skew their business campaign contributions back to their former employers or family members rather than to political leaders that agree with Americans they are legally contracted to represent.

How will the business community's political campaign contributions, and more important, its hiring of trade-association representatives and Washington corporate offices, flow in the next twenty-five years? There are two reasons to believe that the business community will increasingly support Reagan Republicans at the national level.

First, at the national level the two parties have switched their historic positions and the business community has also changed as a result of globalization. The Democrats, once the party of free trade, have become—at the behest of organized labor—the party of protectionism. Republicans have largely moved to support free trade. In the most recent vote on extending NAFTA to Central America (CAFTA) only 15 of the Democrats voted for free trade and 202 of 229 Republicans voted for free trade (2 Republicans did not vote). And a previously protectionist business community is increasingly committed to free trade worldwide.

Trial lawyers have attached themselves to the Democrat Party and the Democrats are firmly attached to trial-lawyer money. This alliance makes it impossible for anyone to speak of a "pro-business" Democrat. Trial lawyers and businessmen large and small are Hannibal and Scipio. Deadly and permanent enemies. You must choose between them. You cannot be friends of both. And the Democrats have chosen the trial lawyers and turned their backs on the entire business community.

The second reason is that when the Democrats lost the House and Senate in 1994, they lost much of their ability to extort money and jobs from the business community through threatened tax hikes and regulations. After the 1994 election, much of K Street, those men and women who work for trade associations and corporate offices, reacted like the silver-faced guards in *The Wizard of Oz* when the Wicked Witch of the West is hit with a pail of water and melts. "Hey, Republicans, we were always with you. We were always rooting for you."

For the following twelve years the business community began to contribute more rationally to candidates and incumbents who shared its vision of free trade, tort reform, low taxes, and deregulation. But progress was slow as many former Democrat staffers from Capitol Hill working as lobbyists were actually loyal to their former Democrat employers in Congress.

Businesses that had regularly sent protection checks to Democrat congressmen who raised their taxes up to and including the 1994 election were now freed to contribute based on their real interests rather than fear.

Agribusiness PACs had contributed roughly equal amounts to Republican and Democrat candidates from 1980 to 1990. They shifted to 60–40 Republican-Democrat from 1990 to 1994, and then to ratios greater than 70–30 after 1994.[4]

Defense PACs contributed roughly equally to the parties of Ronald Reagan and Ted Kennedy in 1990 and 1992 and then shot up to 60–40 in 1994 in favor of the Democrats. To get some idea of how politicians can threaten business into contributing against their interests, note the timing. The defense industry greatly increased its giving to stop a Republican Congress. Freed of these threats the defense industry shifted to ratios above 60–40 to Republicans from 1996 to 2006.[5]

The finance, insurance, and real estate PACS, which should have been fighting for tort reform, lower property taxes, and deregulation, were instead shoveling a majority of their funds to the Democrats in 1990 and gave 50–50 in 1992 and 1994. Only after Tony Coelho's party could not threaten them did their giving shift to 60–40 toward the Republicans from 1996 to 2006.

Bloomberg reported in January 2007 that the top twenty-five business PACS all shifted somewhat toward the Democrats in their giving after Democrats won majorities in the House and Senate in the November 7, 2006, election. This occured despite the fact that the Democrats were after twelve years in the minority—even more antifree trade, pro–trial lawyer, and more supportive of tax hikes. What had changed was they had more power. This shift reflects those businesses that were contributing not on principle, but either paying protection money or hoping to pay to play in return for earmarks and favorable legislation.[6]

Those businesses that after 1994 got used to contributing based on general principle are more likely to continue, and despite the narrow congressional majorities won by the Democrats in 2006, it will be difficult for Tony Coehloism to return in force, as much of the power of the Democrat majority from 1932 to 1994 was the certainty that it was inevitable and that wise businessmen would deal with this reality. Now everyone knows that the majority can and has changed hands and may again.

On the other hand, labor union PACs never dipped below 85 percent support for Democrats and never more than 15 percent for Republicans before or after 1994. Their interests hadn't changed, why should their giving? Lawyers and lobbyists gave 70–30 for Democrats before 1994 and never dipped below 65–35 in favor of the Democrats after 1994.[7] Again, lawyers and lobbyists were contributing to further their interests, not responding to threats.

The business community could go either way. Its activism and contributions could flow to issues and candidates who support free markets, free trade, tort reform, and rule of law. That would bring the business community as a whole into the Leave Us Alone Coalition. Or perhaps some companies and industries will stay or move to the Takings Coalition—those industries that believe they profit from high tariffs, higher taxes, and government regulation and subsidies. The Democrats will work hard to get as many firms and industries dependent on the state as possible. Subsidies for Green Energy. Jimmy Carter's synfuels. Al Gore's high-tech subsidies. Creating political property rights such as "cap and trade" carbon regulations. Subsidies for favored industries, factories, or regions. They hope that corporate welfare will make businessmen as dependent on the state as Aid for

Families with Dependent Children did to many inner-city poor families. And while corporate welfare costs taxpayers more money, the payoff to politicians is greater. Not simply a vote every two years, but truly large and frequent campaign contributions.

The business community will be divided between those who fight for principle and those who fearfully pay protection money or greedily prefer to contribute rather than compete as a business strategy.

The Leave Us Alone Coalition must hunt down and reduce or eliminate all corporate welfare, all tariff barriers, earmarks, and pork spending: all economic rents. The Takings Coalition will strive to invent new reasons for new forms of corporate welfare. The race is on.

## CHAPTER FIFTEEN

# RACE AND POLITICS

The Hispanic and African-American votes are a tantalizing and important target for both parties. A look at the demographics of both groups and the issues and interests that are important to them shows that a surprising number of both groups might very naturally gravitate to the Leave Us Alone Coalition. But it's not that simple. The Republicans have a lot of work to do—but the payoff could be great.

## "The Hispanic Vote" Is Many Votes

The number of Hispanics living in America is growing, the number of Hispanics eligible to vote and actually voting is growing also but not as rapidly, and the Hispanic vote is "in play," not owned by either party.

Hispanics have increased from 9.5 million, or 4.7 percent, of the population in 1970 to 42.7 million, or 14 percent of the population in 2006.[1]

Hispanics were 5 percent of the presidential vote in 1988 and 8 percent of the vote in 2004 when they voted 53 percent for Kerry and 44 percent for Bush.

In the congressional elections of 1994, Republicans won 39 percent of the Hispanic vote. But twelve years later, following a year of anti-immigration rhetoric, the Hispanic vote in 2006 shifted dramatically toward the Democrats, who won 69 percent of the off-year Hispanic vote.[2]

We know our demographic future.

In 2004, there were 4,115,590 births in the United States. Of those, 944,993 births, almost 23 percent, were to Hispanics.[3] Therefore in 2022, 23 percent of those eighteen-year-olds available to vote for the first time will be Hispanic. Everyone born in the United States is a citizen. Their children are citizens.

The question is not whether America should become more ethnically Hispanic. It will. The question is how the two coalitions will react to this stubborn fact.

The Democrat Party's preferred narrative is that Hispanics will become like African Americans. They will increasingly tend to vote Democrat, and nothing the Republican Party can do will alter this. As the number of Hispanics grows, they create an inevitable Democrat majority.

But several factors may change that script for the future.

First, the future is slow in coming. The growth in the number of Hispanics in America is not matched by as rapid an increase in the Hispanic vote as a percentage of the voting population. This is because some Hispanics are not legally in the country and thus not eligible to vote; new legal immigrants are often slower to register and vote even when here legally; and the Hispanic population is younger than the rest of America and many Hispanics are below the age of eighteen. The Leave Us Alone Coalition has time to reintroduce itself to Hispanic Americans.

Second, there is no such thing as "the Hispanic vote." There are Cuban Americans, Puerto Ricans, Mexican Americans, and Latin Americans from Central and South America. Hispanics came to America from many different places over a several-hundred-year period. They do not share one religion or culture.

Despite the hopes and hard work of the modern Democrat Party,

Hispanic Americans have not become the new blacks. They are not lost to the Republican Party. There are several reasons. First, the approximately one million Cuban Americans tend to vote Republican. It was a weak Democrat president who gave their country to the Communists, and American liberals like to praise the Communist dictator, Fidel Castro, who murdered so many Cubans and enslaved the island nation. Democrats speaking to their domestic-left constituency have insulted Cuban Americans by belittling their suffering and cheering the dictator who destroyed their former homeland. The same can be said of Nicaraguans and El Salvadorans as the Communist government of the Sandinistas and the Communist guerrillas of FNLA were praised, defended, and apologized for by leading Democrats.

Some Republicans point out correctly that many Hispanics are religious and social conservatives. Therefore, they reason, once across the border they should vote like religious and traditional native-born Americans—Republican.

One caveat: If the vote-moving issue for a Mexican was the ability to practice his Roman Catholic faith and raise his children in that faith, it is unlikely he would travel one thousand miles north, cross a hostile border, and enter a country that is secular or at best Protestant. An Hispanic immigrant may well be a believing Roman Catholic, but the motivating force in his life is economic advancement. (Or, for some immigrants, it is fleeing Communism in Cuba, Nicaragua, or El Salvador.) Here Republicans have the advantage. The first thing anyone paying attention to the political debate in America for the past fifty years learns is that Democrats hate the rich. Republicans want you to get rich.

Many Hispanics are devout Christians. In addition to an attraction to the Republican Party as the party of economic advancement rather than welfare and leveling, they are likely to be repelled by the aggressive secularism of the modern Democrat Party and its hostility to both religious Catholics and evangelical Protestants. The National Association of Evangelicals estimates that six hundred thousand Hispanics become evangelical Protestants each year.[4] This trend may continue for structural reasons, as *Crisis* magazine reports that there

are only 2,500 Latino priests and only 500 Latinos are currently study-
ing to become priests.[5]

This has political implications as Protestant Hispanics vote Republican more than Roman Catholic Hispanics. The Pew Center's exit
polls in 2004 show that among voters at least 55 percent of Hispanics
were Roman Catholic, 32 percent were Protestant/other Christian, 8
percent were of no religion, 1 percent were Jewish, and 4 percent were
something else. The Protestant number of 32 percent was up from 25
percent four years earlier.[6]

While all Hispanics voted 44 percent for Bush in 2004, up from 35
percent in 2000, Hispanic Protestants voted 56 percent for Bush in
2004, up from 44 percent in 2000. Pew writes, "Hispanic Protestants"
were both a growing and increasingly pro-Republican constituency
between the two elections. Latino Protestants were 23 percent more
supportive of Bush than Latino Catholics. (This is twice the partisan divide between white Protestants and Catholics—12 percent in
2004.)[7]

A wise Republican Party might not be sending so many border
guards to the southern border, but, rather, more Protestant mission-
aries.

On political philosophy, the Pew poll found Hispanics self-reported
26 percent liberal, 45 percent moderate, and 30 percent conservative.
On a partisan basis, Hispanic voters in 2004 self-reported 49 percent
Democrat, 27 percent Republican, and 24 percent Independent.[8]

The left hopes that the Democrat Party will be helped in competing for the Hispanic vote by two forces. First, the seductive attraction
of government benefits—free health care, welfare, government jobs—
and second, the repulsion of the rhetoric of the Tom Tancredos of
the world that, oddly enough, is seen as immigrant bashing and
anti-Hispanic.

Why do the Republicans do better with the Hispanic vote in Texas
and Florida than in California and New York? First, welfare benefits in
Texas and Florida are lower. Few immigrants come to Texas or Florida
expecting something for nothing and fewer still are offered free stuff
when they arrive. In California and New York welfare benefits are

higher, rules are looser, and the hardest-working immigrant is suscep-
tible to the temptation of something for nothing. (Note that most
people who become dependent on welfare in New York and California
were born here.)

Texas and Florida have Republican leaders whose rhetoric is pro-
immigrant—President Bush, Florida governor Jeb Bush, Texas governor Rick Perry, and Senator Mel Martinez. California Republicans
helped put initiative 187 on the ballot to cut off welfare to immigrants. The campaign for this initiative and Pete Wilson running for
reelection that same year were seen as anti-immigrant by many. Certainly the Democrats have created a storyline that makes this seem
true now, even if it was intended to be antiwelfare at the time. You are
not always in control of defining your motives. The other team gets a
time at bat also.

The lesson of the 2006 congressional election is that anti-immigrant
rhetoric and votes in favor of walling off the southern border did not
win votes for Republicans. What seemed so exciting when bandied
about on right-wing talk radio was not a vote winner on Election Day
2006. Not only was there no "upside" with the white or African-
American vote for focusing on immigration, there was a downside as
the Republican vote among Hispanics fell to 30 percent. Those congressional Republicans who ran primarily on an anti-immigrant platform, Randy Graf and J. D. Hayworth of Arizona and John Hostetler
of Indiana, all lost. The silver bullet of restrictionism backfired. Jon
Kyl, the Republican senator from Arizona ran on restrictionist policies as opposed to John McCain's, won in 2006 with a margin of 9
percent compared to McCain's winning margin of 55 percent in 2004.[9]
Anti-immigrant advocates cannot point to an election in 2006 where
their policies helped Republicans. The casualties were all on their
side.

One challenge to the idea that the Hispanic vote can be channeled
to one party is that there is no Jesse Jackson for the Latinos. No one
person or even an oligarchy claims to speak for all Hispanics. Who
would inform Hispanics that they "have" to vote Democrat?

And just who are you calling Hispanic? What good are projections of the Hispanic vote when, as Ben Wattenberg points out, 37 percent of all Hispanics marry someone of another ethnic group? That number is 13 percent for the first generation, 34 percent for the second generation, and 54 percent for the third generation. By comparison, Asian Americans intermarry at a rate of 64 percent, non-Orthodox Jews at 50 percent, and African Americans at 9 percent.[10]

If the Republicans can maintain more than 40 percent of the Hispanic vote, they get to run the country for the next twenty-five years. If they fall below 25 percent, they don't. If Republicans can avoid chasing away Hispanics as they did European Catholics with the rhetoric of "Rum, Romanism, and rebellion," they can speak to a growing Hispanic vote just as they address other successful Americans, hoping to make more of them investors, self-employed, tax-conscious, non-welfare-dependent or government-employed . . . Republicans.

## CAN THE BLACK VOTE BE MOVED?

In 1790, there were 757,208 blacks in the United States, 59,527 free and the rest enslaved. That was 19 percent of the American population. In 1860, just before the Civil War, there were 4,441,830 blacks, 14 percent of the population, of whom 488,070 were free. The 1990 census counted thirty million African Americans, 12 percent of the population.[11]

Blacks cast 11 percent of the vote in 2004 and gave Bush 11 percent of their votes, up from 9 percent in 2000. In the last nine presidential elections the Republican presidential candidate has won an average of 11.9 percent of the African-American vote. Richard Nixon in 1972 did best with 18 percent.

I went to public school in Massachusetts, but recently I was watching the History Channel and learned that Abraham Lincoln, the first Republican president in American history, fought a civil war to end slavery and that the Democrat Party was uncooperative in this effort. Why then are black Americans voting overwhelmingly in all fifty states for the Democrat Party?

Michael Zak, the author of *Back to Basics for the Republican Party*, has made a one-man industry of trying to remind all Americans— starting with the Republicans—of the accurate history of Republicans and civil rights. Bruce Bartlett has added to the intellectual ammunition with the hard-hitting book *Wrong on Race: The Democratic Party's Forgotten Racist Past.*

The Republican Party was formed in 1856 in support of free labor and free land. Republicans opposed the extension of slavery and led the abolitionist movement. Frederick Douglass was a Republican. Democrats supported slavery in the slave states and fought to extend it westward.

After the Civil War, the Republican Party passed the Thirteenth, Fourteenth, and Fifteenth Amendments ending slavery, guaranteeing civil liberties and voting rights for black Americans. Republicans fought against lynching and for grants of land to African Americans. But perhaps more recent history is driving the black vote with a focus on the Civil Rights Act of 1964, allowing full access to "public accommodations" like hotels and restaurants, and the Voting Rights Act of 1965. But here too Republicans provided a higher percentage of their party in support than Democrats. The Civil Rights Act of 1964 passed with 290 votes, 138 Republicans and only 152 Democrats. Of the 130 votes against the Act, there were ninety-six Democrats and only thirty-four Republicans.[12] The 1965 Voting Rights Act had the support of Republican Senate leader Everett Dirksen and House Republican leader Gerald R. Ford, Jr. Sixty percent of Republicans but only 40 percent of Democrats voted for the Act.[13]

Perhaps African Americans focused on the national leadership, where Democrat president Johnson and vice president Hubert Humphrey led the fight for civil rights and Republican senator and 1964 presidential candidate for the Republicans, Barry Goldwater, voted no on the grounds of states' rights and freedom of contract.

The modern Republican Party looks at the African-American vote and wonders why it cannot attract more than 10 percent. Blacks are more likely to be churchgoers. They are largely Protestant churchgoers, theologically the kin of Ralph Reed and Jerry Falwell. African

Americans support school choice by large margins. They want prayer in school overwhelmingly. They suffer more than others from violent crime and at the hands of the liberal judges who release criminals back onto the street. They are disproportionately in the armed forces. They are not particularly excited about tax increases.

Seen in profile they should be likely Republican voters.

Is it a leadership-led vote? Perhaps ministers tell congregations how to vote? Does Jesse Jackson or now Al Sharpton stand between Republican elected officials or candidates and filter their message so that Republican ideas valued by black voters cannot be heard? Maybe, but when in 2004 a Republican governor of Alabama placed a billion-dollar tax hike on the state ballot promising that he was shifting taxes from the poor onto the rich, he lost the entire state 68–32 and lost the black vote, even though many black pastors and all black newspapers endorsed the tax hike.[14]

The black vote has consistently supported recent statewide initiatives to ban gay marriages. Black men are the group that polls most strongly pro-life/antiabortion. Black Americans can and do support many conservative positions.

But the African-American vote for candidates remains stubbornly Democrat.

One challenge may be that black support for the Democrat Party is swayed by the higher percentage of blacks who work for the government. Many higher-income African Americans with college degrees work for the government. They are unlikely candidates to vote Republican.

Some Republicans write the black vote off and take the position that "we have tried repeatedly to win the vote and we just cannot do it. We don't know why we cannot, but rather than focus on winning more than 10 percent of 10 percent of the vote we should focus on winning a bigger share of the 90 percent of the vote that is not African American." Doubling the percentage of the black vote for a Republican candidate from 10 percent to 20 percent is the equivalent in number of increasing the percentage of the white vote Republicans win by 1.3 percent. We don't know how to win that many black votes. Republicans do know how to increase margins among other voters by 1.3 percent. No sweat.

Another factor is that a majority of African Americans live in the eleven Southern states of the old Confederacy.[15] In the close elections of 2000 and 2004, the Republican presidential candidate swept all eleven states both times. In those eleven states Republicans hold 17 of the 22 Senate seats and 77 of the 131 congressional districts. Perhaps only one half of the black vote is therefore really in play. Why don't the Democrats spend more time trying to win the Mormon vote? Much of it is in safely Republican states.

The black vote is important in swing states like Wisconsin, Pennsylvania, Illinois, Ohio, and Michigan. If the Republican Party ever figured out how to make the black vote competitive in elections, the modern Democrat Party would be broken. The South would be gone, as would the industrial Midwest. The same is true if the Republicans could win a majority of the Hispanic vote, pass tort reform and defund the trial-lawyer money flowing in to the Democrats, win parity in Jewish-American campaign contributions, and/or end the use of compulsory union dues in politics. Any one of those five changes would make the Democrats uncompetitive in presidential and congressional races. It may be a rational decision to focus on one of the four targets other than the black vote, but there is no excuse for not knocking at the door each election and coming by to visit and ask politely for African-American support while reiterating again and again that on school choice, crime control, respect for people of faith and traditional values, the Republican Party agrees with the black community. One day the wall keeping the Republican Party and African Americans apart may crumble.

## CHAPTER SIXTEEN

# THE SENATE, THE HOUSE, THE PRESIDENCY

## THE SENATE

The Senate offers two advantages to Republicans. First, the nice folks who drew the state lines created a whole bunch of square states out west that are thinly populated. Some have three people in them. Two are Republican senators and one is the Republican congressman. The second advantage the permanent gerrymander of the Senate provides to Republicans is that unlike redistricting in the House, which threatens to change the rules once every ten years, there is no ungerrymandering the Senate. Those lines are fixed. There are only two provisions in the Constitution that cannot be amended. One, the process for amending the Constitution. And two, the relative power of the states in the Senate.

In the 50–50 election that was Gore/Bush, the Republicans carried thirty states and the Democrats twenty. In the evenly matched 2004 election with Bush at 51 percent and Kerry at 49, Republicans carried thirty-one states and the Democrats carried nineteen. Over time, as the nice citizens of North and South Dakota realize that they are voting for conservative Republicans for president and unreconstructed Bolsheviks for the Senate, they may reconsider, as they did in 2004 by replacing Democrat Daschle with Republican John Thune. (Here we are not imagining that Republicans do as well in winning Senate seats as they do with a strong presidential candidate like Reagan in 1980 and 1984, who carried forty-four and forty-nine states, respectively, and Nixon in 1972, who carried forty-nine states.) Republicans carried thirty and thirty-one states in the weak presidential elections in 2000 and 2004 and even carried a majority of states, twenty-seven, when Gerald Ford lost in 1976.

Today there are twenty Democrat senators in states that voted for Bush in 2004 and seven Republicans in states that voted for Kerry. If over time voters rationalize their Senate and presidential votes, the Senate will have sixty-two Republican senators. This is enough to override a filibuster attempt even if John McCain and Ohio's George Voinovich are playing gin rummy in the Democrat cloakroom.

For years political observers have wondered why the Senate and the House operated so differently. Fire-breathing bomb throwers of either party who began in the House move up (or over) to the Senate and behave like neutered bulls. Why? While the House plays team ball, the Senate rules do not give a great power to a simple majority. The Senate is every man for himself. Many senators believe they could or should be president. This appears odd, as presidents have come largely from the ranks of governors.

But senators see presidents up close and say to themselves, immediate family, and anyone willing to listen, "I could do that better." And often they are telling the truth. If everyone else in the Senate, of your party and the other party, are potential rivals there is less interest in playing well with the other senators in team efforts. Americans outside Washington are surprised to hear that prominent senators of both parties, often those who are serious contenders for the presidency in the past and future, are disliked by their fellow senators.

One difference between the House and Senate has become more pronounced in the past decade and is perhaps as permanent as anything is in politics. This is the fact that to run the House of Representatives, to enact legislation, you simply need a majority of the House.

There you can brush aside any amendments. The minority has little ability to obstruct. In the Senate we are all aware of the filibuster from *Mr. Smith Goes to Washington* and stories of the filibusters of civil rights legislation. But beginning with Tom Daschle of South Dakota and continuing with Harry Reid of Nevada, Democrats changed the rules to require sixty votes for almost everything including sending conferees to House-Senate conferences where bills are finalized. Now that the Republicans find themselves in the minority in the Senate, one presumes that Republican senator Mitch McConnell of Kentucky as their leader will respect this new definition of minority rights demanding sixty votes for anything vaguely important.

This rule of sixty votes does not affect the two parties equally. A Republican party that nationalizes elections and wins Senate seats where it carries the presidential vote can and should have sixty senators on many occasions, not just after landslides. With the Solid South no longer in the Democrat column and even weak Republican presidential candidates carrying thirty and thirty-one states, the Republicans will hold sixty Senate seats from time to time. This means that "movement breaking" legislation that would damage the Republican Party can be stopped by a Republican Party holding only forty seats in the Senate even if the Democrats command the House and presidency. This would certainly include changes in labor law, liability law, and election rules that would do permanent damage to the Leave Us Alone Coalition. And a Republican Party that can run a national effort such as the Reagan campaigns or the 1994 "Contract with America" campaign will periodically find itself with sixty Senate votes and the ability to change the correlation of forces in politics. For instance, with sixty Republican senators—and only with sixty or more Republican senators—one can pass the personalization of Social Security, giving every American control over his or her personal savings accounts in a fully funded and individually held Social Security system. School choice at a national level, the end of compulsory unionism, and the personalization of Medicare, as with Social Security, will also certainly require sixty Republicans.

Reid's "Rule of Sixty" gives the Leave Us Alone Coalition a "ratchet"-effect advantage because Republicans will periodically hold sixty Senate seats and have the ability to pass legislation weakening the Takings Coalition, but it is extremely unlikely that the Democrats will ever again hold sixty Senate seats and be able to cripple the component parts of the Leave Us Alone Coalition.

The response of some conservatives to Daschle and Reid's changing of the rules was like the *Far Side* cartoon where the cavalryman inside the Western fort observes, "The Indians are lighting their arrows on fire. Can they do that?" The proper response to the Democrats' decision to require sixty votes for everything is to go get the sixty votes.

## 20 DEMOCRAT SENATORS IN BUSH 2004 STATES

| U.S. SEN. | STATE | BUSH % | CAND.% | DOB |
|---|---|---|---|---|
| Ben Nelson | NE | 67 | 63.88 ('06) | 5/17/1941 |
| Kent Conrad | ND | 63 | 68.83 ('06) | 5/12/1948 |
| Byron Dorgan | ND | 63 | 68.28 ('04) | 5/14/1942 |
| Evan Bayh | IN | 60 | 61.65 ('04) | 12/26/1955 |
| Tim Johnson | SD | 60 | 49.62 ('02) | 12/28/1946 |
| John Tester | MT | 59 | 49.16 ('06) | 8/21/1956 |
| Max Baucus | MT | 59 | 62.74 ('02) | 12/11/1941 |
| Mary Landrieu | LA | 57 | 51.70 ('02) | 11/23/1955 |
| Robert Byrd | WV | 56 | 64.49 ('06) | 11/20/1917 |
| John Rockefeller | WV | 56 | 63.10 ('02) | 6/18/1937 |
| James Webb | VA | 54 | 49.59 ('06) | 2/9/1946 |
| Blanche Lincoln | AR | 54 | 55.90 ('04) | 9/30/1960 |
| Mark Pryor | AR | 54 | 53.90 ('02) | 1/10/1963 |

| U.S. SEN. | STATE | BUSH % | CAND.% | DOB |
|-----------|-------|--------|--------|-----|
| Claire McCaskill | MO | 53 | 49.58 ('06) | 7/24/1953 |
| Bill Nelson | FL | 52 | 60.30 ('06) | 9/29/1942 |
| Ken Salazar | CO | 52 | 51.30 ('04) | 3/2/1955 |
| Sherrod Brown | OH | 51 | 56.16 ('06) | 11/9/1952 |
| Harry Reid | NV | 51 | 61.08 ('04) | 11/2/1939 |
| Jeff Bingaman | NM | 50 | 70.16 ('06) | 10/3/1943 |
| Tom Harkin | IA | 50 | 54.18 ('02) | 11/19/1939 |

Republicans do not have sixty senators. But when they simply perform to par—win as many Senate seats as the number of states carried by their second-tier presidential candidates—the idea of a Republican supermajority in the Senate will yield as strong a legislative advantage as a simple majority yields in the House.

## 7 REPUBLICAN SENATORS IN KERRY 2004 STATES

| U.S. SEN. | STATE | KERRY % | CAND.% | DOB |
|-----------|-------|---------|--------|-----|
| Olympia Snow | ME | 53 | 74.01 ('06) | 2/21/1947 |
| Susan Collins | ME | 53 | 58.44 ('02) | 12/7/1942 |
| Gordon Smith | OR | 52 | 56.21 ('02) | 5/25/1952 |
| Norm Coleman | MN | 51 | 49.52 ('02) | 8/17/1949 |
| Arlen Specter | PA | 51 | 52.62 ('04) | 2/12/1930 |
| John Sununu | NH | 50 | 50.82 ('02) | 9/10/1964 |
| Judd Gregg | NH | 50 | 66.18 ('04) | 2/14/1947 |

## The House of Representatives

The natural seat of power for conservatives today is in the House of Representatives. A simple majority in the House gives one control of the political agenda. There is no filibuster in the House. No minority rights. It is winner take all.

This is the true post-Gingrich revolution of 1994. Not simply because the Republicans won and held the House for six elections in a row, but because when Gingrich became Speaker he changed the nature of the House of Representatives under Republican control by term-limiting committee chairmen and bringing power into the hands of the Republican caucus—exercised, on their behalf, by the Speaker.

In the past the House was not run by the caucus of the majority party, but by a collection of chieftains, squabbling nobility, and powerful barons—the committee chairmen. John Dingell, Dan Rostenkowski, and Jack Brooks ran their fiefdoms, brooking little interference from Democrat presidents like Carter or even the Democrat Speaker.

The Republicans lost the majority in the House on November 7, 2006. The Democrats will work hard to hold on to their present majority of 233 to 202. They face several challenges. The first is that sixty-one of those Democrats won in districts that voted for Bush in the weak presidential year of 2004. If the Republicans won those districts that voted 51 percent or more for Bush in 2004, they would win a majority of 252 seats. If they won only those seats carried by 55 percent or more for Bush, they would have a stronger majority than in 2004, 236 seats.

The Republican history from 1994 to 2006 shows how tenacious the 1994 majority was.

The Republican majority won in 1994 was not expected to last. On November 8, 1994, Republicans gained a total of fifty-four House seats and then five Democrat House members switched parties to join the new majority. The previous Republican interregnums in 1947–1949 and 1953–1955 have each lasted only one House term. Official

## 8 REPUBLICAN REPRESENTATIVES IN DISTRICTS
## CARRIED BY KERRY IN 2004

| U.S. REP. | DISTRICT | KERRY % | CANDIDATE% IN 2006 | DOB |
|---|---|---|---|---|
| Christopher Shays | CT-4 | 52% | 50.96% | 10/18/45 |
| Mark Kirk | IL-10 | 53% | 53.38% | 9/15/59 |
| Michael Castle | DE-AL | 53% | 57.20% | 7/2/39 |
| Dave Reichert | WA-8 | 51% | 51.46% | 8/29/50 |
| Heather Wilson | NM-1 | 51% | 50.21% | 12/30/60 |
| Jim Gerlach | PA-6 | 51% | 50.64% | 2/25/55 |
| Charlie Dent | PA-15 | 50% | 53.60% | 5/24/60 |
| James Walsh | NY-25 | 50% | 50.79% | 6/19/47 |

Washington expected the world to right itself and restore the Democrats to their natural control of the House in 1996. The GOP House majority did fall by 9 seats, from 235 to 226, while a popular Bill Clinton used his White House in most innovative ways to raise campaign cash and defeat a hapless Bob Dole 49 percent to 41 percent.

Two years later, in 1998, Republicans lost another 5 House seats, shrinking the caucus to 223, while holding steady in the Senate. The focus on Clinton's personal failures and talk of impeachment did not help Republicans in congressional races.

Republicans lost 2 House seats in 2000 while George W. Bush was losing the popular vote to Al Gore, and the House caucus stood at 221.

In 2002, the year of the Enron scandal, recession, and the tense interval between the toppling of the Taliban government in Afghanistan and the later war in Iraq, Republicans gained 7 seats in the House, giving them a majority of 228. This GOP gain took place even

## 61 DEMOCRAT CONGRESSMEN IN DISTRICTS CARRIED BY BUSH IN 2004

| U.S. REP. | DISTRICT | BUSH % | CAND.% IN 2006 | DOB | U.S. REP. | DISTRICT | BUSH % | CAND.% IN 2006 | DOB |
|---|---|---|---|---|---|---|---|---|---|
| Chet Edwards | TX-17 | 70% | 58.11% | 11/24/51 | Ruben Hinojosa | TX-15 | 55% | 61.77% | 8/20/40 |
| Gene Taylor | MS-4 | 68% | 80.00% | 9/17/53 | Solomon Ortiz | TX-27 | 55% | 56.77% | 6/3/37 |
| Jim Matheson | UT-2 | 66% | 58.99% | 3/21/60 | Steve Kagen | WI-8 | 55% | 50.89% | 12/12/49 |
| Ciro D. Rodriguez | TX-23 | 65% | 54.32% | 12/9/46 | Harry Mitchell | AZ-5 | 54% | 51.00% | 7/18/40 |
| Ike Skelton | MO-4 | 64% | 67.90% | 12/20/31 | Jerry McNerney | CA-11 | 54% | 53.30% | 5/4/05 |
| Nick Lampson | TX-22 | 64% | 51.79% | 2/14/45 | Tim Mahoney | FL-16 | 54% | 49.50% | 8/15/56 |
| Earl Pomeroy | ND-AL | 63% | 65.68% | 9/2/52 | Allen Boyd | FL-2 | 54% | N/A | 6/6/45 |
| Brad Ellsworth | IN-8 | 62% | 61.00% | 9/11/58 | Sanford Bishop | GA-2 | 54% | 67.90% | 2/4/47 |
| Bud Cramer | AL-5 | 60% | N/A | 8/22/47 | Bob Etheridge | NC-2 | 54% | 66.00% | 8/7/41 |
| Chris Carney | PA-10 | 60% | 52.90% | 3/2/59 | John Hall | NY-19 | 54% | 51.00% | 7/23/48 |

| U.S. REP. | DISTRICT | BUSH % | CAND.% IN 2006 | DOB | U.S. REP. | DISTRICT | BUSH % | CAND.% IN 2006 | DOB |
| --- | --- | --- | --- | --- | --- | --- | --- | --- | --- |
| Stephanie Herseth | SD-AL | 60% | 69.09% | 12/3/70 | Kirsten Gillibrand | NY-20 | 54% | 53.00% | 12/9/66 |
| Bart Gordon | TN-6 | 60% | 67.09% | 1/24/49 | Jason Altmire | PA-4 | 54% | 51.99% | 3/7/68 |
| Baron Hill | IN-9 | 59% | 50.00% | 6/23/53 | Gabrielle Giffords | AZ-8 | 53% | 54.00% | 6/8/70 |
| Nancy Boyda | KS-2 | 59% | 51.00% | 8/2/55 | Bart Stupak | MI-1 | 53% | 69.00% | 2/29/52 |
| Dan Boren | OK-2 | 59% | 72.74% | 8/2/73 | Mike Arcuri | NY-24 | 53% | 54.00% | 6/11/59 |
| Rick Boucher | VA-9 | 59% | 67.76% | 8/1/46 | John Tanner | TN-8 | 53% | 73.18% | 9/22/44 |
| Ben Chandler | KY-6 | 58% | 85.50% | 9/12/59 | Henry Cuellar | TX-28 | 53% | 67.61% | 9/19/55 |
| Charlie Melancon | LA-3 | 58% | 55.00% | 10/3/47 | Nick Rahall | WV-3 | 53% | 69.36% | 5/20/49 |
| Tim Holden | PA-17 | 58% | 64.50% | 3/5/57 | Marion Berry | AR-1 | 52% | 69.15% | 8/27/42 |
| Lincoln Davis | TN-4 | 58% | 66.45% | 9/13/43 | Vic Snyder | AR-2 | 51% | 60.54% | 9/27/47 |

| Name | District | | | Date | Name | District | | | Date |
|------|----------|------|--------|---------|------|----------|------|--------|--------|
| Alan Mollohan | WV-1 | 58% | 64.33% | 5/14/43 | Mike Ross | AR-4 | 51% | 74.54% | 8/2/61 |
| Heath Shuler | NC-11 | 57% | 54.00% | 12/31/71 | Tim Walz | MN-1 | 51% | 53.00% | 4/6/64 |
| Zack Space | OH-18 | 57% | 62.00% | 1/27/61 | Carol Shea-Porter | NH-1 | 51% | 52.00% | 12/2/52 |
| John Spratt | SC-5 | 57% | 56.90% | 11/1/42 | Charlie Wilson | OH-6 | 51% | 62.08% | 1/18/43 |
| Melissa Bean | IL-8 | 56% | 50.90% | 1/22/62 | Dennis Cardoza | CA-18 | 50% | 65.50% | 3/31/59 |
| Joe Donnelly | IN-2 | 56% | 54.00% | 9/28/55 | Loretta Sanchez | CA-47 | 50% | 62.40% | 1/7/60 |
| Mike McIntyre | NC-7 | 56% | 73.00% | 8/6/56 | Leonard Boswell | IA-3 | 50% | 52.00% | 1/10/34 |
| John Salazar | CO-3 | 55% | 61.59% | 7/21/53 | Darlene Hooley | OR-5 | 50% | 53.99% | 4/4/39 |
| Jim Marshall | GA-8 | 55% | 51.00% | 3/31/48 | Brian Baird | WA-3 | 50% | 63.12% | 3/7/56 |
| Dennis Moore | KS-3 | 55% | 64.60% | 11/8/45 | Tim Bishop | NY-1 | 49% | 61.00% | 6/1/50 |
| Collin Peterson | MN-7 | 55% | 69.66% | 6/29/44 | | | | | |

though the total stock market capitalization had declined by nearly 50 percent from March 2000 though October 2002, losing $7.3 trillion in shareholder wealth in a nation where a majority of voters now owned stock directly.[1]

In 2004, Bush's job-approval rating was below 50 percent, the war in Iraq was troubling, and the Democrat billionaires like George Soros understood this was an election for both the presidency and the Supreme Court. Bush squeaked by with 51 percent of the vote, and the Republicans picked up four seats in the House, with an assist from Texas governor Rick Perry and the newly minted Republican majority in the Texas legislature, which redistricted Texas between 2002 and 2004.

The preceding history suggests that the Republican majority in the House was not fragile or accidental or a one-time event in 1994. They survived a recession, two wars, trillions in lost stock-market wealth, a late-breaking DUI announcement, a popular-vote-losing Republican president, the Enron scandal, and the best Bill Clinton had to throw at them. They could not survive the Iraq occupation and Bush's promise/threat of no change.

In 2006, there were two challenges that cost the Republicans their majority and are unlikely to be repeated. The first was the Iraq occupation, which was a boat anchor on the popularity of the president. The president promised that nothing would change in the occupation, that Rumsfeld would stay, and that he would change nothing, even, he said, if he was alone in his views. Voters believed him. But the same voters who saw his tenacity in 2004 as strength saw now an unwillingness to learn from or admit error and an inability to change direction.

The second, and the White House's favorite argument, was that self-inflicted wounds did most of the damage. Tom Delay should have resigned in time to choose a replacement who would have appeared on the ballot rather than a write-in. When Bob Ney resigned as a result of the Abramoff scandal, he waited so long that his replacement was hurried and flawed. Pennsylvania's Don Sherwood was accused of throttling his mistress. Curt Weldon was an appropriator under investigation. Foley had the e-mail sex scandal. But those scandal-related races will most likely be won back in a normal year and they alone would not have cost the Republicans their majority.

On the issues of corruption and overspending: Does the most optimistic Democrat really believe that either of those issues will cut for the Democrats in 2008 or 2010? Putting the spotlight on federal government spending is an asset for Republicans. In 2006, the average Republican running for office co-sponsored legislation that would increase spending by $14 billion. The average Democrat co-sponsored legislation that would increase spending by $500 billion.[2]

If Iraq is in the rearview mirror, then the Republicans will strengthen in the House in 2008. If Iraq remains in the windshield, as it was in November 2006, then the Democrats will gain in both the House and Senate.

American politicians are fond of seeing every international event as either World War Two or Vietnam. This is because these are the only foreign events they remember or have seen on TV. Iraq is not World War Two, but Bush should have remembered that in 1972 Richard Nixon was withdrawing from Vietnam. He had a plan to leave, Vietnamization, training the Vietnamese to run their own defense. American troops were being reduced from the high-level mark of 537,377 under Lyndon Johnson to 35,292 by Election Day 1972. In 1972 alone, U.S. troop level in Vietnam fell by 177,633 soldiers.[3] We were leaving Vietnam.

McGovern looked like a "cut and run," weak "peacenik" because he wanted to surrender when Nixon simply wanted to leave. Nixon won overwhelmingly not as a vote to stay the course or change nothing, but as a vote to manage the withdrawal and achieve "peace with honor." In 2006, Bush offered no change. The killing would continue without end or victory or a plan in sight. If there was a plan it was not articulated to the American people. (The "surge" and losing Rumsfeld both came after the 2006 election.)

Assuming a presidential candidate who nationalizes the campaign on standard Reagan Republican issues rather than a promise to occupy Iraq indefinitely, the Democrats will have a hard time defending sixty-one congressional districts that even Bush won in 2004. Republicans will only have to defend eight congressional districts that voted for Kerry in 2004.

## THE PRESIDENCY

With the end of the cold war and the strengthening of the Republican Party in the House and Senate, the presidency is no longer the central goal of a competent center-right movement. Nor is it as easy a target.

Republicans used to believe that the Senate and certainly the House were irretrievably lost to the Democrats. Republicans could and had to win the presidency on foreign-policy issues to keep the Soviet Union from taking over the planet and to stop the Democrat Congress from socializing America.

After the 1980 election there was brave talk about the "Electoral College lock" on the presidency where Republicans would always carry California, the Rocky Mountain West, and the South, and enough of the Midwest to maintain a firm grip on the presidency. From our presidential redoubt we could try and slip reasonable Supreme Court justices past the Democrat Senate, keep the Soviets at bay, and veto really bad ideas that flew out of the Capitol like shots on goal.

The Republicans and the conservative movement became very president-centric. This changed when the world changed with the fall of the Soviet Union. Ross Perot was a luxury many disappointed center-right voters could flirt with—despite Bill Clinton's "draft dodging" past—only because there was no longer a Soviet threat.

When Gingrich demonstrated that Republicans could win a national campaign for the House and Senate just as we had won national campaigns for the presidency, the movement actually focused more on keeping the House and Senate in 1996 than electing Dole.

It is reasonable and correct for the Republican Party and the Leave

Us Alone movement to abandon their quest for and support for the presidency at the expense of everything else. This was painfully high-lighted when Nixon promised dozens of Democrats who supported him on Vietnam that he would not support Republican attempts to defeat them in 1972. He made sure his victory was a lonely one also by flying over Colorado where he could have dropped by and reelected Senator Gordon Allott. Or Nixon could have ordered his campaign not to turn out voters that were identified as Nixon voters who were planning to vote for Democrats for Congress and Senate in key states like Ohio where he had a comfortable lead.

Presidents have come to see the party and sometimes the movement as working personally for them. Bush 41 ordered the NRCC, the cam-paign fund for House Republicans, not to encourage Republicans to speak against his tax hike in 1990 in order to help elect themselves. Bet-ter to have the emperor think no one opposed him than to elect more Republicans for Congress. And the NRCC, which is paid to elect Re-publicans to the House, caved to the presidential pressure. Even Reagan sent out a letter to the RNC donor base in 1982 telling them that the 1982 tax increase was not a tax hike. It was a year before fund-raising for the party recovered from this "stop telling the emperor he isn't wearing any clothes" memo. Reagan even spent time flying to Minne-sota because his campaign was focused on him only and he was hoping to win a historic fifty-state victory in 1984 (for which the reward is nothing) rather than view his time as available to other campaigns. Reagan commanded the RNC to appoint his daughter as co-chairman.

Bush in 2006 was not campaigning to help elect Republicans to the House and Senate but was defending his own decisions on Iraq. He spent the summer of 2006 giving talks about how it is inconceivable that he had learned anything that might make him change Iraq policy in the slightest.

Worse, under Bush's direction, Republicans did not support their Senate candidate in Connecticut against the divided left of Senator Joe Lieberman running as an independent, and antiwar activist Ned Lamont running on the Democrat ticket. This left only two players on the field and both were turning out Democrat voters, one for the traditional LBJ liberal and one for the anti–Iraq War liberal. Because President Bush wanted to thank a liberal Democrat, Lieberman (who is left-wing on everything except the war in Iraq), he doubled the strength of the Democrat turnout and gutted Republican turnout, in the process giving two Republican House seats away.

Presidents will always think that this is all about them. Clinton took this attitude. Those of us in the center-right greatly appreciate that Clinton did. But the modern center-right party and movement must be as interested in governorships and the Congress as the presidency and should start by requiring any candidate for president to keep a hands-off policy toward the Republican National Committee, the governing body of the party. The overall party began this process following Abraham Lincoln's presidency when the radical Republicans in the House set up the NRCC to raise money for House Republicans independent of Lincoln's Democrat vice president, and then the new president, Andrew Johnson.[4]

The 168 members of the RNC can and should elect the chairman of the RNC. And run the budget. This is the party's machinery, not the president's piggy bank and nepotism niche. Yes, the president writes direct mail letters and appears at fund-raisers. That should be committed to by any candidate for the Republican Party nomination as a condition of auditioning for the job. A president should not use the party to get elected and then demand to run the party. Loyalty should flow to the party and its principles, not to an individual candidacy.

## CHAPTER SEVENTEEN

# THE STATES

The great economic thinker Ross Perot predicted that a free-trade agreement among Canada, the United States, and Mexico would create gaint sucking sound as jobs, capital, and wealth flowed out of the United States to Mexico.

But low labor costs are only one part of an investor's decision of where to build factories, create jobs, and put wealth at risk. If labor costs determined everything, all jobs would be in Bangladesh. Within the United States every factory would have moved to rural Mississippi.

Labor, capital, and management move reasonably freely within the United States. The rule of law, at a national level, is consistent. But there are differences among the states in how they treat capital and labor. One critical difference is the tax burden they impose. In 1990, New Hampshire residents paid 8.6 percent of their personal income in state and local taxes. A short drive west, citizens of New York State paid 13.5 percent of their personal income in state and local taxes.[1]

The establishment press has sometimes suggested that migration south and west is driven by a desire for "dry heat" and snowless winters. But weather does not explain why every state in New England lost citizens to outmigration, except equally cold and snowy—but low tax—New Hampshire.

Between 1990 and 1999, 1.109 million Americans moved into Florida, a state without a state income tax. In the same decade 2.171 million Californians moved out of sunny California. During the 1990s California's top income-tax rate was above 9 percent.

New York State, with a top state income tax as high as 7.8 percent between 1990 and 1994, saw 1.889 million citizens leave.

Florida, winning 1.1 million new citizens, was joined by Texas, which gained 570,000; Tennessee, up 357,000; Washington State, up 382,000; and Nevada, up 433,000. These states have no income tax.[2]

From 1990 to 1999, the ten highest-tax states lost 890,000 citizens to emigration and the ten lowest-tax states gained 2.052 million tax refugees.

Looking just at the state income-tax burdens, the ten lowest-tax states gained 2.8 million between 1990 and 1999 and the ten highest-income-tax states lost 2,151,300 in the same decade.

This trend continued in 2000 to 2002, when the top ten high-tax states lost 371,000 to domestic migration and the ten lowest-tax states gained 729,000 in net in-migration. Immigration from other nations sometimes masks the scale of internal migration. But even including all immigration from foreign countries in those two years, the numbers show the ten highest-tax states gained only 108,000 people and the ten low-tax states gained a net 1,709,000.[3]

## STATE-BY-STATE MIGRATION AND INCOME, 1996–2004

| STATE | MIGRATION GAIN/LOSS | INCOME GAIN/LOSS ANNUAL ($ MILLIONS) |
|---|---|---|
| Alabama | 18,984 | $44.8 |
| Alaska | −24,204 | −$824.7 |
| Arizona | 457,181 | $13,791.2 |

| STATE | MIGRATION GAIN/LOSS | INCOME GAIN/LOSS ANNUAL ($ MILLIONS) |
| --- | --- | --- |
| Arkansas | 42,858 | $931.4 |
| California | −871,655 | −$13,181.0 |
| Colorado | 185,027 | $4,519.8 |
| Connecticut | −84,597 | −$2,713.6 |
| Delaware | 31,588 | $764.6 |
| District of Columbia | −83,225 | −$1,647.0 |
| Florida | 1,137,912 | $57,208.5 |
| Georgia | 420,656 | $3,892.7 |
| Hawaii | −73,885 | $430.3 |
| Idaho | 61,897 | $1,820.2 |
| Illinois | −538,004 | −$18,185.3 |
| Indiana | −10,128 | −$3,192.6 |
| Iowa | −59,642 | −$2,765.2 |
| Kansas | −56,564 | −$2,601.7 |
| Kentucky | 47,916 | $122.2 |
| Louisiana | −128,255 | −$3,075.1 |
| Maine | 34,472 | $1,955.0 |
| Maryland | −6,747 | −$1,915.8 |
| Massachusetts | −192,542 | −$7,133.1 |
| Michigan | −141,863 | −$6,094.6 |
| Minnesota | 15,536 | −$2,611.4 |

| STATE | MIGRATION GAIN/LOSS | INCOME GAIN/LOSS ANNUAL ($ MILLIONS) |
|---|---|---|
| Mississippi | 4,281 | $20.9 |
| Missouri | 54,130 | −$1,710.8 |
| Montana | 9,115 | $1,100.9 |
| Nebraska | −40,792 | −$1,708.3 |
| Nevada | 352,524 | $11,218.0 |
| New Hampshire | 60,298 | $2,768.1 |
| New Jersey | −236,045 | −$9,476.8 |
| New Mexico | −23,074 | $162.1 |
| New York | −1,258,322 | −$33,121.7 |
| North Carolina | 371,686 | $8,269.0 |
| North Dakota | −40,068 | −$893.3 |
| Ohio | −220,051 | −$10,461.3 |
| Oklahoma | −6,702 | −$1,608.3 |
| Oregon | 99,862 | $2,007.8 |
| Pennsylvania | −140,829 | −$4,489.4 |
| Rhode Island | −10,573 | $269.3 |
| South Carolina | 158,981 | $5,667.7 |
| South Dakota | −13,261 | $133.9 |
| Tennessee | 174,683 | $2,386.2 |
| Texas | 307,329 | $4,202.7 |
| Utah | −39,724 | −$606.0 |

| STATE | MIGRATION GAIN/LOSS | INCOME GAIN/LOSS ANNUAL ($ MILLIONS) |
|---|---|---|
| Vermont | 3,998 | $576.5 |
| Virginia | 136,171 | $2,897.8 |
| Washington | 102,548 | $2,972.6 |
| West Virginia | −5,843 | −$262.9 |
| Wisconsin | 26,000 | −$481.5 |
| Wyoming | −9,038 | $627.2 |

Source: Internal Revenue Service, Americans for Tax Reform Foundation[4]

Individuals and businesses that move from high-tax states to low-tax states are by definition "tax sensitive." This makes them more likely Republican-trending voters as they find their new homes in red and growing redder states.

When people move they bring their wealth and their annual incomes with them. This transfer of populations and the income and wealth they bring strengthens the low-tax and redder states. They bring to those states more congressional districts and more electoral votes.

More taxpayers flowing into Florida allowed Jeb Bush to cut taxes each year of his eight-year governorship (1998 to 2006) and to have a surplus of $4.99 billion in 2006.[5] As taxpayers fled New Jersey, Governor Jim McGreevey had his state borrow $14 billion, much of which went to operating expenses, and he raised taxes again, which will continue to repel businesses and taxpayers.

## FREE MEN, FREE LAND, FREE LABOR

Taxes are a major factor in where Americans choose to live. Labor laws also have an effect. The Wagner Act of 1936 passed by Congress

# 2007 Right-to-Work States

| | States without RTW |
| | States with RTW laws |

Source: Alliance for Worker Freedom: www.workerfreedom.org

greatly empowered labor unions and their leaders against both employers and individual workers. The number of Americans who were members of labor unions jumped from 3.3 million in 1935 to 6.8 million in 1940 and 11.6 million by 1945.[6] When Republicans swept the House and Senate in 1946 they were able to pass, over the veto of posthumously anointed "moderate" Democrat Harry Truman, section 17(b) of the Taft-Hartley Act, the "Right-to-Work Law," which allows each state to decide if it wishes to allow or disallow compulsory unionism. In a "right to work" state a worker cannot be required to join a labor union as a condition of employment. Given the level of labor-union violence, joining a union can be a condition of remaining healthy, but in nonright-to-work states, the government plays the role of the baseball bat–wielding union organizer and the government itself makes the worker an offer he cannot refuse: Pay union dues or don't work in the factory, mine, or construction job.

At first, mostly Southern states, lightly industrialized and not strongly unionized, passed right-to-work laws. Those laws made right-to-work states more attractive to businesses, and over time, investment, businesses, and jobs poured into those states. As the benefits of being a right-to-work state became clearer, more states passed right-to-work laws. In 1948, eighteen million Americans lived in 10 right-to-work states. By 2004, there were 108 million Americans living in 22 right-to-work states.[7]

By 1994, there were twenty-one right-to-work states. Oklahoma became the twenty-second right-to-work state in 2001 through a referendum.

From 1994 to 2004, nonfarm private-sector employment grew 21.1 percent in right-to-work states and only 12.4 percent in nonright-to-work states. Average real household income in metropolitan areas was $50,571 in right-to-work states and $46,431 in non-RTW states. Construction employment grew 42.2 percent in RTW states versus 38.3 percent in non-RTW states. Manufacturing businesses grew 4.9 percent in RTW states and fell 8.3 percent in non-RTW states. Real personal income grew 37 percent in RTW states and only 27 percent in forced unionism states. Adjusting for cost of living, per-capita personal income in metro areas was $25,900 for RTW states and $22.926 in forced unionism states.[8]

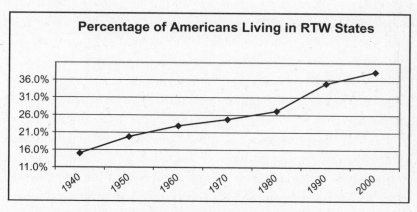

*This chart shows the increasing percentage of Americans living in right-to-work states since the 1940s.*
*Sources: Census Bureau and Alliance for Worker Freedom*

More flexible labor laws that do not turn the state into an enforcer for organized, um, labor create conditions for more job creation, higher real wages, more business, and even more home ownership (71 percent versus 68 percent).

Every year people, capital, and companies move disproportionately into the twenty-two right-to-work states. In 2000, every single one of the twenty-one right-to-work states voted for Bush. In 2004, the now twenty-two right-to-work states were unanimous for Bush.

The guardian of the right-to-work laws, just as the NRA is the protector of the Second Amendment, is the National Right to Work Committee based in Virginia, founded in 1954, and run by its founding president, Reed Larson, from 1954 to 1994. Mark Mix, previously director of legislation, has been president since 1995.

Protecting workers from exploitation by compulsory union laws attracts more workers, more businesses, more wealth, and a growing population. This leads to more House seats and more electoral votes.


*Red States Growing Faster than Blue States.* Looking at the thirty-one states that voted for Bush in 2004 and the nineteen states that voted for Kerry in 2004, we find that the red states had in-migration of 3.3 million residents from the Kerry blue states in the years 1996 to 2004. The blue-state migrants carried with them $100 billion of annual personal income into red states.[9]

Red states have 38,355,472 children under eighteen.

Blue states have 35,001,675 children under eighteen.[10]

Red states have more children and more people are moving into them.

This will affect the Electoral College and the partisan distribution of the House of Representatives.

If the 2000 election had been based on the census of 2000 instead of the ten-year-old census of 1990, Bush would have won not 271 electoral votes but 278. Every state that gained seats, except California, voted for Bush: Arizona, Colorado, Florida, Georgia, Nevada, North Carolina, and Texas.

## LABORATORIES OF DEMOCRACY:
## THE REPUBLICAN PILUM

Roman soldiers carried a pilum, a spear unlike those carried by their enemies. The pilum had a sharp pointed end to pierce through shields or people. It was barbed so that if it went through you and/or your shield it got stuck and could not be pulled out and thrown back at the Romans. In addition, the metal end of the spear was weaker than the wooden shaft. This was deliberate. A thrown pilum that struck a person, shield, or the ground would bend. It would no longer be useful as a spear. It could not be thrown back at the Romans. It was a weapon useful in only one direction.

Many political tactics can be thrown back at you. When the Democrats got the jump on Republicans in turning out voters in 2000, the Republicans responded with their own increased voter turnout in 2002 and 2004. Democrats returned fire in 2006 with increased turnout in key states like Michigan. Both parties can register and turn out voters.

If Republicans can make their states more attractive by reducing taxes, abolishing the state income tax and state death tax, and having flexible labor laws such as right-to-work laws, perhaps the left can draw businesses, investment, and quality citizens through passing progressive legislation? They have tried. It doesn't work.

The Leave Us Alone Coalition has one great advantage over the left. Its policies, when enacted into law, attract citizens. People want to live in low-tax, small-government, tough-on-crime states that do not hand over their citizens' lives and paychecks to the trial lawyers, the labor-union bosses, and City Hall. This is not an assertion. It is observable, quantifiable fact. Good policy is good politics.

At the national level, however, it is difficult to separate out the effects of various policies. We pass tax cuts, the economy booms, and the Democrats argue it would have happened anyway. How can you prove that your policies work and the other team's policies are counterproductive? Things would have to get pretty awful before folks started moving to France. Or stopped coming from Mexico.

But there are fifty states. And increasingly we are moving toward one-party dominance in many of those states. There are red states. There are blue states. The modern Democrat Party can do anything it wants with and to the citizens of New Jersey and West Virginia and Massachusetts. On the other side, Florida, Texas, Georgia, and South Carolina have solid Republican majorities. This will increasingly allow each party to govern through example.

At first, the left thought this might provide them an opportunity. Writing in *The Nation* magazine, Thomas Geoghegan argued for just this strategy for the left. "Maybe Labor Should Give Up on Washington in Favor of Friendlier Terrain," headlined an article in the weeks after the 2004 election. In it, he wrote, "Let's govern from the blue states. If we govern from the blue states, it may be possible to bring the labor movement back. What do I mean by 'governing from the blue states'? Use state law as much as possible to set up the kind of social democracy we should like to see for the country as a whole."[11]

The modern Democrat Party can whine that it has been kept out of the halls of power in Washington or, post 2006, is now thwarted by Bush's veto. But Democrats do have the ability to create their own version of utopia in those states with Democrat governors who will sign legislation passed by Democrat majorities in the legislatures. Open for experimentation are: New Jersey, New York, New Mexico, Illinois, Maine, Massachusetts, Washington State, and West Virginia.

Republicans can create their policy nirvana in twelve to fourteen states including large ones like Florida and Texas. Just as states and congressional districts that vote Republican for president are increasingly voting Republican for House and Senate—and vice versa for blue states and congressional districts—there is an increasing tendency for states to go all one way or the other in their voting patterns for governor and legislature.

The challenge to Geoghegan's strategy is this: if you make a list of what the Democrat coalition wishes a state government to do, it is very similar to a list of what drives individuals, families, businesses, and capital out of a state. Give labor unions more power. Raise taxes. Allow trial lawyers more leeway in suing companies and doctors.

Raise taxes. Increase pensions and health care for state and local government workers. Raise taxes. Have lots of fun environmental regulations. Be understanding of the needs of drug addicts and muggers. Make it easier to get on welfare and stay there. Raise taxes.

The Democrats in California followed Geoghegan's strategy working to turn California into a social democracy. One problem: California has the recall and initiative process and voters recalled Governor Gray Davis and elected Arnold Schwarzenegger. But those Democrat-controlled states without recall and initiative can be pushed toward social democracies without so much as a speed bump to slow down "progress." Dissenters will have only one choice: Submit or leave.

The Leave Us Alone Coalition and Republican elected officials have their own list of projects at the state level: Cut taxes. Play smash mouth with trial lawyers. Cut taxes on businesses. Regulate less. Keep pay and pensions for government workers in line with the private sector. Reduce gold plating on mandates for health insurance. Give parents control over their children's education. Pass right-to-work laws. Put criminals in prison. Execute murderers. Make it difficult to get on welfare and uncomfortable to stay there. The Republican "to do" list attracts new investment and attracts citizens, particularly citizens who work and pay taxes and have and create wealth.

The more Democrats and Republicans are successful in "capturing" control of their respective states, the faster private-sector workers and tax-sensitive individuals will transfer from blue states to red states. And conversely, the more those wishing government jobs and pensions and welfare benefits will stay in blue states and perhaps move there.

It is possible that Democrats believe that paying teachers more generous pensions will excite young couples who wish to raise their children in public schools with high rates of teacher pay and shorter working hours. Comparing teacher pay and per-capita spending on children with in- and out-migration shows that citizens are fleeing the states that have tried this approach.

The top ten states in teacher pay had *3.6 million* residents leave those states from 1996 to 2004, taking with them $97 billion in annual income. The "state" with the highest amount spent per capita is Washington, D.C. Washington, D.C., lost 83,225 residents from 1996 through 2004 and these residents took with them $1.6 billion.[12]

The ten lowest-spending states on "education" per pupil are Utah, Idaho, Arizona, Oklahoma, Mississippi, Nevada, Tennessee, Alabama, North Carolina, and Arkansas. These ten states had net immigration of 1.43 million from 1996 to 2004.[13]

Education spending alone does not attract citizens or voters. Americans value a quality education. Their personal migration patterns show that parents do not view increasing total spending on the education bureaucracy to be the same thing as producing real education.

One notes that federal spending reduces the competition between states based on sound policy. States with destructive policies can find themselves reaping federal subsidies to "fix" or alleviate the problem that bad state and local government causes. And "revenue sharing" plans divorce state revenue from competent economic policies.

Competition among states will help America see which policies work. Americans can move their families, their businesses, and their wealth and property to more successful states. We will have competition among states to provide the best government at the lowest cost.

Success at the state level helps promote winning ideas to the federal level. The success of welfare reform in Wisconsin and Michigan made the welfare reform of 1996 at the national level possible. The reduction of crime in states where citizens are given the right to carry weapons concealed has convinced legislators in numerous states to pass similar laws, and after September 11 Congress gave all policemen the right to carry concealed not just in their own states but in all states. Legislation to extend that right to all citizens is before Congress.

There is all the difference in the world between promoting an idea that has succeeded in one or two states and proffering a theory that has never been tried. It is also a good shield against bad ideas—"Hey, why not try that out on Vermont first and come back and let us know how it did?"

## STATES TRUMP CITIES

Paper wraps rock. Rock breaks scissors. Scissors cut paper. And states trump cities. In most states, local governments—cities, towns, and counties—are political creations of the state. States can merge cities. Divide them in half. Create counties or not. They can deny local governments the power to tax income. They can limit how much any subdivision of the state can spend. They mandate expenditures. They put limits on state funding. States have even more power over cities than the federal government has over states.

This is an asset for the Republican Party, which has much greater control over states than cities. In 2007, Republicans held twenty-two governorships out of fifty and had control of the governorship and both houses of the legislature in ten of fifty states. And this was a recent low point. Before the 2006 Iraq election, Republicans held twenty-eight governorships, controlled forty-nine of the ninety-nine state legislative bodies, held both the House and Senate in twenty states, and held the governorship and both houses—full control—in twelve states. Democrats had full control in eight states. Today, of the largest fifty cities, Republicans have nine mayors. Of those cities, Republicans hold the mayor and control of the city council in exactly none.[14]

Republicans like to whine about the Democrat political machines in Detroit, Philadelphia, and Austin. Those cities are overwhelmingly Democrat. They use tax dollars to get out the Democrat vote. They shield and perhaps organize voter fraud.

State governments are not impotent. They can stop sending state tax dollars disproportionately to cities where those tax dollars fund excessive bureaucracies that are used as political shock troops by the Democrat Party.

Washington can help states combat corruption in cities. When Republicans nationally control the House, Senate, or presidency, they should refuse to use federal funds to finance Democrat precinct workers through "aid to cities."

Many of the federal grant programs thought up by the Johnson administration flow through cities and local governments or directly to government schools and universities. They bypass the state legislature or go through the legislature with such restrictions that they are not really under its control.

A competent Republican Party would use its strength at the state level to stop transfers of tax dollars into cities that use them for political purposes. All excess funds turn into the financing of bureaucracies that are the modern Democrat political machines in cities.

The Gordian knot can best be severed by block-granting all federal aid for welfare, food stamps, housing assistance, and health care directly to the state government with minimal restrictions. Democrats fight against such block grants, claiming they fear a cut in welfare benefits. The actual history of welfare reform shows that the block grants were increased to cover inflation since enactment in 1996. What declined was not the total funding, but the number of citizens made dependent on the government.

Sending federal aid to states—not political subdivisions—cuts out much of the corruption and politicization of such "free monies." And yes, eventually Congress should trade such block grants for tax cuts that allow states to raise and spend their own money on projects they deem worthy.

As with the Roman pilum, fifty states competing to provide the best government at the lowest cost to taxpayers is a one-way weapon. There are no Republican political machines at the city and county level being funded with federal and state money. And if there were, the Leave Us Alone Coalition should cheerfully crush it, as any political organizing on "the right" driven by tax dollars is politically corrupting.

*Purple States: Lincoln Republicans vs. Reagan Republicans.* The Leave Us Alone Coalition has an opportunity and a very real danger when looking at the broad swath of Lincoln Republican territory from Long Island to Illinois. One hundred and forty years after the Civil War, when you move west from New York through

New Jersey, Pennsylvania, Ohio, Indiana, and Illinois, you see not Reagan Republican parties, but Lincoln Republican parties.

These are states, some with strong "Republican" histories, where, if you ask Republicans why they are Republicans their answer too often boils down to the fact that Abraham Lincoln was a Republican and their great-great grandparents were for the Union. Their allegiance to the Republican Party is as tenuous as that of the Democrats in the eleven formerly Confederate states who were voting Democrat until recently out of respect for General Lee.

Lincoln Republicans in 1860 believed that slavery should not be extended to the West, and that the Union should remain united. These are, in most counties, settled issues in the United States of today.

Why then vote Republican today? Most Republicans in most states have moved on to become Reagan Republicans, who are best defined as members of the Leave Us Alone Coalition and are committed to limited government. But the Republican Party machines of Long Island, New Jersey, Pennsylvania, Ohio, Indiana, and Illinois have too often relied instead on patronage. This has been a flawed strategy. In Long Island, the Republican machine of Nassau County was repudiated by voters because the taxes to pay for the patronage were too high. In the 1980s there were three Republican congressmen in Long Island and fifteen in all of New York; by 2006, there was one in Long Island and six in New York State. New Jersey in 1993 elected Christie Todd Whitman and solid majorities in both houses of the legislature. They did not govern as Reagan Republicans limiting government, but rather as Lincoln Republicans living inside the government and handing out contracts and jobs and driving government spending and borrowing upward. By 2006, the Democrats had the governorship and both houses of the legislature. Being of the party that won the Civil War was no longer a good reason to vote Republican. Pennsylvania was governed by a Republican governor, Tom Ridge, and both houses were Republican from 1994 to 2002. But they spent their time spending tax dollars to build football stadiums rather than giving parents school choice or lower taxes. Illinois had a Republican governor and both houses were Republican after the 1994 election, but Governor

George Ryan's drive to create a patronage state rather than a Leave Us Alone Coalition delivered the governorship and both houses of the legislature to the Democrats. Ohio and Indiana are hanging on, but Ohio's Governor Taft governed as if he had never heard of Ronald Reagan. Taft raised taxes. He enthusiastically spent other people's money, and his patronage machine of jobs and contracts got tangled up in corruption. And he lost the governorship for the Republicans in 2006.

In Reagan Republican states where the Republican Party is in concert with the Leave Us Alone Coalition, the Republicans have done better.

Will this swath of Lincoln Republican states make the transition to become Reagan Republican states? Much hangs on this question. For Lincoln Republicanism—relying on people voting for a party based on a 150-year-old allegiance driven by issues long ago settled—has turned into patronage and contract corruption that cannot attract and hold the Leave Us Alone Coalition voters. Such historical allegiances might work in Serbia or Albania, but Americans are blessed with shorter memories for history's slights. Lincoln Republicans cannot continue for very long to govern major states in America. They will become Reagan Republicans or they will lose power. They cannot become a competent alternative to the Takings Coalition. They are the Takings Coalition with a top hat and beard.

# PART FOUR

# TAXES, AND WHAT WE MUST DO ABOUT THEM

---

"The power to tax is the power to destroy."

—*John Marshall*

"We're going to take things away from you on behalf of the common good."

—*Hillary Clinton, June 28, 2004*

IF YOU SEND IT, THEY WILL SPEND IT.

—*Bumper sticker*

## CHAPTER EIGHTEEN

# TAXES: THE LIFEBLOOD OF THE STATE

In politics, taxation is not the most important thing. It is the only thing.

It is the cutting edge of the state, its point of contact with citizens, its means of control, punishment applied or withheld. Everything changes except the two constants: Death and Taxes.

The Rosetta Stone was carved in Egyptian hieroglyphics, demotic characters, and Greek so that all would understand and time could not erase its message: an agreement on which Egyptians were taxed and how much. The Magna Carta was about taxes. The French Revolution began when the king called the national assembly to discuss taxes. (Bad move.) The American Revolution began as a tax revolt. When Rome wanted to destroy Rhodes they gave tax-free status to a nearby competing port. It worked.

Taxes control everything.

When Reagan took office in 1981 the top marginal income tax rate was 70 percent. When he left it was 28 percent. In 1980, an American paying the top marginal tax rate of 70 percent who earned an extra $100 got only $30 in after-tax take-home pay. When Reagan left office you got to keep $72 of that $100. The reward to working doubled. The cost of sleeping in doubled. Taxes can and do change everything.[1]

The power to tax is the power to destroy. The power to tax is the power to determine how much a product, service, or good costs to produce, to buy, to use. Taxes determine your take-home pay. The value of your retirement portfolio. The value of your home.

High taxes have destroyed great civilizations. Lower taxes have created economic miracles on the rocky island of Hong Kong after World War Two, and Ireland in the 1990s.

The power to tax is, quite simply, the power.

The goal of Americans who love liberty is not to wield that power but to reduce it. To control it. To bind it down with the chains of the Constitution and popular will. To destroy much of that power lest it fall back into the same old hands. The goal is not to try and use the ring of power for good, but to hurl it into the fires of the pits of Mordor.

Before we look forward to how we can reduce the power of the state to tax, control, and destroy, we can learn a great deal from our own history of our government's exercise of the power to tax.

## A Brief History of American Taxation

America won its independence in a revolution opposing tax increases. Small tax hikes. The stamp tax imposed a levy of less than a few pence on any official document. The tax on tea that inspired the Boston Tea Party was only three pence on each pound of tea.[2]

The British tax burden on Americans was about 1 percent of income. This was completely unacceptable, and Americans fought from April 19, 1775, in Lexington and Concord until victory at Yorktown, Virginia, on October 19, 1781, to put an end to this. Since then there has been some backsliding.

The Whiskey Rebellion ended poorly for the good guys. The Civil War was driven both by conflicts over the extension of slavery westward and the North's insistence on high tariffs that funded the overwhelming majority of the federal government. When elected, President Lincoln originally promised not to interfere with slavery in the slave states but the high tariffs were nonnegotiable.

During the Republican dominance following the War Between the States, it was the Republican Party that supported high tariffs and Democrats who supported lower tariffs.

The Sixteenth Amendment to the U.S. Constitution, which allowed Congress to impose an income tax on the American people, was passed by a Republican Congress early in the Taft administration and was ratified by the states in 1913 while Taft was just leaving the White House to incoming Woodrow Wilson.[3]

The federal income tax began at 1 percent on net personal incomes above $3,000. There was a 6 percent surtax on incomes above $500,000.

During the First World War, America's officially worst president, Woodrow Wilson, raised the maximum income tax rate to 77 percent.[4] This was reduced under the Harding and Coolidge administrations from 75 percent to a top rate of 25 percent. Federal income tax revenues shot up from $300 million in 1920 to $600 million in 1928 when Coolidge left office.

Herbert Hoover defined his presidency by announcing on June 17, 1930, that he would sign the Smoot-Hawley Act raising tariffs to new highs. The stock market reacted by dropping 53 percent. In the fine tradition of governments "fixing" problems they created in the first place, Hoover decided to raise the income tax back to a top rate of 63 percent for incomes above $1 million (or $ 9 million today), which collapsed both the economy and tax revenues. Higher tariffs, simply raising taxes at the border, and higher income taxes saw tariff revenue fall 40 percent, and income tax revenues fell from $1 billion to $527 million.[5] Supply-side economics works in both directions. Higher marginal tax rates depress economic activity just as lower tax rates reduce the drag of government on the economy.

U.S. imports from Europe declined from a 1929 high of $1.3 billion to just $390 million in 1932, while U.S. exports to Europe fell from $2.341 billion in 1929 to $784 million in 1932. We have lived in Lou

Dobbs's America, freed from the horrors of icky foreigners selling us stuff at low prices. It was called the Great Depression.

Herbert Hoover gave us the nice Depression by raising taxes on the border and helped drive what might have been yet another short-lived panic—there had been seven panics or recessions since the end of the Civil War—to become the Great Depression lasting ten years. Government *can* do great things.

The Democrats were elected in 1932 on a platform promising small government at the national and state levels. "We advocate an immediate and drastic reduction of governmental expenditures by abolishing useless commissions and offices, consolidating departments and bureaus, and eliminating extravagance to accomplish a saving of not less than twenty-five percent in the cost of the federal Government. And we call upon the Democratic Party in the states to make a zealous effort to achieve a proportionate result."[6]

But the new Democrat Party rejected its Jefferson and Jackson traditions and ended the Roosevelt/Truman twenty years of Democrat dominance as the party that brought federal income taxes to a top rate of 94 percent, took total government employment from 3,331,000 in 1932 to 10,043,000 in 1952,[7] established a peacetime draft that would continue for twenty-five years after the end of World War Two, passed a compulsory national pension plan modeled on Bismarck's Germany and Ponzi's scheme, and advocated nationalizing the healthcare industry.

Amity Shlaes has written the definitive history of Hoover and Roosevelt's joint efforts to control the American economy and its devastating costs in her 2007 book, *The Forgotten Man*. Roosevelt used the term to suggest that the "forgotten man" was in need of being discovered and "helped" by the government. But this phrase was knowingly stolen from William Graham Sumner, who correctly pointed out that the true "forgotten man" was the taxpayer who was expected to pay for the false philanthropy of politicians.[8]

Eisenhower was elected in 1952 running against "Communism, Corruption and Korea." Eisenhower opposed Robert Taft and the Republican Congress's desire to bring down the high tax rates from the New Deal and World War Two.[9] Eisenhower increased federal spending from $79.7 billion to $122.9 billion from 1952 to 1960.[10] He presided over the 1958 recession and lost the presidency for the GOP to John F. Kennedy, whose call to get America moving again would include a 22 percent across-the-board cut in tax rates that was enacted in February 1964.[11] Barry Goldwater voted against the Kennedy tax cut, as did most Republicans. In the early 1960s, the Democrats were not committed opponents of tax cuts and Republicans were not consistent champions of lower taxes.

This tax cut, the supply-siders point out, created the strong economic growth in the 1960s that increased GDP from $664 billion in 1964 to $985 billion in 1969. The growth did not end until Richard Nixon imposed a surtax of 10 percent on July 9, 1969.[12] Some Democrats who supported the tax cuts believed they were enacting a Keynesian tax cut that would stimulate the economy through increasing demand. Kennedy himself understood and argued that the tax-rate reduction would change incentives to produce and save. He said,

> Our true choice is not between tax reduction, on the one hand, and the avoidance of large Federal deficits on the other. It is increasingly clear that, no matter what party is in power, so long as our national security needs keep rising, an economy hampered by restrictive tax rates will never produce enough revenue to balance the budget—just as it will never produce enough jobs or enough profits.
>
> In short, it is a paradoxical truth that tax rates are too high today and tax revenues are too low—and the soundest way to raise revenues in the long run is to cut rates now.[13]

Richard Nixon increased taxes to pay for the War in Vietnam and the War on Poverty; he also signed into law a proposal cooked up by the Johnson Treasury Department and passed by the Democrat-controlled House and Senate called the "Alternative Minimum Tax" to "fix" the problem that some individuals who earned a great deal of income from tax-free municipal bonds were not paying federal income taxes.

In the Carter years the supply-side argument was pushed by the *Wall Street Journal*, the U.S. Chamber of Commerce, led by chief economist Richard Rahn, and New York congressman Jack Kemp. The Kemp-Roth legislation to cut individual income tax rates by 33 percent across the board became the campaign slogan for the Republican House members in 1978 with the bumper sticker REPUBLICAN TAX CUT 33 PERCENT.

Jimmy Carter and his secretary of the Treasury, Michael Blumenthal, wanted to increase the capital gains tax rate from 39.9 percent to 50 percent:[14] Congress, however, was trying to move in the other direction. The Steiger amendment, authored by liberal Republican William Steiger, cut the capital gains tax from a top rate of 39.9 to 28 percent. It passed both houses, and Jimmy Carter grudgingly signed the capital gains tax cut.

Way back then, supply-side tax cuts enjoyed bipartisan congressional support. As a result of the lower tax rates—and the Reagan 1981 tax cut further reduced the capital gains tax rate to 20 percent—capital gains tax receipts to the government increased from $9.1 billion in 1978 to $53 billion in 1986.[15]

The Kemp-Roth tax-cut legislation passed the Senate 65 to 20 and won a majority vote in the House on May 3, 1978, as the Holt Amend-

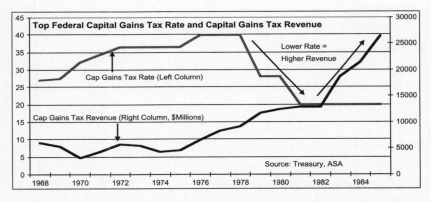

As the capital gains tax rate was reduced in 1978 and 1981, the actual capital gains revenue to the government increased. This is what the left says never happens.

ment. The Democrat leadership forced 8 members to change their votes so the legislation never went to Carter for signature. Still, what would later become the "partisan Reagan tax cut" passed the Democrat-controlled House and Senate in the 1970s.

On June 6, 1978, California voted to pass Proposition 13, an initiative proposed by taxpayer advocates Howard Jarvis and Paul Gann that cut property taxes and required a two-thirds vote to raise taxes in the future. This vote stunned the nation.[16] That fall other states quickly put similar tax-slashing measures on state ballots, and the "tax revolt" joined the property-rights-driven "sagebrush revolt" as vote movers in the 1980 election.

Ronald Reagan, who had passed a significant income tax hike as governor and in 1976 campaigned on spending restraint without specific tax cuts, led his 1980 campaign with the Kemp-Roth tax cuts. Elected with 51 percent of the vote to Jimmy Carter's 41 percent and Independent John Anderson's 7 percent, Reagan carried forty-four states—all but Georgia, West Virginia, Minnesota, the District of Columbia, Maryland, Rhode Island, and Hawaii.[17]

Reagan signed his tax cut into law on August 13, 1981, at his California ranch. The legislation dropped the top income tax rates by 25 percent over three years. The top rate was dropped from 70 percent to 50 percent. Reagan Republicanism was identified with supply-side tax rate reductions, but not yet with opposition to tax hikes.

The Reagan tax cuts paid off in turning the economy around. Four million jobs were created in 1983 alone and America rebounded from an inflation-ravaged recession to a low-inflation period of growth.[18] *Wall Street Journal* editor Robert L. Bartley defined this period in his book of the same name, *The Seven Fat Years.*

Republican Senate Leader Bob Dole was a pre-Reagan Republican who focused not on economic growth, cutting taxes, or restraining government spending, but rather on the federal deficit. Dole talked Reagan into signing a tax increase in 1982 that was supposed to raise $90 billion over five years by reducing or eliminating tax credits and deductions. Reagan was promised, but never received, three dollars in reductions in federal spending in trade for agreeing to the tax increase. He was double-crossed on the promised spending reduction by both a Democrat House and a Republican Senate. Reagan is reported to have cited this tax hike as the biggest mistake of his administration.

Taxes were hiked again in 1984 on gasoline.

The Tax Reform Act of 1986 reduced the number of marginal tax rates from fifteen rates ranging from 11 percent to 50 percent to two rates: 15 percent and 28 percent. The tax base was broadened by eliminating many tax credits and deductions in an attempt to make the overall legislation revenue-neutral.[19]

It was during the 1985–1986 campaign to enact Reagan's tax reform legislation that Americans for Tax Reform was created to build grassroots support for the effort. The board included Kraft CEO John Richman, Focus on the Family leader James Dobson, and the head of the Knights of Columbus, Supreme Knight Virgil C. Dechant. I was asked to serve as executive director and then president.

As the legislation neared passage in the summer of 1986, some conservative members of Congress expressed the fear that lowering the marginal tax rates and eliminating "loopholes" might make it easier for future politicians to let the tax rates drift upward and taxpayers would have surrendered those credits and deductions that had sheltered them in the past from the damage done by high tax rates.

## THE TAXPAYER PROTECTION PLEDGE

To avoid just this problem, Americans for Tax Reform created the Taxpayer Protection Pledge, which was a written commitment by those running for the House of Representatives, the Senate, and the presidency to oppose any and all increases in the personal or corporate income tax by either hiking tax rates or further eliminating deductions, unless such changes were revenue-neutral.

The actual pledge follows.

The first year that the pledge was offered to all candidates for federal office was 1986. By Election Day, one hundred incumbent House members and twenty senators cheerfully signed the pledge. The

### AMERICANS FOR TAX REFORM

United States House of Representatives candidates

# Taxpayer Protection Pledge

I, _____, pledge to the taxpayers of the _____ district

of the state of _____, and to the American people that I will:

ONE, oppose any and all efforts to increase the marginal income tax
rates for individuals and/or businesses; and

TWO, oppose any net reduction or elimination of deductions and
credits, unless matched dollar for dollar by further reducing tax rates.

Signature _____     _____ Date

Witness _____     _____ Witness

Pledges must be signed, dated, witnessed and returned to:
AMERICANS FOR TAX REFORM
1920 L STREET NW, SUITE 200, WASHINGTON, DC 20036

Chamber of Commerce and the National Federation of Independent
Businesses urged candidates to sign the pledge.

Reagan had his veto, and the Republicans had enough votes in the
House and Senate to sustain that veto.

In the 1988 presidential election, the only Democrat calling for
higher tax rates was Jesse Jackson. The eventual winner of the Democrat nomination, Massachusetts governor Mike Dukakis, suggested
he could increase tax revenues by improving enforcement, not by
raising tax rates. (This Dukakis strategy of higher taxes through
tougher enforcement of present law would resurface in 2007.)

On the Republican side every major candidate for president
signed the pledge—except Senator Dole. Governor Pete du Pont of
Delaware opened his New Hampshire campaign by signing the
pledge on the steps of the state capitol. Vice President Bush wanted
to say to other groups asking for such commitments that he didn't

sign pledges, so he signed a letter that was verbatim the pledge. Same difference.

Bob Dole won the Iowa primary on March 8, 1988. He was on his way to winning the Republican nomination. Two weeks later, the candidates were debating in New Hampshire one day before the New Hampshire primary and Pete du Pont handed Dole the pledge, saying, "We have all signed the pledge. Will you?" Dole recoiled as if he were a vampire confronted with a crucifix and said that he did not sign things he had not read. This was intended as a criticism of George H. W. Bush, who had endorsed some as-yet-unwritten treaty. But as a snappy comeback it fell short. Dole had actually read the pledge many times in the past.

The next day, Bob Dole lost the New Hampshire primary to Vice President Bush 38 percent to 28 percent, and the momentum of the primary shifted permanently to Bush.[20] The tax issue had downed a front runner in Dole and created a winner in Bush.

Bush made the centrality of the tax issue clear to the nation when he said in his acceptance speech at the Republican National Convention in the Louisiana Superdome on August 18, 1988, "Read my lips: no new taxes."[21] It was the most memorable line in the entire campaign, and before he said it, he was seventeen points down in the polls against Dukakis. Assuming the mantle and policies of Reagan, Bush climbed steadily upward to a final victory margin of 53.4 to 45.7.[22]

Bush appointed John Sununu as chief of staff and Dick Darman as head of the Office of Management and Budget. By the summer of 1990 he agreed to a summit with the Democrat majorities in the House and Senate with the fateful announcement that "revenues" would be on the table in the negotiations. The man who won his election promising never to raise taxes announced that this principle was negotiable and his word meant nothing.

This was the Munich moment for the Bush presidency. He had been elected promising to be a Reagan Republican. Reagan was elected promising to reduce marginal tax rates. Bush was elected promising to stop any tax rate increase and to continue to cut taxes (specifically rolling back the capital gains tax that had been increased from 20 percent to 28 percent in the Tax Reform Act of 1986).

But Bush broke his promise to the American people, and his tax hike raised the top income tax rate from 28 percent to 31 percent and increased the AMT rate from 20 percent to 24 percent.[23] And of course, Congress increased spending in appreciation of the higher taxes, and the deficit soared.

In hindsight, this willingness to raise taxes was the moment Bush lost the 1992 election. He would come to enjoy unprecedented and faux popularity ratings of 90 percent with the commencement of the war to drive Saddam Hussein's Iraq out of Kuwait. But already his political neck was broken. He was a dead man walking. It was otherwise a successful presidential term: Inflation was kept down, the collapse of the Soviet Union was managed with very little blood on the floor, and Bush built an international coalition of the willing that included France and much of the Arab world to drive Iraq out of Kuwait. He did not get talked into occupying Iraq. There was no scandal.

And yet, Bush only won 38 percent of the vote up against someone he called a "failed governor from a small state," Bill Clinton. Without the betrayal on the tax issue, the idea that the fellow with large ears from Texas could have pulled 18 percent of the national vote would be a joke. Clinton's winning total of 43 percent of the vote was below Dukakis's humiliating 46.6 losing percentage and barely above the losing percentages of Carter in 1980 (41 percent) and Mondale in 1984 (41 percent). The presidential vote that tended left remained a distinct minority.[24]

Because he signed the Taxpayer Protection Pledge against tax hikes, Bush won the presidency. He highlighted this with his "Read my lips: no new taxes" battle cry. Because he broke his pledge and raised taxes, he lost to a second-tier Democrat candidate with a very flawed character.

Many Republicans in the House were saved from voting for the Bush tax increase because they chose to honor their pledge. Bob Dornan (R-CA) had been one of the first conservative congressmen to endorse Bush 41 in the Republican primaries and he had a four-foot-by-five-foot blowup of the pledge hanging on his congressional office wall. He very much wanted to support his president on this test vote, but could not and would not break his pledge. Newt Gingrich, then the Republican whip, was under tremendous pressure to vote with other Republicans in leadership such as Bob Michel. Had Gingrich bowed to this pressure he could never have led the Republican resurgence in 1994.

If George H. W. Bush had won in 1992, the Taxpayer Protection Pledge would have been demoted to just another promise that candidates make and break like piecrusts. But because the political class watched Bush throw away a perfectly good presidency with this one "mistake," Republicans learned the following lesson: Take the pledge, win the primary. Take the pledge, win the general. Keep the pledge, win reelection. Break the pledge, lose the next election.

When George H. W. Bush was losing the 1992 election with only 38 percent of the vote—roughly equaling Goldwater's losing 38.47 percent in the debacle of 1964—Republicans actually *gained nine seats* in the House of Representatives.[25] Nixon had a lonely victory in 1972. Bush had a lonely loss.

Bill Clinton misread his 43 percent election as a mandate for his four major domestic planks: raise taxes on the rich; spend billions on the nation's infrastructure (read: union-controlled construction projects in big Democrat-controlled cities); government-controlled health care; and more expensive environmental regulation.

Clinton should have known better.

On Election Day 1992, four large-state initiatives spoke directly to these four themes. Voters in California voted on Proposition 167, an initiative that would have raised taxes on businesses and individuals making more than $250,000. It was defeated by an eighteen-point margin, 59 percent to 41 percent.[26] Also in California, a "Clinton-esque" mandatory government health-care regime was defeated 69 percent to 31 percent.[27] In New York State, an infrastructure bond that promised thousands of government jobs in return for additional state debt was defeated with 56 percent. And while carrying Massachusetts, the green ticket of Clinton-Gore watched a mandatory-recycling bill go down to defeat 55 percent to 38 percent.[28]

Voters in Colorado rejected a 1 percent sales-tax increase to pay for education billed as "pennies for the children," and enacted a constitutional amendment requiring that all tax increases be voted on by Colorado citizens. Arizona passed an initiative to require a two-thirds vote of the legislature to raise taxes.

In all, ten out of eleven statewide ballot questions that would have raised taxes were defeated. Six of eight measures to cut or limit taxes and spending were passed. The coming electoral message of 1994 could already be seen in 1992. It was simply obscured by the Perot vote, which made Bill Clinton's 43 percent win appear to be a mandate for big government.

Despite these warnings Bill Clinton and the Democrat Congress in 1993 increased the top marginal tax rate from 31 percent to 39.6 percent and increased the top AMT tax rate from 24 percent to 28 percent. Not a single Republican legislator voted for the Democrats' tax hike.[29]

After the election of 1994 there were 215 pledge signers in the House and 32 in the Senate.

In 1996, Bob Dole did sign the Taxpayer Protection Pledge prior to the New Hampshire primary, as did all the other presidential candidates. And Dole did pick up a sound policy idea of economist Bruce Bartlett's—an across-the-board tax cut of 15 percent for income tax rates and a cut in the capital-gains tax. This is the tribute vice pays to virtue.

Dole had spent his entire political life focused on the deficit rather than economic growth and on the government's finances rather than the budgets of American families. When the government had enough money, things were good. When the government was short of cash, we needed to raise taxes, as in 1982. Dole ridiculed the supply-side growth argument, often telling the joke that there was good news and bad news. "The good news is that a busload of supply-siders had run off a cliff. The bad news is that there were three empty seats."

In 2000, George W. Bush signed the pledge, as did John McCain and every one of the republican presidential candidates. Bush and a Republican Congress passed and enacted a tax cut each and every year from 2001 to 2006. In total Bush has enacted $2 trillion of tax cuts since entering office.

## BRANDING THE REPUBLICAN PARTY AS THE ANTITAX PARTY

The Republican Party had branded itself as the party that would not raise your taxes. No Republican member of the House or Senate had voted for a tax hike since 1990. Every Republican voted against the Clinton tax hikes of 1993 and most Republicans voted for the annual tax cuts put forward by the Republican majorities beginning in 1995.

You could walk into the voting booth dead drunk and know that if you simply voted for the candidate with the "R" after his or her name there was a 94 percent certainty that he or she would never vote to raise your taxes. (In 2007, only seven Republicans in the Senate and only eight in the House had not signed the Taxpayer Protection Pledge. One Democrat in the Senate and four in the House had signed the pledge.)

## RAT HEADS IN A COKE BOTTLE: BAD FOR THE BRAND

Businessmen understand the importance of a brand. When you walk into a grocery store and pick up a bottle of Coca-Cola you don't have to open it. You don't have to read the label, or ask a friend what he thinks of the product. You just pick it up and put it in your shopping cart. You trust the quality control of Coca-Cola because you understand that Coke lives off the reputation of the quality of their brand and that they will police that quality in their own self-interest.

Should you bring a bottle of Coca-Cola home and drink half the bottle and then look down and notice a rat head in what is left in the bottle, your first thought would not be, "Well, I may not finish the rest of this particular bottle of Coke." You would begin to wonder if you would ever drink Coke again. You would call your friends and tell them about your experience. You might go on the local TV news and point at the rat head in the Coke bottle. All across the country consumers would have doubts about Coca-Cola.

Republican-elected officials who vote for tax increases are rat heads in a Coke bottle. They damage the brand for everyone else. This is not a victimless crime. A Republican who votes for a tax increase brings all Republicans into disrepute. It makes voters wonder. It makes the choice of voting Republican more difficult and less automatic. It confuses small children about the ways of the world. "Mom, you told me that Republicans never raise taxes, and look at that man over there."

When George Herbert Walker Bush destroyed his presidency by raising taxes, one might have expected this lesson to be learned by all Republicans in the United States. It was certainly learned by most congressmen, senators, and would-be presidents. But surprisingly, at the state level it appears that this lesson must be learned anew in each state. Watching someone else burn his fingers is not good enough for Republican governors and state legislators.

*The No-Tax-Hike Movement Moves to the States, Slowly. Haltingly.* Of the 7,382 state legislators in the United States there are 3,321 Republicans and 3,989 Democrats. All have been asked to sign the Taxpayer Protection Pledge. As of January 2007, 1,080 Republicans and 127 Democrats had signed the pledge. Whereas 95 percent of Republicans in the U.S. House of Representatives had signed the pledge, only one-third of Republican state legislators had signed the pledge.

State by state, the Republican Party is working to earn the antitax brand enjoyed by the national Republican Party. The two largest Republican states, Florida and Texas, have built up their Republican majorities and maintained Republican governors with a no-tax-hike promise. Florida's Jeb Bush actually cut taxes every one of his eight years as governor. In California, led by State Senator Tom McClintock, every single state senator and state assemblyman (minus one, Assemblyman Roger Niello) signed the Taxpayer Protection Pledge in 2007 and held a joint press conference to announce that they had the one-third plus in each house that is enough to stop any tax hike in a state that requires a two-thirds vote to raise taxes.[30]

Still, the lessons must be relearned at the state level in some cases.

Alabama elected conservative Republican congressman Bob Riley governor in 2002. He surprised everyone by immediately demanding that the state raise taxes by two billion dollars. This required a change in the state constitution and therefore went before a vote of the people. The Republican Party of Alabama, led by Chairman Marty Connors, opposed the tax hike. Riley brought the national chairman of the Christian Coalition into Alabama to support his tax hike. Together they explained that Jesus of Nazareth would have supported this tax. It was a Christian tax increase. On Election Day (perhaps due to the growing number of Hindus in Alabama) the tax hike was defeated 68 to 32.[31] Because the party never lost its principles, even when the Republican governor did, the GOP brand was not damaged. Four years later, a chastened governor promising never to raise taxes was reelected.

In Oregon and North Carolina, the Republican Party itself held fast even when a handful of Republican legislators joined with Democrats to try to raise taxes. Because the party did not bend, it protected the no-tax brand. It helped that voters defeated a number of the Benedict Arnolds in each state in the next election.

Ohio and Illinois Republican governors Robert Taft and George Ryan abused the Republican brand by pushing for higher taxes and more spending. Taft gave the governorship to the Democrats and Ryan gave away both houses of the legislature, and the governorship, to the Democrats.

In Colorado, Governor Bill Owens had been one of the front-runners for the Republican presidential nomination in 2008. He was even featured on the cover of *National Review* as "America's Best Governor" in April 2002.[32] Owens demonstrated the power of the tax issue when he inexplicably changed teams and led a fight to increase state taxes in Colorado. The Republican Party of Colorado was not able to be independent and oppose this tax hike. As a result taxes were raised in Colorado and voters gave the governorship and both houses of the legislature to the Democrats in 2006. Would-be presidential candidates around the nation watched a front-runner end his chances of becoming president by supporting a tax hike.

No one's life is ever a complete waste. Some serve as bad examples.

The good news for Republicans and the Taxpayer Protection Pledge is that as the pledge has moved from the national level to the state level, state legislators have become less willing to raise taxes in response to an economic slowdown and more willing to cut taxes in times of growth. And when they do raise taxes it has been increasingly targeted on consumption taxes that do not spike upward with a recovering economy as income tax hikes do. The number and severity of tax hikes after each recession have declined.

## CHAPTER NINETEEN

# TAX
# REFORM

Okay, Republicans will not raise taxes. That is necessary but not sufficient.

Tax reform must follow.

Immediately after the 1994 GOP capture of Congress, the idea of a flat tax was debated vigorously. The Steve Forbes presidential campaign of 1996 introduced the flat tax to the national scene. It was met with a friendly counterproposal for a national sales tax that had the added populist appeal of abolishing the IRS. The Forbes campaign also introduced Social Security privatization to the national agenda, or at least the GOP agenda.

All this was followed by silence. Many activists wondered if the party or its leaders had abandoned tax reform. Perhaps it was political red meat for the base but not a serious effort.

To the contrary, the reason the flat tax receded from the national debate after 1996 was precisely because Republicans were dead serious about tax reform, and they knew that no real tax reform could survive a Clinton veto. There was no point in passing legislation that would hypothetically sacrifice some cherished tax credits and deductions in return for pro-growth tax rate reductions if Clinton would veto the bill. The benefits would never appear and those who feared for their tax credits would be stampeded to Clinton fund-raisers in self-defense.

Bringing the flat tax forward for a vote before it was possible to enact would ensure no progress in the short run and might well damage the long-term prospects of reform.

The debate on tax reform disappeared from talk radio and congressional debate precisely because Steve Forbes, Dick Armey, and Jack Kemp had won a Republican consensus on tax reform. What was there to debate? Rather than waste breath debating the exact wording of the perfect reform, the movement correctly worked to build the political strength necessary to enact it. It will undoubtedly require sixty senators and more than a simple majority in the House of Representatives.

The consensus, however, was clear: Real tax reform means taxing consumed income one time, at one rate, and it also means constitutional protection against tax increases in the future.

The strategy for tax reform was to take those steps toward taxing income one time at one rate that could be enacted into law. Some political movements disdain half-measures and view every small step in the right direction as a betrayal of the ultimate goal. They make the perfect the enemy of the good. The tax reform movement has not succumbed to this temptation. It has taken its work seriously enough to think through not only where it wants to go, but how to get there.

Let's look at the three components of the goal of tax reform and then the seven steps necessary to accomplishing this political journey.

## THE THREE PRINCIPLES OF TAX REFORM

*The First Principle: Tax Income One Time.* Today, the federal government taxes your paycheck when you earn a dollar. It takes out 10, 15, 25, 28, 33, or 35 percent depending on your income.[1] Then if you save what is left of your dollar and invest it in a company, the government taxes the company's income through the corporate income tax. When the company pays a dividend to you, the government steps in and taxes that dividend income again. And if the value of the stock goes up over time, the government will politely ask for its cut. This is called a "capital gain" and is subject to a "capital gains tax." Save your dollar in a bank and the government will take a percentage of the interest the bank pays you. And if you are foolish enough to die, the government takes as much as half of all your life savings. This is the death tax. When you die your kids get to count up everything you own: bank accounts, your car, your house, land, and the gold in your teeth. Uncle Sam takes as much as half.

Not only does this serial taxation result in the government taking more and more of your income away, it is a terrible violation of your privacy.

It is no fun having the government watch you when you earn a dollar or watch you when you spend a dollar, but each of these would be an improvement over having the government watch you earn a dollar, watch you save it, watch you invest it, watch you spend it, and then insist on a complete accounting of what is left—all your life savings—for the death tax. Sting's eerie ballad "Every Step You Take (I'll Be Watching You)" could be the theme song for today's IRS.

A flat-rate tax on consumed income—your income minus savings—would allow the government to watch you earn a dollar and then go away. The "FAIR Tax," a retail sales tax to replace the income tax as recommended by Congressman John Linder of Georgia, would take a pass at looking over your shoulder when you earn a dollar or invest a dollar and instead would hang around and watch every single thing you buy and tax those transactions.[2]

So one reason for moving to a tax system that taxes income only one time is to increase your family's privacy. Another is to stop the double and triple taxation of capital—your savings. Once the government has taken its vig out of your paycheck, you should be free to take your money and buy groceries, drink it, stick it under the mattress, give it to charity, invest it in Microsoft, or anything your little heart desires. It should no longer be any of the government's business and they certainly should not tax any of these decisions. They had their bite at the apple. And it hurt enough the first time.

Taxing income one time means ending the death tax and abolishing taxes on your savings and investments such as capital gains taxes or taxes on dividends and interest income. Taxation would fall only one time on consumed income.

*The Second Principle: Tax Income at One Rate.* This is not a question of fairness. Taxation is when the government takes money from people who earned it and often gives it to people who did not. Fairness does not enter into this equation.

The most important reason for a single rate is that it treats all Americans the same. Equality before the law is central to a free and just society. A single-rate tax is transparent. If the tax rate is 10 percent for everyone, then everyone knows what everyone else is paying. No one need fear that someone else is getting favors. The guy next door is paying 10 percent. So is your brother. And the rich Kennedys.

If everyone is paying the same rate the politicians cannot divide taxpayers and set them against one another. The Commonwealth of Massachusetts has a constitutionally mandated single-rate income tax. The politicians cannot have a higher tax rate on one person than another. Five times the advocates of larger government have put a proposed constitutional amendment on the ballot to allow a graduated or "progressive" income tax system. Five times the citizens of Massachusetts—Ted Kennedy, Mike Dukakis, and John Kerry's Massachusetts—have refused to abandon the flat tax: in 1962, 1968, 1972, 1976, and 1994.[3]

There has been a very sophisticated discussion each time. Citizens for Limited Taxation organized by Edward F. King in 1978—and led now by the Amazon of the taxpayers' movement, Barbara Anderson, Francis "Chip" Faulkner, and Chip Ford—has led a statewide conversation through letters to the editor and talk radio. Citizens came to realize that if the politicians are allowed to divide the taxpayers of Massachusetts into several groups based on income, they might reduce "my" taxes the first year, but when my interests are divorced from Ted Kennedy's and I then allow his tax rate to be raised because he is rich, who will defend me when the same politicians come to raise my tax rates? United we will stand together. Divided we will be taxed one at a time.

This was the very strategy of divide and conquer that Clinton employed in 1993 when he promised that he would only raise taxes on the top 2 percent of American earners. Clinton might as well have said, "This doesn't affect you. This will only hit a rich few. So you go into another room. You don't want to hear this. It won't be pleasant, but it doesn't hurt you. Just them." Then after he finished raising income taxes on the top 2 percent—which frequently turned out to be small businesses rather than individuals—he turned on those who drive cars and raised gasoline taxes and then raised taxes on those who receive Social Security checks. This is the Richard Speck theory of tax increases. If you cannot take on everyone in the room at once, you take your victims out of the room one at a time.

A flat tax forces the politicians to face every citizen and speak to them honestly and at the same time. With a flat tax, if a politician has a good idea and he wants to raise taxes to pay for it, he must confront all taxpayers at once and explain, "I have a good idea and you will all help pay for this." If it is a good idea he may win support. But it had better be a *really* good idea. In the other direction, tax cuts will benefit all taxpayers as they all pay the same rate and will see a lower rate as helping all taxpayers. No more attacking tax cuts as only for the rich.

The Third Principle: Create Constitutional Protections Against Taxes Creeping Back Upward. This can come in the form of a constitutional amendment making it more difficult to raise taxes. California, Arizona, and Nevada have all enacted constitutional amendments requiring a two-thirds vote of both houses of the legislature to raise taxes. California's constitutional requirement for a two-thirds supermajority for higher taxes was part of Proposition 13 promoted by Howard Jarvis and Paul Gann in 1978.

The two-thirds requirement in Arizona, enacted through an initiative in 1992, has stopped all legislative tax hikes since then. Nevada elected Congressman Jim Gibbons governor in November 2006. His

claim to fame was leading the campaign that put the two-thirds supermajority for tax hikes in the Nevada Constitution.

In 1992, Colorado passed TABOR, the Taxpayer Bill of Rights,
which requires any tax hike to be put before the people for approval
by popular vote. Some towns and cities have voted to raise taxes, but
many more have decided to avoid risking irritating voters by reining
in spending instead.

All advocates of a national sales tax (aka the "FAIRTax") agree that
it is only safe to switch the present income tax for a sales tax if the
Sixteenth Amendment that allowed the creation of the income tax in
1913 is abolished and a new amendment specifically forbidding the
taxation of income by the federal government is enacted. Otherwise
during any transition period of ten years, ten months, or ten minutes
there remains the danger that America could be saddled with both a
national income tax and a national consumption tax and we would be
right where France is with both an income tax and a VAT, or value
added tax, a sales tax at every level of production.

If every Republican agrees that we should move to a single-rate tax
that taxes consumed income only once and this should be protected
from future generations of politicians with constitutional safeguards,
what is holding up the show? We had a Republican majority in the
House and Senate from 1995 to 2007 with only an eighteen-month
hiatus in the Senate from June 2001 to January 2003. And from January 2001 to the present there has been a Republican president who
says he wants tax reform. The sticking point has been the Democrat
Party's willingness to invoke the filibuster and require a sixty-vote
majority for tax reform or in fact any significant legislation.

Facing this frustration, the taxpayers' movement figured out that
there are seven steps to a flat-rate tax on consumed-income. And then
one more step, moving from taxing income when you earned it to
taxing it when you spend it, to arrive at a single-rate retail sales tax—
the "FAIRTax."

Each of the steps has serious political support. Each step can be accomplished by itself. In fact each step has greater political support
than fundamental reform itself. Why? Because Americans rightly do

not trust politicians to make multiple changes at once, but will more comfortably watch a single change that they understand. Fewer moving parts. Less likelihood that reform could—under cover of political white noise—morph into a tax hike.

If you follow the Bush administration's annual tax cuts, you will see a method in their meandering. They have taken baby steps and some significant steps forward in each of these seven steps to a single-rate tax that taxes consumed income one time.

## The Seven Steps to Tax Reform

*1. Abolish the Death Tax.* Alongside the first income tax, the death tax was created in 1862 to help pay for the North's costs of the Civil War. It was a tax on inheritances that ranged from 0.75 percent to 5 percent and then raised again in 1864 to 6 percent.[4] Following the Civil War, the tax was abolished in 1870 only to reappear again in 1898 as one tax instituted to pay for the Spanish-American War. This time the rate was 15 percent on estates of over $1 million ($22 million in 2005) and was repealed in 1902. The death tax was reinstituted for World War One in 1916 at a 10 percent rate on estates over $5 million ($96 million today) alongside the newly created income tax and raised again in 1917.[5] When WWI ended, the tax was not repealed. The tax shifted from one to finance temporary wartime needs to a tax designed to redistribute income, and by 2001 it taxed your life savings above $675,000 at a 55 percent rate.

It was a perfect tax from the standpoint of politicians. It only hit the wealthiest Americans. In 2004, only 2 percent of estates were paying the federal death tax.[6] And it was paid by dead people, who in most cases were no longer voters.

Any effort to reform taxes so as to tax consumed income one time at one rate starts with abolishing a graduated tax on the accumulated savings of Americans at death. The federal tax collectors raised $14.8 billion through the death and gift tax in 1995, $29 billion in 2000, and $24.8 billion in 2005, or 1.1 percent, 1.4 percent, and 1.2 percent of the total federal tax revenues.[7] Taxes paid on the wealth saved by your father and mother are taxes levied on money that has already sailed between the Scylla and Charybdis of federal and state income taxes, business taxes, dividend taxes, and capital-gains taxes. While the American tax code has long punished capital accumulation more violently than many other nations, the death tax is the final insult.

In 1999 and 2000, the Republican House and Senate voted to abolish the death tax. Clinton vetoed it each time. In 2001, the House and Senate voted to phase out the death tax, taking the top rate from 55 percent to 45 percent in 2009 and to zero in 2010, and the legislation increased the amount of your savings exempted from the tax from $675,000 in 2000 to $3.5 million in 2009.[8] Because the abolition of the death tax came inside a reconciliation package, the tax cuts were only good for ten years, and in 2011 the original death tax of 55 percent snaps back into place.

Among those Democrats voting against repealing the death tax in 2005 were several Democrat senators who had promised their voters they would support abolition. On his official website Arkansas senator Mark Pryor twice stated his commitment to abolish the death tax. (He changed his website—not his vote—after the press in Arkansas pointed this out.) Oregon's senator Ron Wyden voted for abolition in the year before his 2004 election. When safely reelected he gave his vote to Democrat leader Harry Reid. Reid had a strategy of moving around Democrat votes on the death tax so that those up for reelection could vote for abolition and those in safe seats or not up for several years would be ordered to vote no despite their public commitments or previous votes.

This has stopped death-tax repeal to date, but it is a dangerous game, as Senator Tom Daschle found out. Daschle was elected in 1986, 1992, and 1998, and lost in 2004 by only 4,508 votes after voting three times against abolishing the death tax. He was the Democrat leader and led the party's support to keep the death tax but this forced him to vote against the people of South Dakota, who had voted 80–20 to abolish their own state death tax in 2000. The South Dakota Legislature passed resolutions demanding that Daschle vote to abolish the death tax. The two Democrat senators from California voted to protect the death tax despite the 60–40 vote to abolish the state's death tax in 1982.[9] In Washington State, Dick Patten, the leader of the American Family Business Institute, placed an initiative to abolish the death tax on the November 1981 ballot and citizens voted to kill the death tax 60–40.[10] Despite this, the two Democrat senators from Washington State have also voted to keep the federal death tax.

Why did the move to abolish the death tax come so close to victory in a short time period and why did it fall short despite more than sixty senators promising to vote for abolition?

Several reasons.

Jim Martin, the president of 60 Plus Association, the conservative answer to the politically left American Association of Retired People (AARP), popularized the name the "death tax" rather than the left's preferred "estate tax," arguing that there should be "No Taxation without Respiration."

The campaign against the death tax also benefited from a change in tactics from arguing for reductions in the death tax to outright abolition. Efforts to reduce the death tax or increase the amount of savings exempted from taxation had failed for many years, as they were seen as special pleadings for higher-income taxpayers. But a campaign to abolish a tax that taxes income that has already been taxed is an argument on principle.

And in America a more radical demand based on principle and fairness trumps a more "reasonable" request that looks like special treatment for a few.

Democrats long felt that they had a political winner. Why should anyone care about high taxes on a few rich people? Clinton had won against Bush in 1992, admitting that he would raise taxes on the richest 2 percent. But Clinton was only able to do that because Bush had destroyed his credibility on the tax issue with the 1990 tax and spending increase "deal" of $125 billion in new taxes over four years. (It was sold as a deficit reduction package, but spending increased by $209 billion during the same period.)

But envy is not a winning political strategy in the modern United States. In a *Time*/CNN poll of October 27, 2000, Americans were asked: "Do you think you will be in that top group that will benefit from Bush's proposed tax cut right away?" Nineteen percent of Americans said they believed they would benefit "right away" from a tax cut described in the poll as targeted only at the top 1 percent of Americans. Twenty percent said they would benefit "in the future." Fifty-five percent, introduced to the tax cut after hearing only Al Gore's characterization, felt they "will not benefit."[11]

The polling data on the death tax is even starker. Even though the death tax today directly hits only the top 2 percent of Americans, nearly 67 percent of Americans support ending the death tax.[12]

The left has responded poorly to the news that class division and hatred and envy were not the powerful political weapons they believed they would always be in America. The left's economic and envy analysis was stuck in the 1930s with FDR's attacks on economic royalists and bankers.

The left understands this is not just a fight over money. They know that the Kennedys and Rockefellers can spend the necessary millions to avoid paying the death tax through family foundations and insurance purchases that pass money to the next generation, avoiding the death tax. The death tax costs so much to administer, and estate planning to avoid the tax is so damaging to the economy, that it is probably a net loss to the government coffers. Liberals probably lose money with their favorite tax.

## CLASS WARFARE REPLACES RACIAL DIVISIONS

Both sides understood that the fight over abolishing the death tax was an up-or-down vote on whether discrimination based on wealth is acceptable. This was a contest to decide whether envy is an acceptable political strategy or one of the seven deadly sins. Much would flow from this debate. A nation that will not tolerate discrimination against the wealthy would not long tolerate graduated or progressive income tax rates. The path to a flat tax begins with the abolition of the death tax.

It speaks very much to the health of the nation that a strong majority of Americans want to abolish the death tax because they see it as fundamentally unjust. The left pushes an argument playing on the politics of hate and envy and class division saying, Why should you care what we do to "them"? They, the rich with taxable estates, are a small minority. This doesn't affect you. That, of course, is the morality that could justify the Holocaust. This mistreatment of the other does not affect you. Just a few of the "others."

The left recoils in horror at equating discrimination by the state on economic grounds with discrimination on the basis of race or religion. They want to argue that discrimination by race in South Africa was wrong, but discrimination on economic grounds in East Germany or in the Soviet Union's starvation campaign against the Kulaks—independent, land-owning farmers—was somehow okay. No. East Germany and the anti-Kulak campaign were not an improvement over South Africa. State discrimination against any group, for racial, religious, or economic reasons is wrong.

But of course the left has to believe that East Germany was an improvement over South Africa. For one hundred years the Democrat Party was competitive in national politics only because it enacted and exploited Jim Crow laws that divided Americans by race. Eventually the Democrats had to shed that tool, and they lost the South to the Republicans just as racism was ruled an unacceptable way to organize politically. The Takings Coalition, the modern Democrat Party, can only come to power and rule if they divide the natural majority of Americans who should be members of the Leave Us Alone Coalition. The Democrats used to divide Americans by religion and race. More recently, they have aimed at dividing Americans by income and wealth. The state, under their benevolent control, will manage the conflict they created. Should the Democrats find class envy and hatred ruled similarly obnoxious and illegitimate as racial discrimination, they will have a hard time maintaining the discriminatory tax structure they believe they need to finance their Takings Coalition.

## The Art of the Possible

The abolition of the death tax also began moving forward only when it was seen as possible. Serious men and women do not focus on the unattainable no matter how much it is desired.

Congressman Chris Cox introduced legislation to abolish the death tax in 1996. It won a handful of co-sponsors. Then 60+ and Americans for Tax Reform announced that they would rate co-sponsorship as a key issue in their annual ratings. Thus a congressman with a voting record that justified a 75 percent rating would, should he or she co-sponsor the Chris Cox legislation, gain an 85 percent rating and earn a "Hero of the Taxpayer Award." Sponsorship jumped to one hundred House members, and abolishing the death tax became part of the Republican agenda.

At an Americans for Tax Reform's annual press conference in support of a constitutional amendment to require a two-thirds vote to raise taxes, then-Speaker Gingrich announced that abolishing the death tax and abolishing the capital gains tax were now officially goals of the Republican Party. We would work to achieve each as soon as possible.

Death-tax repeal also won supporters as congressional candidates reported back that calling for the abolition of the death tax was the strongest applause line in their speeches. Candidate George W. Bush in 2000 got the loudest applause when he called for ending the death tax. Senator Bill Frist, speaking to CPAC in 2005, rattled off the litany of coming votes on key conservative issues: protecting marriage, protecting the flag. His call for abolishing the death tax won the "applause meter."

## Destroying Wealth

Abolishing the death tax is not just a political trophy. Neal B. Freeman, chairman of the Foundation Management Institute, has calculated that in the next forty years as much as fourteen trillion dollars will pass from grandparents and parents to children and grandchildren. If the federal government takes and consumes half of that accumulated savings, it will be a body blow to our economic growth in the future. Capital is the seed corn needed for investing in jobs, technology, and new businesses.

## No More Ford Foundations

The second challenge is political rather than economic. If a 55 percent tax looms over every American who has accumulated savings during his or her working life, it will drive much of that wealth into tax-sheltered foundations. Think how much damage the Ford and Rockefeller foundations have done. They have hired hundreds of tough and hardworking activists of the left to spend wealth created by Republicans to promote the agenda of the left. The Pew and MacArthur foundations are further examples of how foundations are reverse alchemists, turning free-market wealth into left-wing funding. Despite the hard work of activists such as Neil Freeman of the Foundation Management Institute and Adam Meyerson of the Philanthropy Round Table, there are few trained conservatives interested in or capable of running such foundations. The world is full of liberals willing to spend the money accumulated by conservative Republicans. That is what liberals do for a living, whether in the federal, state, or local governments or by running foundations brimful of cash forced by tax laws into their waiting hands.

If the death tax is allowed to continue, the next twenty-five years will see the creation of hundreds of such foundations. They will all be taken over by liberal activists. They will spend dead entrepreneurs' wealth to ensure that future entrepreneurs cannot thrive. Think how much less damage is done by the Kennedy kids, who—largely avoiding death taxes with clever lawyers—simply drink up granddad's money and only damage those near them.

Abolishing the death tax is a key component of defunding the left.

And abolishing the death tax will eliminate more than 54,095 words of the IRS tax code.[13]

*2. Expand IRAs/401(k)s and Enact Universal Savings Accounts.* Step two in moving to a tax code that taxes consumed income one time at one rate is creating a universal IRA—to set all savings free from taxation. Once income has been taxed it is up to you what to do with it. If you wish to spend it on wine, women, and song or invest in Microsoft, that should be your call and the government loses any legitimate interest in following you around and asking how what is left of your paycheck is doing.

Individual retirement accounts created in 1974 allowed all Americans to save up to $1,500 in pre-tax dollars in an account that would over the years accumulate tax free but could not be withdrawn until one was fifty-nine and a half, and one had to begin drawing down the account by age seventy and a half. If you saved $2,000 one time at age twenty-one, you would have $42,000 when you hit age sixty five. If you put away $2,000 each year, earning the average of 7 percent interest, you would have over $520,000 when you retired at sixty-five.[14] Albert Einstein called the power of compound interest the most powerful force in the universe.

Also in 1978, 401(k)s were created, allowing companies to contribute to a personal savings account held by their employees—originally up to $10,000, or 10 percent of one's salary.

In one of the bad bits of the Tax Reform Act of 1986, IRAs were limited to Americans earning less than $50,000 unless not covered by a pension. But many taxpayers simply heard that IRAs were restricted and their use fell significantly even among those Americans still offered the original deal.

Former assistant secretary of Treasury Pam Olson mentioned in a 2003 speech that contributions to IRAs rose nearly tenfold, from $4 billion to $38 billion between 1980 and 1986. When Congress restricted the deductibility of IRA contributions in 1986, the level of IRA contributions fell sharply to $15 billion in 1987 and $8.4 billion in 1995.[15]

A portion of this decline is the result of previous higher-income contributors being excluded from participating, but savings also dropped among families retaining full eligibility. In fact, participation

declined by 40 percent between 1986 and 1987 for families still eligible, despite the fact that the change in law did not affect them.
The number of IRA contributors with income of less than $25,000
dropped by 30 percent in that one year.[16] *Here we have the politicians trying to limit savings benefits to the "rich" and their largest
effect was to scare away the middle class from a powerful saving
tool.*

IRA contribution amounts were expanded in 2001 (but not income
eligibility), and while most of President Bush's tax-cut ideas were opposed by most Democrats, the IRA expansion passed 400 to 23. This
at a time when the death-tax repeal won support from only forty-
three Democrats. Income-tax-rate cuts were supported by even fewer
Democrats.

Both the IRA and 40l(k) expansions originally passed for only a
ten-year period were made permanent in the 2006 pension reform
bill. At the time of this writing this is one of the few Bush tax cuts
made permanent.

The automatic enrollment feature of the Pension Protection Act of
2006 could raise worker participation in 401(k) plans from 66 percent
of eligible workers to 92 percent of eligible workers. Assuming the

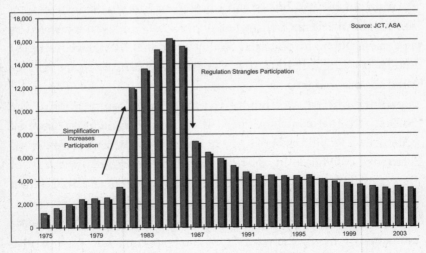

Number of IRA Participants (in the Thousands)

same number of 401(k)-eligible employees (a number which itself should grow with these changes), the number of 401(k) participants would rise from fifty-five million in 2006 to sixty-nine million if every 401(k) plan had these auto-features.[17]

A second major component of the Pension Protection Act of 2006 allowed workers to be automatically enrolled in a "lifecycle fund," which gives employees greater exposure to stocks and bonds. This should move more retirement savings from low-return money market accounts toward higher-returning stocks, further increasing the wealth of American workers.

Finally, the legislation makes employers realize the true cost of antiquated defined-benefit plans, which will lead to more companies using defined-contribution plans in the future. These three factors led Morgan Stanley analysts to conclude that annual defined-contribution inflows will increase 150 percent when the provisions take effect, jumping from $12 billion to $30 billion annually.

The next step in tax reform is to consolidate the existing hodgepodge of tax-free savings accounts with lifetime and retirement savings accounts (LSAs/RSAs).

A retirement savings account (RSA) would allow every American to put aside $5,000 of after-tax income each year toward retirement. Earnings on the $5,000 would accumulate tax free.

A lifetime savings account (LSA) allows every American to set aside $5,000 in after-tax savings to accumulate until needed for housing, education, health care, or whatever. It is a vehicle for tax-free building of savings. The enemies of the LSA are the big insurance companies who sell whole life insurance to people with only a passing interest in insurance, but who want to benefit from the tax-free buildup inside the insurance. We hope that if we can make it easy for insurance companies to sell such LSAs, they will drop their protectionist opposition to the creation and then expansion of LSAs.

There is a debate between those who wish to "force" taxpayers to save for education, retirement, or health care in individual silos that cannot be used for other purposes and those who would make all savings tax free without restrictions.

Eventually one would like to treat Americans as adults and allow them universal tax-free savings, which they could decide to access as needed for housing, health, education, retirement, or other needs. But at present the federal and state governments guarantee to pay for health and retirement if you show up old and impoverished even if this is through your own bad decisions. Given this political reality, it is an acceptable compromise to "require" citizens to save for these future needs so they do not end up on the government's doorstep demanding that their grasshopper behavior be financed by additional taxes on the ants.

Passing LSAs and RSAs would eliminate 117,151 words of the tax code by rolling all the various tax-free investment programs into these two easily portable accounts.

3. *Abolish the Capital Gains and Dividend Tax.* Capital gains are created when you take what is left of your paycheck after state and local income taxes and buy land or a home or invest in stocks or a mutual fund, and as the land, house, or stock increases in value you have a capital gain. Naturally the government wishes to tax this.

Congress began taxing capital gains during the Civil War with the creation of the temporary income tax, and capital gain at that time was viewed as "ordinary" income, meaning the capital gain was added to wage income and taxed at the standard income tax rate. The income tax was declared unconstitutional and there was no effort to tax capital gains until the creation of the present income tax in 1913.[18] Recognizing that income was being taxed for the second time and that high capital gains taxes were particularly damaging to economic growth, politicians usually set the capital gains rate lower than the regular income tax rates, which eventually reached 90 percent.

Richard Nixon increased the capital gains tax from 25 percent to 36 percent in 1969 in the same tax-increase package in which he increased marginal income tax rates with a surtax of 10 percent.[19] The value of stocks collapsed. An analysis by the American Shareholders

Association found that from 1968 through 1977 total shareholder wealth dropped by 48 percent in inflation-adjusted dollars, declining from $1.6 trillion to $824 billion (1978 dollars).[20] (One is hard pressed to understand why the Democrats hated this tax-and-spend liberal. In fact, should Richard Nixon come back to life and get elected to Congress as a Republican he would be the most left-wing Republican member of the House.)

When the Steiger amendment reduced the top capital gains tax rate from 39.9 percent to 28 percent in 1978, tax revenue from capital gains taxes increased from $9.1 billion to $11.9 billion in 1979.[21] Before Democrats learned to oppose Ronald Reagan's tax cuts by shouting that tax-rate reductions would never "pay for themselves" in higher economic growth and higher tax revenue, they actually proved that supply-side economics is very real. To understand how economically illiterate George H. W. Bush truly was, his comment that supply-side economics was "voodoo economics" came one year after the demonstration of the supply-side success of the Steiger amendment.

When Reagan further cut the capital gains tax to 20 percent as part of the 1981 tax-rate reduction that also saw the top income tax rate fall from 70 percent to 50 percent, capital gains revenue grew from $12.8 billion to $18.7 billion.[22]

The Tax Reform Act of 1986 dropped the top income tax rate from 50 to 28, but simultaneously increased the capital gains rate from 20 to 28. Higher taxes on capital gains led total capital gains tax revenue to fall from $52.9 billion in 1986 to $33.7 billion in 1987 to a low of $25 billion by 1991.[23]

Supply-side economics works in forward and reverse.

George H. W. Bush urged a reduction in the capital gains tax rates during the first year of his presidency, but turned and signed an income tax rate increase from 28 percent to 31 percent. Clinton raised the top rate to 39.6 percent. Neither tax increase moved the capital gains tax rate of 28 percent.

In 1997, Clinton signed a cut in the capital gains tax rate—after vetoing it in 1995 and 1996 (shades of welfare reform). At that point total shareholder wealth stood at $11.5 trillion and capital gains revenues were $66.4 billion. By January 1, 2000, total shareholder wealth stood at $17.3 trillion (a 50.4 percent increase). The Dow Jones had increased from 8,194 to 11,497 (40.3 percent) and the NASDAQ had increased from 1,594 to 4,069 (155 percent). As a result, capital gains tax revenue nearly doubled, rising to $79.3 billion in 1997, $89.1 billion in 1998, $111 billion in 1999, and $127.3 billion in 2000.[24]

Bush 43 waited until 2003 to reduce the capital gains tax rate from 20 percent to 15 percent in legislation that also cut the double taxation of dividend income from a high of 38.6 percent to 15 percent.

In 2003, capital gains tax revenue was expected to be $42 billion that year, $46 billion in 2004, $52 billion in 2005, and $57 billion in 2006. The Joint Committee on Taxation predicted that capital gains revenue would fall $5.4 billion over three years if the capital gains tax rate was cut from 20 percent to 15 percent. Instead, capital gains tax revenue doubled in two short years. By the end of fiscal year 2006, the government realized an "unexpected" revenue windfall of $133 billion.[25] (Just because the government doesn't believe in supply-side economics doesn't mean it ain't true.)

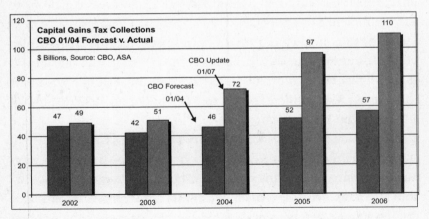

The dark bars show the Congressional Budget Office (CBO) estimate of capital gains tax revenue and the light bars shows the actual revenue. Following the capital gains tax cut from a 20 percent rate to a 15 percent rate, the CBOs estimates were particularly underestimated. Even more wrong than usual.

At the same time, the sharp reduction in taxes on dividends paid reversed the twenty-five-year decline in the number of dividend-paying companies. Prior to the tax cut, dividend income was taxed as normal income and at a rate as high as 38.6 percent. But this number is misleading, since corporations already paid taxes on the income before returning the money to shareholders. As a result, dividend income was taxed twice, resulting in an effective tax rate as high as 60 percent.

With such a punitive tax rate of 60 percent on dividends, the use of dividends declined steadily. In fact, the number of S&P 500 companies paying a dividend dropped from 469 in 1980 to 351 in 2002.[26]

But once the tax cut went into place, companies immediately began initiating and increasing their dividends for shareholders; 2005 marked the third consecutive year of more S&P 500 companies paying dividends than the previous year, and dividend income has increased at an 11 percent annual rate since the tax cut. As a result, the Congressional Budget Office (CBO) frankly admitted the dividend tax cut did not "cost "as much as previously believed.

The debate over the estate tax/death tax is truly a fight over whether envy is a legitimate political impulse. The debate over the capital gains tax today has a history. We know that higher capital gains taxes slow growth and actually reduced tax revenue: 1969 and 1986. We have seen a lower tax rate on capital gains strengthen economic growth and increase capital gains tax revenue: 1978, 1981, 1997, 2003.

The Democrats who knew this in the 1970s have moved to a position where they oppose a tax cut they know will bring in more revenue for the government. Why? They are so wedded to the politics of envy and class hatred that they pass up the opportunity to create jobs and actually gain more tax revenue for the government. But they are paying an even higher price for their devotion to envy.

The refusal to learn from history costs them credibility in the one part of the economy from which they might win supporters. No high-tech businessman or venture capitalist can take the Democrats seriously on economics as long as they remain blind to the economic costs

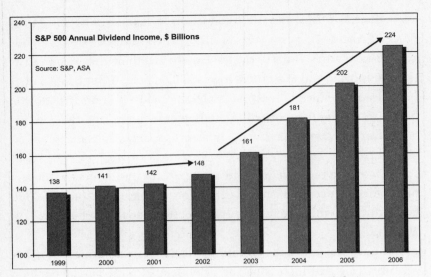

After the tax cut of 2003, American companies increased their
dividend payout.

of capital gains taxes. Raising the capital gains tax rate would greatly
harm the high-tech community. Democrats have been trying to appeal to this demographic since they created the fiction of the Atari
Democrats. At the behest of environmentalists and labor unions, the
Democrats have long acted as if they wish to destroy the steel, auto,
and coal industry. But they had a chance to appeal to the "nonpollut-
ing" and nonunionized high-tech industry. It is a measure of how
handcuffed they are to the politics of envy that they repel this last best
hope of the Democrats for business support that is not coerced.

Democrats attacked the Reagan tax cuts and the argument of
supply-side economics that high tax rates reduce job creation, income, and investment. They now feel wedded to this position even on
capital gains taxes where they know Reagan was right. They cannot
stand having been wrong. A smarter Democrat Party could have insisted that many of them got it in 1978 and used this tax cut to spur
the economy while their other policies slow it down.

The growth of the number of Americans who own stock directly
has increased the constituency for abolishing the capital gains tax.
Now that the capital gains tax rate and the double taxation of corpo-

rate income—the tax on dividends—are both set at the same rate of 15 percent there is increased political support for ending both.

Abolishing the capital gains tax would eliminate 54,278 words of the tax code.

*4. Expensing.* The next step toward a tax system that taxes consumed income one time at one single rate is to replace the complicated system of long depreciation schedules for business investment and replace it with immediate expensing of all investment.

Under present rules, when a company buys a new machine, the government in its infinite wisdom declares that it can be depreciated over, say, three, five, seven, or ten years. The useful life of a computer, a computer program, or a building is unknown but to the gods, but the IRS will tell you what—for tax purposes—is the "useful" life of any investment.

Under present rules if you buy a machine for the assembly line of an auto company for $1 million and the government determines that the machines can be depreciated over ten years, then each year for ten years the company can deduct $100,000 from its income for purposes of paying income taxes. You have to pay for the machine in year one. You are out the remaining $900,000 in cash in year one. But you will be paying taxes on money you don't have for ten years.

Expensing would mean that if you buy a machine in year one for $1 million, you would deduct that $1 million from your income that year for tax purposes. You would not pay taxes on that $1 million—because you don't have it anymore. You spent it. This is fair. This is simple. This is understandable and doesn't require any lawyers.

Moving from long and arbitrary depreciation schedules to simple and immediate expensing simply moves the timetable for any company to pay its taxes. It doesn't affect how much you pay, just when you pay. It takes the deduction immediately rather than over time. The same amount of taxes is paid. Just later. Because in the real world—as opposed to government finances—there is a time value to money; moving to expensing and away from depreciation greatly reduces the cost of capital investment.

Throwing away all the depreciation tables and moving to expensing would remove roughly 17,000 words from the tax code. It would eliminate the backroom corrupt politics where politicians get campaign contributions in return for changing the depreciation schedules here and there. Everyone would have the same depreciation schedule: 100 percent in year one. No politics. No corruption. No pages and pages of tax code and expensive lawsuits over just how to define this investment versus that one.

Expensing would be a tremendous boon to the economy. Particularly those industries with high capital costs: steel, autos, chemicals. All the manufacturing businesses that politicians say they care about. Now they can put up or shut up.

And we don't have to take this on trust. This is not an untested theory. The Bush tax cut of 2002 allowed 30 percent "accelerated depreciation" or, in English, 30 percent of the purchase could be expensed immediately. Subsequently, in 2003, Bush increased the amount from 30 percent to 50 percent for one year and allowed small-business investment of less than $100,000 to be fully and immediately expensed. Investment boomed.

Legislation introduced in the 110th Congress would move America to full expensing of business investment.

Static tax revenue estimates suggest this initiative would "cost" the federal treasury hundreds of billions of dollars over ten years. Enacting expensing for a single year would only "cost" the federal government tens of billions of dollars and would provide undeniable testimony to the power of this tax reduction for those who missed the partial expensing and its success in 2002.

These estimates fail to take into account two effects. First, expensing, rather than depreciation, is really just a timing difference and has no "cost" to the government over time. Second, empirical studies suggest expensing can provide an enormous bang for the buck. Economist Gary Robbins found that for every $1 of foregone tax revenue from expensing provides $9 of additional Gross Domestic Product (GDP). This suggests that the increased investment resulting from expensing actually generates $3 of tax revenue from the new investment for every dollar in taxes that is cut.[27]

The failure to allow companies to expense is placing America at a competitive disadvantage with the rest of the world.

There is another advantage to full expensing. It is the one tax cut that Democrats have not opposed in the past. In 1981, Dan Rosten-kowski actually offered full expensing in the Democrat alternative to President Reagan's tax-cut package. Reagan's legislation moved the depreciation schedules to a simpler and less costly "Accelerated Cost Recovery System" that was the "economic" equivalent of full expensing. But because it was still complicated and discriminated between and among industries and types of investment it was soon unraveled and politicians found they could raise taxes by simply lengthening depreciation schedules. A nice stealth-tax increase felt by everyone, but understood by few.

Democrats have yelled and screamed against cutting the top marginal tax rate for individuals and companies, against cutting the capital gains tax, and against eliminating the death tax. Moving to expensing is a pro-growth tax cut that Democrats could support without public humiliation. We could be generous and let them lead the parade.

5. *Abolish the AMT.* Moving to a tax system that taxes consumed income one time at one rate requires that Congress deal with the Frankenstein's monster they created in 1969: the Alternative Minimum Tax.

The history of the AMT is instructive. Its story is similar to that of many new taxes. The Johnson administration leaked out that 155 high-income Americans paid no income taxes at all in 1967. Much of this was due to the fact that interest paid by city and state and federal bonds is not taxed. Anyone, rich or poor, can buy a city bond and pay no tax. You get a lower rate of return because of the tax-free status. Governments like this. It reduces their costs when they borrow. It makes building a school or road less expensive. Congress could have ended this "subsidy" for investing in government. But they didn't. The politicians created the tax structure that advantaged investing in government rather than the real economy. Then the same politicians incited hatred and envy and called for a pogrom against all these rich people who didn't pay taxes on tax-exempt activity.

So Congress passed the AMT requiring that many Americans calculate their tax burden twice, using two forms, the regular income tax and the Alternative Minimum Tax (AMT), even if their deductions and credits were all perfectly legitimate. This "clawed back" some of the value of deductions and credits.

Now, the politicians who clamored for the AMT are hearing from the younger siblings and children of those American taxpayers who demanded the AMT hit "someone else." The tax that was promised to hit big business and rich people hit two million tax filers in 2002 and that number grows to thirty million by 2010, or 20 percent of households. This number grows to 30 percent of households in 2020 and 50 percent of households by 2030. These numbers do not include the millions of taxpayers who are forced to fill out the Alternative Minimum Tax forms but eventually do not pay the tax.

Who pays the AMT? Primarily taxpayers in states with high state income taxes, high property taxes, and high home costs that drive large interest payments on mortgages. States like New Jersey, New York, Connecticut, California. Blue states.

In 1993, Bill Clinton and the Democrat House and Senate increased the top AMT rate from 24 percent to 28 percent. The Republican House and Senate voted to abolish the AMT in 1999. Clinton vetoed this bill.

In Congress in 2007, there are 107 Democrats who voted to increase the AMT in 1993 and 177 Democrat congressmen and senators who voted against repealing the AMT. No Republican voted in 1993 to hike the AMT. Just four Democrats in the House of Representatives and none in the Senate voted to repeal the AMT. This is a tax invented, raised, and protected by the Democrats.

Republicans should stand ready to—once again—abolish this liberal tax passed on the lie that rich folks were cheating the system. But before we help bail out liberal Democrat senators we should insist on the equivalent of the South African Truth and Reconciliation Board. The history of the tax must be publicly acknowledged. We must get our history straight *now*. This must become the object lesson that stops liberals from playing this game again—promising to tax imaginary rich people with a new tax that over time loots the middle class while the guilty stand on the side and shrug their shoulders as if someone else did this.

The AMT is simply the largest and most recent example of this ancient scam. Americans are still paying a federal excise tax on phone bills also known as the Spanish-American War tax. This was imposed in 1898 as the perfect tax. It was for an emergency. The New York tabloids had to sell newspapers and they had whipped the nation into a fury to launch a war against Spain's control of Cuba. It would be temporary. The tax would end with the war. And best of all it was a tax that would be paid by "other people"—rich other people who owned the newfangled and very expensive toys called telephones. In 1898, roughly 1 percent of households actually owned phones and would pay this new tax.

Fast-forward one hundred years and any American who wishes to has a phone. Some have several. Poor people have phones. Everyone is paying a 3 percent tax to the general revenues of the federal government on their phone bill. While I went to public schools, I do get the History channel on cable and have recently learned that the Spanish-American War has been over for some time.

Congress voted by voice vote to abolish this tax in 2000. Bill Clinton vetoed the legislation. Perhaps it should now be named the Bill Clinton tax.

Courts have now struck down some of the tax, but it remains as an irritant and a reminder that liberals who tell you a tax will be temporary and paid by other people, other rich people, are not only lying, they are repeating an old and tired lie.

The politics of the AMT is odd. It is a Democrat tax, invented, passed, raised, and protected by Democrat presidents and congressmen. But it hits most painfully in blue states with high income taxes, high property values, and high housing costs. Democrat strategists have bragged that they would appear good on taxes to their base by loudly calling for shifting this tax onto other shoulders. This effort has been checkmated, to date, by Chuck Grassley, the Republican leader in the Senate Finance Committee who has called for abolition of the AMT rather than moving its costs elsewhere. The AMT, Grassley explained, was a mistake. You end mistakes, you do not replace them.[28]

Abolishing the AMT would eliminate 9,159 words of the IRS code.[29]

6. *Make Taxes "Territorial."* Usually when someone begins a sentence with the phrase "The United States is the only government that . . ." we are about to hear a demand that America do something truly stupid "like everyone else." The United States is the only country that doesn't have a ministry of the interior, a national ID card, a government-run airline, a ministry of youth, government-run rationing of health care, or a value-added tax. True. America *is* alone in having a pathologically stupid tort system designed to make annoying nonproductive people rich by suing everyone. But there is one other area where America is unique in a self-destructive way.

We have worldwide taxation. French people living in France must pay French income taxes. French people working in the United States pay American income taxes but not French taxes on top of that.

Americans working overseas pay income taxes to that host government, and, on top of that, they pay American income taxes. American businesses that earn money in Britain pay British taxes and American taxes. They compete with German and Japanese firms that pay only British taxes. This puts all American companies at a disadvantage and all American expatriates at a disadvantage. America claims the right to tax you, not just for what you do in America, but wherever you have sneaked off to to create wealth. Uncle Sam wants a cut. His vig. On top of whatever the local government takes from you. No matter how much it hurts individual Americans, individual companies, and our economy as a whole. This is true for individuals and companies. This is why you read about American companies choosing to be Irish companies. They then are not double taxed. Democrats call this being a Benedict Arnold business.

Would you like to pay taxes twice or once? This is an IQ test, not a test of patriotism. Now if you are an American company that earned $1 billion in Ireland, the American government will not tax your earnings until you bring them home to America. So our brilliant federal government allows you to build a $1 billion factory in Ireland with all that lovely money, but if you are stupid enough to try and bring it back to America to build a factory, then you must pay the difference between Ireland's 12.5 percent corporate tax rate and the 35 percent U.S. corporate tax rate on that $1 billion. So just who is the Benedict Arnold around here? It is our tax code that works as if it were written by Julius and Ethel Rosenberg to damage the American economy.

How much money has this rule cost America? We had a little test when Phil English of Pennsylvania led the successful effort to enact the "Invest in USA Act" as a provision in the 2004 American Jobs Creation Act. The law said that for one year, 2005, an American company that previously designated its foreign profits as permanently reinvested overseas (translation—the money was never coming back to America) could bring that money to the United States at a tax rate of 5.25 percent tax rather than at a rate as high as 35 percent. Companies responded by bringing more than $275 billion to America that might never have been invested in the United States to create American jobs. For all the talk about outsourcing, this tax cut has become the greatest story never told. According to data by the Federal Reserve Board of Governors, foreign earnings retained abroad were negative in the final two quarters of 2005 for the first time on record (which goes back to 1952). In the third quarter of 2005, foreign earnings retained abroad were a negative $62.3 billion followed by $80.6 billion in the fourth quarter.[30]

In 2005 alone, the amount of cash being returned was the equivalent of the total amount of money Bush had returned to taxpayers through all his tax cuts in the first four years of his administration.

Again, the official tax "revenue loss" of this tax cut was severely overestimated. Members of Congress were informed this legislation would increase tax revenues $2.8 billion in FY (fiscal year) 2005, lose $2.2 billion in FY 2006, and then lose money in the following eight years for a total $3.2 billion loss over ten years.[31]

Based on the estimated $300 billion of repatriations, the provision generated $17 billion in corporate tax revenues for fiscal years 2005 and 2006 combined. This indicates the government revenue forecast missed by $16.4 billion in the first two years, which more than wipes out the expected $3.2 billion, ten-year "loss" to the federal treasury that the Joint Committee on Taxation expected. This increase in revenue also does not include the increase in tax revenues from an additional $300 billion of new investment in America, which has led to more income, payroll, and corporate tax collections as well.[32] Territoriality would go much farther than this one-time experiment by setting a zero rate for American corporate overseas profits entering America and the provision would be permanent.

Reducing the tax burden on individual Americans working overseas would make it more likely that American and foreign companies would hire Americans for work around the world. Today, the double taxation of Americans working overseas often prices Americans out of such work. And Americans working overseas tend to buy and subcontract from American firms. Germans working overseas buy and subcontract from German firms. Our present tax policy harms not only our overseas citizens directly, but also American companies at home lose work and income.

7. *Enact a Flat Tax.* Once we have abolished the death tax, the capital gains tax, made all savings tax free through universal IRAs, ended the Alternative Minimum Tax, and created a territorial rather

than worldwide tax structure, we can put a single tax rate on taxable income and we have a flat-rate consumed-income tax. Voilà.

The flat tax will have the greatest resistance from the modern Democrat Party, drenched in envy and class hatred. They want to divide Americans into as many tax brackets as possible in order to convince each one that someone else is paying more and therefore they should shut up and stop complaining. You should be happy that we are cutting off one of your fingers, because we are cutting off two fingers of the guy who works on Saturdays. Yes, you are short one finger, but someone else is being more mistreated.

The pressure for a flat rate will come from principled Americans who reject envy and believe in equality before the law. Pressure to move to a flat tax will also come from competition from other nations. America is not used to having other nations compete with us through lower taxation. We have become complacent, thinking that no matter how silly our tax code gets, everyone would rather invest here in America than in France or Germany or Sweden. But times have changed and the flat tax is sweeping the world. The former Soviet colonies of Eastern Europe find that they can only attract more capital and investment with low simple tax rates. They do not wish to price their workers out of the world market. They wish to compete with Germany and its high tax rates on workers—not emulate it.

Poland has a flat tax rate of 18 percent. Russia, for crying out loud, has a flat rate of 13 percent. Slovakia has a 19 percent rate. Albania is moving to a 10 percent flat-rate income tax. These changes have put pressure on the countries of Old Europe to make improvements in their tax systems.[33]

When Secretary of State James Baker, about to travel abroad, was asked if he had ever been to a Communist country, he explained that he had been to Massachusetts. Well, Massachusetts has a flat-rate income tax of 5.3 percent. As Communist countries go, it was an "early adapter."[34]

So to the question: Will Americans vote to move to a single-rate tax away from the present progressive, graduated income tax structure? We find a strong hint as to the answer through the example of

| COUNTRY | INDIVIDUAL TAX RATE | CORPORATE TAX RATE |
|---------|---------------------|--------------------|
| Estonia | 22% | 24% |
| Georgia | 12% | 20% |
| Hong Kong | 16% | 17.5% |
| Iceland | 36% | 18% |
| Kyrgyzstan | 10% | 10% |
| Latvia | 25% | 15% |
| Lithuania | 27% | 15% |
| Macedonia | 12% | 12% |
| Mongolia | 10% | 25% |
| Romania | 16% | 16% |
| Russia | 13% | 24% |
| Slovakia | 19% | 19% |
| Ukraine | 15% | 25% |
| Serbia | 14% | 14% |
| Poland | 18% | 18% |

liberal deep blue Massachusetts, which has five times refused to move away from its constitutionally mandated flat tax. If Massachusetts is ready for a flat tax and will repel efforts to end it, the rest of America is likely to be able to handle this change.

Investment will, over time, flow to those nations with lower taxes on labor and capital. America will have a flat tax. It will get there driven by the twin pressures of international competition and the domestic desire for justice and equality before the law.

The hate-and-envy crowd will fight against treating all Americans the same. They like taxing people who work on Saturdays at punitive rates. A further source of opposition to a flat tax comes from those who fear losing specific deductions or credits.

This second, understandable concern can be met with a transition feature recommended by Steve Moore which is an optional flat-tax system that runs parallel to the present existing structure. If you would prefer to pay higher tax rates and keep your deductions and credits, fine. Everyone else is invited to move to the low single-rate income tax that would likely have fewer, though by no means zero, deductions. This may well be the best way to introduce the flat tax with the least disruption and minimizing opposition from those used to the old system.

A flat tax has other advantages. It will eliminate the marriage penalty tax. At present a single woman earning $150,000 and a single man earning $150,000 pay a total of $72,000 in federal income taxes. If they marry and continue in their jobs they would find their new income of $300,000 subject to a higher graduated income tax rate and their total tax burden would rise to $78,201.

One tax rate. No marriage penalty tax. The Democrat Party rationally opposes the flat tax and also opposes ending the marriage penalty tax as married men and women are more likely to vote Republican. Some have argued that once we get to a single-rate income tax that taxes only consumed income—not savings—we should then move to a national sales tax, the "FAIRTax."

This might well be a good idea.

Economists will point out that the two taxes are economically equivalent. Both tax income only once. Both exempt savings and investment from taxation.

At first glance it seems that if we wade through the political struggle necessary to bring about a flat-rate income tax of, say, 15 percent, and we have any energy left over, why not simply push to bring the rate down to 10 percent rather than moving the tax from payday to spending day? Luckily, or sadly, we are quite a ways off from having to make this decision.

There is however, one, very serious danger to moving to a retail sales tax.

Any change as dramatic as moving from taxing income to taxing consumption will require a transition period. Even a short transition period creates a risk that an election might bring in politicians who see the virtues of having *both* an income tax and a consumption tax. This would not be surprising. Every single country in Europe has saddled their subjects with individual and corporate income taxes and a value-added tax, which is a sales tax at every level of production.

This would be the worst of all possible worlds. All taxes are increased to their breaking point—i.e., the point at which the careers of politicians are broken by taxpayer/voter unhappiness. The more kinds of taxes, the higher the total burden. This is why New Hampshire, which forbids both a state income tax and a broad-based sales tax, has high property taxes—property taxes raised to the breaking point—but lower total taxes than those states with property, sales, and income taxes that are each brought to the breaking point. Visit New Jersey for a case in point.

Every country in Europe is a reminder of the danger of having both a national income tax and a national consumption tax.

## Ten Small Steps Forward

The seven significant reforms that will bring us to a consumed-income tax that taxes income one time all command strong political support in the electorate. I offer ten baby steps forward that move in the direction of full tax reform and may be opportunistically pursued as day-to-day politics changes at the federal and state level.

## An Annual Tax Cut

**First,** pro-taxpayer legislators at the federal and state levels should learn from and follow the successful model of the Bush administra-

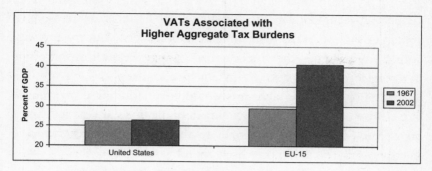

Source: Daniel Mitchell, The Heritage Foundation

tion and cut taxes each and every year. This has had several benefits. First, if citizens believe that there will only be one tax cut in the foreseeable future, all the possible tax cuts become competitors. In 1981, President Reagan cut taxes. There was not another tax cut until 1996. Fifteen years between tax cuts. Is it any wonder that the business community fought to reduce the value of the individual tax cuts of Kemp-Roth from 33 percent to 25 percent and made them phased in over three years? They feared that the reductions in the corporate income tax they needed would never have been addressed if they didn't elbow others aside.

In 2001, the Bush administration proposed a tax cut that was almost wholly aimed at individuals, not businesses. But Bush was wise enough to explain that there would be an annual tax cut. And the way for any company to be first in line for the tax cut of 2002 or 2003 would have been to be helpful in enacting the 2001 tax cut. Those trying to cut in line in 2001 were less likely to be cheerfully received in 2002. An annual tax-cut strategy keeps all advocates of tax cuts on the same side, as allies rather than as competitors.

## OFFER "TAX ME MORE" ACCOUNTS

**Second,** all states can follow the lead of eight states that have enacted "Tax Me More" accounts. This allows citizens who agree with the left that the government can spend their money better than they can to put up or shut up. If the government can best spend your money, why would you only pay the amount that a stingy Republican governor and state legislature require. Why not spend more?

The "Tax Me More" accounts would be an additional line on the state income tax form that says, "I believe my taxes are too low and I wanted to send additional money to the state government which I believe would spend it more wisely than I would."

Any politician who votes for higher taxes should be asked if they have been contributing to the "Tax Me More" account. A politician who doesn't think he should send the government more—but you should—is saying something very interesting.

To date, the states that have "Tax Me More" accounts are Arkansas, Massachusetts, Kansas, Minnesota, Montana, New Hampshire, Oklahoma, and Virginia. In the case of Massachusetts the option is right on the income tax form. The other states have accounts liberal taxpayers can send the money to.

## No Taxation Without Representation, Really

**Third,** national and state leaders should keep an eye out for the constant temptation to "tax those who cannot vote." Politicians love to load taxes on hotels and car rentals. The theory is that New York politicians know that few New York voters stay at New York hotels. They live at home. Tourists and businessmen from Los Angeles pay this tax. Of course, when New York City taxpayers visit Los Angeles, they are mugged with hotel taxes and car-rental taxes passed by Los Angeles politicians who have figured out that New Yorkers don't get to vote against them in the next election. Thus their pockets can be safely picked.

The only way to stop this mutual mugging society is through the federal government extending the "Four R" law that presently protects railroads and pipelines from discriminatory taxes by state and local governments. The state of Utah has noticed that railroads and pipelines passing through it are unlikely to be moved except at great cost. They tend to be owned by voters in other states. Hence the temptation to load property taxes on railroad property at higher rates than for, say, Utah farmers or homeowners. To stop this government-run bush-whacking the federal government passed a law banning discrimina-tory taxes on railroad or pipeline property. This should be extended to hotels, car rentals, and telecommunications. All targets of state and local governments that like to hide their tax burdens. This will allow any state to tax property or sales of railroads or telephone companies, at the same rate as everyone else, but not at higher rates.

The present ban on discriminatory taxes on Internet access fees is an example of protecting citizens from having state and local govern-ments clog up interstate commerce with discriminatory taxes.

## No Taxing Sales on the Internet: Hands Off eBay

**Fourth,** another effort to tax those on the other side of the state line who cannot vote against their looters is the constant attempt by loser states to tax Internet or catalog sales. Present law is that a state can only tax those companies that are based in their state, who have a store or factory that provides "nexus" in the state. If you live in Ala-bama and buy online or through the catalog from L. L. Bean based in Maine, there is no "nexus," and Alabama cannot require L. L. Bean to levy the Alabama state sales tax on your purchase. This is only fair. L. L. Bean receives no services from the state of Alabama. When UPS delivers your order, they pay gas taxes for whatever roads they use.

If North Dakota—or any state for that matter—is allowed to force L. L. Bean or Amazon to collect taxes for them, one can only imagine the corruption that would flow. Think how your state government abuses the businesses based in your state. Then think how rough they could get with a business without workers/voters in the state. Out-of-state retailers might receive a letter suggesting that the state believes they really owe tens of thousands of dollars in sales tax. They could pay or instead hire North Dakota lawyers for hundreds of thousands of dollars to contest the issue—in North Dakota courts. Of course, a letter might follow explaining that the tax commissioner of North Dakota is thinking of running for, say, senator, and if the company that received the harsh note going on and on about back taxes would simply make a nice contribution to the Senate campaign, perhaps the previous letter could become "inoperable."

Here one spots politicians who think they live in "loser" states looking for ways to tax people who have moved out of their state and/ or would never think of moving in. The more confident a state is that its businesses are healthy and growing and likely targets for "loser" states, the less tempted their politicians are to push for rules that allow such crossborder raids.

## REDUCE THE CORPORATE INCOME TAX RATE

**Fifth,** while we work to get a flat tax and reduce the double taxation of all income, we can start by reducing the corporate income tax from its present high of 35 percent to 25 percent, the average corporate income tax rate in Europe. A 25 percent tax on companies creating jobs and wealth is dumb, but 35 percent is dumber. We used to be able to count on the Europeans, who had a 38 percent average corporate income tax rate. Now even Germany is cutting the top rate from 40 percent to 30 percent. We should begin by not kneecapping our own companies in international competition.[35]

## NO COLLABORATION WITH FOREIGN TAX COLLECTORS

**Sixth,** we should resist the kind request from French tax collectors to do their job for them. At present, we do not tax foreign investors in the United States. If they are nice enough to invest an estimated $2.2 trillion in America, we are thankful enough not to tax them or ask a bunch of silly questions about what country they come from. The French would like a list of all Frenchmen investing in America on the off chance that they would like to pay France taxes on their investments in America.

America should make itself the friendliest country in the world for investments that create jobs and wealth. We should do nothing to send away foreign investors or chase away American investors to send their lovely money elsewhere. And if the French wish to mistreat their own citizens we should not help them.

## LEAVE OUR MUTUAL FUNDS ALONE

**Seventh,** 52 percent of American households own shares of stock. They are disappointed to learn each year that Uncle Sam taxes the capital gains that accrue in the various stocks that make up their mutual fund. Legislation has been introduced to stop the government from taxing whatever capital gains build up each year inside a mutual fund. Capital gains taxes—until we abolish them—would only kick in, and kick you, when you sell the mutual fund and the capital gain is real.

## ABOLISH THE CAPITAL GAINS TAX
## ON INFLATION

**Eighth,** today when you pay capital gains taxes on land, a house, a building, a stock holding, you pay taxes on the real appreciation in value *and* the inflation that have taken place since you purchased your asset. There is a drive to end the taxation of inflation gains. Legislation has been introduced by Congressman Mike Pence and Congressman Eric Cantor that would index the basis of your property to inflation and you would only pay capital gains taxes on the real growth in value. This would in effect cut in half the taxation of capital gains. Better yet would be for President Bush to do this unilaterally by executive order. The courts have ruled that the executive branch can define the word "cost" in treaties and law as historical cost, real cost—historical cost plus inflation—or even replacement cost if it simply has a good reason for doing so. This would be a revolutionary change Bush could make even with a Congress held by the opposition party. Of course, Bush can and should do this not just looking forward but retrospectively so that all the nice farmers and homeowners with valuable land and homes that have skyrocketed in value due largely to inflation would not have to pay taxes on that government-created inflation. Homeowners, landowners, small-businessmen, and stockholders would make Bush a saint.

## REMEMBER: TARIFFS ARE TAXES

**Ninth,** all free-trade agreements are tax cuts. Tariffs are simply taxes imposed on the border. They are taxes imposed on American consumers. While politicians like to pretend that tariffs are paid by foreigners, in fact, you and I pay every tariff levied by the American government in the form of higher prices. Free trade is Latin for lower taxes.

## CUT THE 35 PERCENT TAX RATE ON CORPORATE CAPITAL GAINS

**Tenth,** when Reagan made the backsliding mistake of eliminating the differential between the capital gains tax and the tax rate on "normal income," he increased the individual tax rate on capital gains to 28 percent and the corporate capital gains tax rate to 35 percent. Despite all the fine efforts to cut the capital gains tax to 20 percent and then 15 percent on individual capital gains, the corporate capital gains tax rate languishes at 35 percent. There is some $800 billion in locked-up capital that would be freed if the corporate capital gains tax rate were set at 15 percent alongside the individual rate.[36]

PART FIVE

# GOOD POLICY, GOOD POLITICS

---

"What is to be done?"

—*V. I. Lenin*

## CHAPTER TWENTY

# SPENDING: WHAT WENT WRONG?

The Leave Us Alone Coalition has a clear strategy on tax policy. Never raise taxes. Cut taxes as the opportunity arises to move toward a single-rate, flat tax that taxes consumed income one time only.

No tax increases is the first step in reforming and reducing government spending at the national, state, and local levels. Preventing higher taxes or new taxes is only the first step in spending reform, but it is the necessary first step. Politicians prefer to take all existing spending as given, add this year's new programs, and simply send taxpayers a bill for the total. If they are not allowed to raise taxes, they have to examine previous decisions, prioritize various spending programs, and make decisions about which programs to reduce, end, or reform. There is a stark choice: govern and make real decisions or simply raise taxes. Understandably most politicians prefer door number two.

Only when the Leave Us Alone Coalition is strong enough to prevent a tax increase are they even on the playing field to demand that elected officials actually govern.

So, how are we doing on the spending front?

Not very well. In the first five years of the Bush administration, government spending increased from $3.1 trillion in fiscal year 2001 to \$4.1 trillion in fiscal year 2006.[1] Except for the twenty months when the Democrats controlled the Senate from June 2001 to January 2003, the Republicans had majorities in the House and Senate in addition to the White House. This was also the period of "bridges to nowhere." Billions of dollars in "earmarked spending." The creation of the largest new entitlement program since Medicaid with the creation of the Medicare part D program at a cost of \$746 billion over the next ten years, the restoration of the Farm Subsidy program at a ten-year cost of \$200 billion, and the No Child Left Behind experiment, that helped propel federal spending on education—a subject infrequently mentioned in the U.S. Constitution—by \$30.8 billion or 92 percent from 2000 to 2007.

What in the world happened?

When the Republicans became the majority party in both the House and Senate in January 1995, federal spending was 21.7 percent of the Gross Domestic Product (GDP). After six years of a Republican Congress and Democrat Bill Clinton in the White House, federal spending had fallen to 19 percent of GDP.[2]

Two things caused this. There was modest restraint in the growth of federal spending. Federal spending had been increasing at a 5.4 percent annual rate from 1988 through 1994. In the six years from

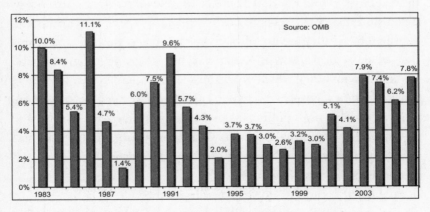

The Chart Shows the Annual Federal Spending Increases from 1983 to 2006.

1994 to 2000, federal spending increased 3.4 percent per year (nominal dollars—not inflation adjusted).

In November 1994, the Dow Jones Industrial Index stood at 3,830, up slightly from 3,252 when Clinton was elected and in line with the historic annual stock market growth. When the Republican victory ended the possibility that Bill Clinton and a Democrat Congress would nationalize heath care in a single stroke or again raise taxes, the stock market began its climb to 4,852 ( a gain of 27 percent) by November 1995, then up to 6,219 (a 62 percent increase from November 1994) by November 1996.

In 1997, the Republican Congress passed a reduction in the capital gains tax from 28 percent to 20 percent. Clinton signed the legislation on August 4, 1997. The economy grew 4.5 percent in 1997, 4.2 percent in 1998, 4.5 percent in 1999, and 3.7 percent in 2000. Stock market capitalization rose from $9 trillion on the day the capital gains tax cut passed to $13.8 trillion by January 2000.[3]

Some modest spending restraint and a pro-growth reduction in the rate of taxation of capital gains reduced the cost of government compared to the total economy. Tax payments grew even faster than the economy, and the budget went into surplus. When Bill Clinton took office, federal government spending was 22.8 percent of the economy. When he left office, it was 19 percent of the economy. Had this downward progress continued uninterrupted during the Bush years, the federal government would have shrunk to 15 percent of the national economy by 2008. This would have been very real progress toward the goal of cutting the cost of government in half as a percentage of the economy in twenty-five years.[4]

Then President Bush was elected on November 8, 2000, and for most of the next six years had a Republican House and Senate. During those six years federal spending as a percentage of the national economy rose from 19 percent to 20.3 percent. This was not progress. This was backsliding.

Of course, taxpayers do not shoulder just the cost of federal taxes. They pay state and local taxes and the cost of regulations imposed by all levels of government. The total cost of all government taxes

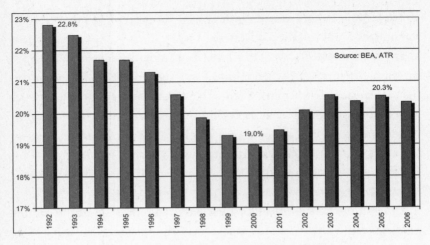

Total Federal Spending as a Percent of GDP

and regulations tracked with the federal government spending growth.

What in the world happened here? The Republicans took over and the size of government increased.

Why? How?

Worse, this was taking place during a period of economic expansion when, historically, spending as a percentage of the economy should be falling.

## COST OF GOVERNMENT DAY 1977–2006

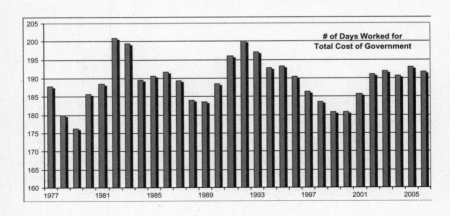

But there is little time to whine about the amount of money spent or wasted between 2000 and 2008. Looking down the track we have a slight problem: The bridge is out, and if nothing changes we are heading for a rather nasty crack-up.

Entitlement spending on Social Security, Medicare, and Medicaid will increase as the baby boomers get older, retire, and develop chronic medical conditions that are no fun for the afflicted or for their children who will be paying the freight. Spending on the big three—Social Security, Medicare, and Medicaid—will increase from 8.7 percent of the economy in 2006 to 15.2 percent of the economy in 2030 and 19 percent of the economy in 2050.

Federal government spending as a percentage of the economy has been relatively stable at around 20 percent for the past forty years. Without any changes in federal law, the present demographics, and entitlement spending that is presently committed, federal spending increases to 22 percent of GDP by 2020, 25 percent by 2030, and 27.6 percent by 2040.[5] We make fun of the French who today spend 50 percent of their economy on government. Adding in state and local spending of 12 percent of GDP—kindly assuming this doesn't increase as a percentage of the economy—to federal spending we become France in 2060. A burden of government this large slows economic growth, turns young entrepreneurs into bureaucrats, and

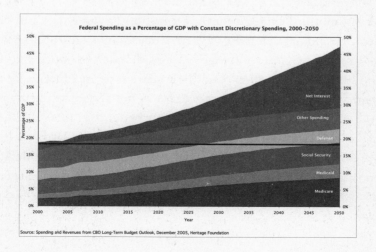

Federal Spending as a Percentage of GDP with Constant Discretionary Spending, 2000–2050

Source: Spending and Revenues from CBO Long-Term Budget Outlook, December 2005, Heritage Foundation

somehow creates shortages of soap and keeps women from shaving their legs.

The challenge for the Leave Us Alone Coalition on spending is clear.

Democrats will oppose all efforts to avoid or reduce this looming spending explosion. They have two preferred options. First choice, they convince the Republicans to raise taxes to pay for a European supersized government. This would destroy the Republican Party's credibility as the low-tax party and Republicans would cease to be a serious alternative to the Democrats. This would be a return to the role played by the Republican Party of the 1950s and 1960s as the "tax collector for the welfare state": Eisenhower opposing tax cuts because he wanted to fund the New Deal intact; Goldwater voting against the 1964 tax cut to keep the funds flowing to Washington. This would, for the Democrats, return the world to its proper orbit. The world had been temporarily turned upside down by the modern Republican refusal to see itself as the "fiscally responsible" guardian of the welfare/warfare state designed and ultimately run by Democrats. If the modern Republican Party refuses to play Charlie Brown to Lucy and fall for the spending cuts for tax increases trick once again, then the second choice for the Democrats will be to allow the spending crisis to unfold and work with what is left of the establishment press to helpfully blame the Republicans for the crackup.

A distant third choice is for the Democrats to win power and raise taxes high enough themselves to turn America into a European social democracy. This third alternative looks a little too much like the 1993–1994 campaign to expand the welfare state in America by nationalizing the half of health care that was not already explicitly run by the government. It might not work any better this time.

All exertions will go into option one: the Andrews Air Force Base ploy. Get the Republicans into a negotiation to "reduce the deficit." This is code for "raise taxes to pay for the coming explosion of spending." Make the Republicans share responsibility for these tax increases.

The Democrat strategy is set. It worked with Eisenhower. It worked with Goldwater. And it worked with George H. W. Bush, whose failure to learn might have been more inexplicable if he hadn't watched Reagan condone a series of small tax hikes following his pro-growth tax cut of 1981. In his defense, Reagan had first passed a significant rate reduction and he was blackmailed into spending on domestic goals to get his military buildup. Bush should have noted that Reagan conceded that his 1982 one dollar of tax increase in exchange for three dollars of promised—but not delivered—spending restraint was the greatest mistake of his presidency. The tax increase was gobbled up, but the spending cuts never happened. Too late, George H. W. Bush did learn. In an interview with Trudy Feldman on September 11, 2004, he admitted that "raising taxes was my worst decision. I think I lost the election because of the economy."[6]

The promise of spending restraint in exchange for tax increases is almost as old as "The check is in the mail," "I'll still respect you in the morning," and "I'm from the government and I'm here to help." When sober, all Republicans claim they will never fall for this. But it is the Democrats' only good option. They have to try.

The Democrat strategy is as obvious and avoidable as the Maginot Line.

So how can the Republican Party sidestep this entirely foreseen trap?

The first step is to understand why government overspending has long been the soft underbelly of the Reagan Republican movement.

## NO ONE VOTES ON TOTAL SPENDING

Visualize the Leave Us Alone Coalition as it meets. Around the table are businessmen and -women who wish to be left alone with their businesses, and would also like the government to spend less. Next to them are taxpayers who voted for Bush because they wanted lower taxes. They would also like lower overall spending. Then there are the gun owners who voted for Bush because they feared gun control and would also like lower spending. Ditto property owners, homeschoolers, the various communities of faith. Everyone in the Leave Us Alone Coalition wants lower spending. However, no one votes on that issue as their primary vote-moving issue. It is, politically, a secondary issue for each group or individual. There is no antispending voting bloc to mirror and complement the antigun control and antitax hike tendencies. This explains (but does not excuse) the counterintuitive failure of Reagan and Bush "43" to reduce spending. During the Bush "43" years, it is a little difficult for someone who votes on the tax issue to say, "Thank you for the tax cut of 2001 that reduced the marriage penalty, increased the per child tax credit, and reduced everyone's marginal income tax rates. And, oh yes, thank you also for the business tax cuts of 2002 and the drop in the capital gains tax rate and the halving of the double taxation of dividend income in 2003 and the 2004 tax cut and the tax cuts in 2005 and 2006 and the close-run thing where we almost abolished the death tax in 2006. But, by the way, I have had it with your overspending, you bloated budget-buster, so from now on I'm voting for the Democrats, who opposed all your tax cuts. Or perhaps I'll stay home, disappointed by your spending problem, and allow the Democrats to win the Senate or House and stop any future tax cuts."

A voter happy with the Republican president or congressional leaders on his or her primary issue cannot credibly, or logically, jump ship on a secondary issue. To say that federal spending is a secondary issue is not to suggest it is unimportant. It is very important. It is, however, for most center-right voters not their primary vote-moving issue.

I have been urged to create a "taxpayer protection pledge" for the spending issue to repeat the success we have had with the pledge against tax hikes. Just how could one create a pledge on spending? "I promise to oppose too much spending"? How much is too much? Who would decide? The power of the taxpayer protection pledge comes from its clear and binary nature. A politician votes for or

against a tax hike. Yes or no. Hero or bum. Friend or foe. The coin
never falls on its edge.

## No Accountability

Congress never holds a vote on whether or not to spend too much
money. Even the overall budget votes mean little. The Bush administration has perfected the strategy of pretending to send up a budget
and then showing up later with "emergency" spending requests to pay
for such "unexpected" costs as pay and equipment for the hundred
thousand American troops in Iraq that have been there for years, but
somehow the guys at OMB forgot this when they wrote their budget.
And floods, droughts, and hurricanes happen every year, but they are
always surprises to the budget.

If you brought a rope to D.C. to hang the guy responsible for
spending too much money, who would you hang? The House of
Representatives voted for one budget. The senators voted to fund
other things for a different total cost. Then each piece of the budget
is passed separately. And surprise: When you add up all the little
bits, the total is larger than promised. When the spending bills go to
the House and Senate for final passage they don't look much like
what was passed earlier in the year. Any congressman can honestly
tell you that he or she opposed much and maybe most of what ended
up in the legislation. Everyone touched the ball, but no one touched
it last. And then the president, who sent up a different collection of
spending priorities with a different total cost, gets to sign the entire
bill or veto the whole thing. No line item veto. Swallow it whole or
starve. It was as if the appropriations process were designed to make
it impossible to hold anyone responsible for the total amount spent.
As if.

Thus the first challenge for the center-right is that there is no competent, credible, and focused pressure on the overall budget. There is
no one guarding the chicken coop. Over time, even originally vegetarian foxes have figured this out.

## IT IS THE SPENDING: NOT THE DEFICIT

The second challenge is that unlike fighters for "pro-life," "taxpayer," or "death tax" issues, the forces of limited spending have given away control of the language. In the 1950s, conservative Republicans—a permanent minority within the permanent minority party—fought against federal spending. But because they believed, perhaps correctly, that their cause would not gain majority support they targeted "deficit spending," hoping to win over all the Methodists who hate debt. "Deficit" was not meant to be a qualifier, but an intensifier. It meant, "really bad."

Liberals responded by arguing that deficits were meaningless because "we owed the money to ourselves." (Which was technically true for liberal owners of Treasury bonds.) Better from the left's perspective in their constant drive to expand state power and government spending, they had a whole theory, called Keynesianism, which proved with cute little equations that for every dollar of government deficit spending the economy was strengthened. There was a "multiplier" effect for deficit spending by the government. Taking a dollar from you and spending a dollar and a half through the government actually made us all richer. It was good for the economy.

The government could also make us all richer by printing additional money. The Great Inflation and the recession of the 1970s poked a hole in the enthusiasm for John Maynard Keynes. (Keynes was born in 1893, the year Marx died, but his theories collapsed a decade before communism went belly up. In the long run all stupid theories are dead.)

By the 1980s, Democrats discovered that deficits were, in fact, very bad. But there was no time to apologize for the past twenty years of cheerleading for deficit spending. Now, the newfound opposition to deficits was, conveniently, an important weapon in opposing Ronald Reagan and his tax cuts. Best of all, Democrats would no longer have to call for higher taxes. Now they would be for lower deficits (through higher taxes, true). Democrats wisely dropped the word "spending" from the Republican formulation of "deficit spending" and returned to the fray to focus on the evil of "deficits" caused by low taxes.

Democrats in the 1950s and 1960s had defended deficits in arguing for higher government spending. Then in the 1980s when Ronald Reagan and Jack Kemp argued that "deficits" didn't matter, they were defending their tax cuts.

This was very confusing for many Americans who heard Democrats and Republicans both denouncing "the deficit." Both Caesar and Pompeii were fighting "for Rome." The fellow with the big ears from Texas, Ross Perot, was so discombobulated by the two parties shouting in tandem against the deficit while pulling in different directions that he actually ran for president promising to "get under the hood" of the budget and fix everything. But the Republicans and Democrats were not in agreement. Republicans opposed "deficit spending" meaning "spend less." Democrats opposed "the deficit" meaning "tax more."

Then in 1995, the newly elected Republican Congress slowed the growth of federal spending just a tad and put a stop to Bill Clinton's stated plans to nationalize health care, private pensions, and further increase taxes, and they cut the capital gains tax. The economy took off and the federal budget went into surplus. Then came a rare moment of clarity. Republicans challenged Democrats: "You said you opposed tax cuts because of the deficits: Now that we are in surplus, will you support our tax cuts?"

"No, no," the Democrats replied. "We were lying. We always oppose tax cuts. Deficit. Surplus. Exactly in balance. Doesn't matter. We support higher taxes and more government, not lower taxes."

The Democrats returned the favor: "Hey, Republicans, you said you were against spending on various attractive domestic spending programs because of the deficit. Now that we have this lovely surplus, will you help us pass new spending programs?"

And the Republicans answered, "No, we were lying. We oppose more spending period, surplus or deficit. We would oppose this spending if it was free money contributed by the French."

And for a few golden months in the late 1990s, the focus remained on spending. And spending as a percentage of the economy fell. It actually fell from 21 percent in 1994 to 18.4 percent in 2000.[7]

In January 2001, the incoming Bush administration had a perfect opportunity to focus on the one real metric that matters for the federal government: how much money the federal government spends as a percentage of the national economy, federal spending as a percentage of GDP. This (plus the cost of federal regulations) is the true cost of the federal government.

The deficit has always been a sideshow. It is the unimportant and uninteresting difference between two important and interesting numbers: how much money the federal government spends and how much it takes by force. The difference between total spending and total taxation is the deficit. It doesn't matter. Total government spending is the amount of money taken from the real economy and spent by the politicians on politically directed rather than consumer directed decisions. It doesn't matter if the money is taken or borrowed. It is spent.

As a thought experiment, imagine the entire federal budget is one hundred dollars. That one hundred dollars is not available to the private sector. One way to finance the one-hundred-dollar budget would be to take ninety dollars in taxes and borrow ten dollars. This would result in a ten-dollar "deficit."

Suppose the Democrats and the national media demand that we eliminate the ten-dollar deficit by raising taxes. Okay. Now taxes are increased by ten dollars and the one-hundred-dollar budget is funded by one hundred dollars in taxes. The deficit is zero.

Have we helped the capital markets because the government no longer has to borrow ten dollars? No. The ten dollars is still missing from the private sector. It is taken rather than borrowed.

At the end of the day, total government spending (plus the cost of the federal, state, and local government regulatory burden) is the true cost of government. The deficit is at best a vivid reminder that costs are running ahead of the government's ability or willingness to tax its citizens.

## THE RIGHT METRIC: GOVERNMENT SPENDING AS A PERCENTAGE OF THE ECONOMY

The Bush administration's greatest strategic error occurred when they failed to focus on government spending as a percentage of the economy as the key number to measure their progress. Instead, going into the 2004 election, Josh Bolton of the Office of Management and Budget announced that the Bush administration's goal was to cut the federal deficit in half in five years.[8] George Bush then confirmed this as his goal in his 2004 State of the Union speech.[9]

Is it any surprise that America has a federal-government spending problem when the center-right movement is not able to credibly provide outside pressure on elected officials to restrain spending—because their primary focus is elsewhere—and the leader of the Republican Party announces that disciplining overall spending is not his goal? He is focused on the deficit, not total spending.

Focusing on the deficit is the equivalent of obsessing on the visible part of an iceberg, the one-tenth that is above the water. Of course, the *Titanic* never hit the part of iceberg that was visible and covered with snow. It was torn apart by the relevant and deadly part of the iceberg under the water. Likewise, the damage done to the economy is not done by the deficit, but by the total size of government spending.

Cynics suggest that the Bush administration knew perfectly well that as the economy continued to grow in response to the better-late-than-never pro-growth tax cut of 2003 the deficit was sure to shrink even as spending continued to career upward. They were claiming their goal was something that they knew was going to happen anyway without any hard lifting on spending restraint. This is exactly what did happen when, totally predictably, the deficit fell in half three years ahead of schedule and the president had a big press conference at the White House on October 11, 2006.[10]

Trivia question: There was a national election on November 8, 2006, less than one month after this wonderful news about the deficit declining by half thanks to higher tax revenues. How did Americans express their gratitude for the lower deficit?

When Bush confirmed that his administration's goal was a mono-maniacal focus on the deficit while ignoring total spending, it was not a clever magician's legerdemain—or misdirection. They empowered their enemies and handcuffed themselves.

When the problem is correctly defined as "overspending," the center-right movement has full control of the conversation and political debate. Democrats cannot credibly compete with Republicans if the fight is over who can control federal spending. Even on a very bad day, halfhearted efforts by incompetent Republicans outpace the Democrats, who are invariably moving in the wrong direction.

And just as with an issue such as the environment or education—where "everyone knows" the Republicans are indifferent at best and the Democrats engaged and well intentioned—the government spending issue comes prepackaged in the minds of voters: Republicans, good; Democrats, bad. The public has good reason to sense this difference in spending proclivities. In 2006, the National Taxpayers Union reported that the average House Republican committee chairmen proposed to increase federal spending by $10.1 billion. The average potential House Democrat committee chairmen proposed $931.2 billion in spending increases.[11]

But if a Republican is stupid enough to switch the public focus from spending to the deficit, why then the Democrats are back on the playing field. There is only one way to deal with overspending: spend less. There are two answers to the deficit: spend less or tax more. And the Democrats have an ally in the establishment press and in the various spending lobbies that will push tax hikes as the preferable option.

One understands why CBS and Ted Kennedy want the discussion to be about "deficits." But it is intellectually dishonest, and in Washington, more important, suicidal for any Reagan Republican to so frame that debate.

The correct focus both from a policy perspective and the politics of the center-right is not only to focus on spending rather than the deficit, but to focus like a laser on "government spending as a percentage of the economy." Why? Because only by comparing the size of government with the size of the economy that has to carry it can we understand if the government is too large. A trillion-dollar government is not a big problem for a ten-trillion-dollar economy and a killer for a two-trillion-dollar economy.

The second reason to focus on spending as a percentage of the economy is that it puts the left farther behind the eight ball. There are two ways to reduce spending as a percentage of the economy: *one,* reduce the growth rate of spending and *two,* cut taxes to create more economic growth and make for a larger denominator. The modern Democrat Party in the thrall of the Takings Coalition has to oppose both spending restraint and pro-growth policies.

How can we reduce the size of government as a percentage of the economy? Republicans have a slew of pro-growth tax cuts to suggest. And are willing to defund bunches of the Takings Coalition's favorite charities. Democrats have no answer as to how to promote growth or cut spending.

Good policy is good politics. And vice versa.

*Now what?* Okay, nice to know where we went wrong and how we can do better in the debate. But we are still on the railroad tracks heading toward a spending crack-up driven by runaway entitlement spending and the inevitable aging of the American population. Now what?

The 2006 election was a wake-up call. The Leave Us Alone Coalition has wisely focused on saying no to tax increases. That is step one. Step two is to reduce total government spending.

Just as Ronald Regan and Jack Kemp led the modern Republican party to its present position on reducing taxes at every opportunity, the emerging leaders of the Leave Us Alone Coalition such as Senator Tom Coburn of Oklahoma and Congressman Jeff Flake of Arizona are focused on limiting spending.

If the Leave Us Alone Coalition is sending its leadership into Republican spending rehab, the first of those twelve steps must be to put an end to "earmarks" where congressmen direct specific spending into their districts—bridges to nowhere, grants to one's alma mater, funds for the local library, museum, public school swimming pool . . .

## EARMARKS: THE BROKEN WINDOWS OF
## THE FEDERAL BUDGET

It is true that earmarks are not themselves the problem. Earmarks cost tens of billions and the problem is measured in the trillions. But earmarks are the broken windows of the federal budget. Just as when we look at a neighborhood and see buildings with broken windows and realize that no one cares, that property is not taken care of in this area, a Congress tolerating the political spending of a few thousand or even a few million dollars of taxpayer monies in earmarks will not police the spending of billions and trillions. If congressmen are busy walking out the door with small shoplifted grants to friends and campaign supporters, will they really call the budget cops on grand larceny?

Ending earmarks is an important first step for several reasons. It eliminates the argument that "everyone is doing it" that first arises in kindergarten and wasn't a good argument then. Second, earmarks are used by congressional leadership to get congressmen and senators to vote for legislation they otherwise would not support: they are often bribes. Earmarks are granted to Republicans to vote for bills that are otherwise too expensive—like the farm bill or the highway bill or a Medicare expansion. That makes them twice as bad; they are little bribes to encourage really big spending. Earmarks for Democrats may be buying support for free trade or the defense budget. (A bribe, true. But a bribe for sound policy.) They may be a case for some earmarks for Democrats; there is no case for earmarks for Republicans.

And Leave Us Alone Coalition members should remember that earmarks are almost always grants to local government and universities. Republicans sending earmarks into their districts are funding the Takings coalition. Why should we tolerate Republican congressmen taxing working men and women in the Leave Us Alone Coalition to send the cash to the Takings coalition? Republicans engaged in this self-destructive behavior are like Munchausen syndrome sufferers who mutilate themselves. It is irrational and counseling is called for.

The Reagan years taught Republicans that it is not enough to be for smaller tax hikes than the Democrats. Citizens watching Republicans call for a smaller tax hike than their Democrat opponents miss the distinction. Likewise, busy citizens cannot distinguish between big spenders and a really big spender. There has to be a difference of direction, not merely of degree, between candidates and between the two parties on the issue of government spending for voters to recognize who stands with the Leave Us Alone Coalition and who fights for the Takings coalition.

The Leave Us Alone Coalition must now focus on reducing government spending as a percentage of the nation's economy. This chapter has described how this has not happened to date, the economic and political costs of this failure, and the looming spending explosion if we continue apace.

The next chapter focuses on five Great Reforms that will prevent a spending crack-up and cut the size of government in half over the next twenty-five years. And incidentally will move almost every American into the Leave Us Alone Coalition and reduce the size of the Takings Coalition to the point of irrelevancy.

Good policy is good politics.

## CHAPTER TWENTY-ONE

# THE FIVE GREAT
# REFORMS

As we saw in the previous chapter, the challenge of reining in government spending is huge. The good news for the Leave Us Alone Coalition is that the solution is simple. Not easy, but easy to understand and easy to enact, given the required political power.

The Leave Us Alone Coalition's good-government policy goal of limiting the cost and scope of government dovetails precisely with its political goal of increasing the number of Americans who are independent of the government: men and women in control of their own lives, their own retirement, health care, and the upbringing and education of their children.

There are hundreds, thousands of government programs. Our federal, state, country, town, and city governments poke us in many different ways. But there are really three big costs of government in America: pensions, health care, and education.

Pensions start with the largest government program in the world, Social Security, which spent $544 billion in 2006, or fully 20.5 percent of the federal budget and 4.2 percent of the GDP.[1] Pensions also include government payments to retired government workers which totaled $343.6 billion in 2005 for federal, state, and local employees.

## PENSION COSTS IN 2005 = $862 BILLION, 22 PERCENT OF ALL GOVERNMENT SPENDING

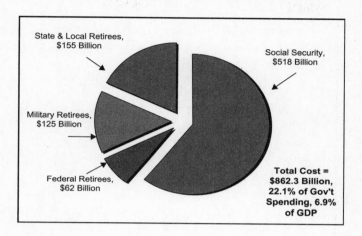

This represented 8.8 percent of all government spending and 2.8 percent of the national economy.[2] With roughly 20 percent of government workers eligible to retire in the next five years, this number will increase substantially in the near future.

Health-care spending by federal, state, and local governments in 2005 was $780.6 billion, 6.3 percent of the American economy.

Education is the third major component of spending, and totaled $730.7 billion in 2005, including K–12 and higher education. Spending on education at the federal, state, and local levels represented 18.7 percent of total government spending and represents 5.9 percent of the national economy.[3]

Looking at just K–12, taxpayers spent $443,198,760 in the academic year 2003–2004. This was $9,052 per student enrolled.[4] Public K–12 schools employed 5,657,090 staff, of which two-thirds, or 3,048,549, were teachers. State universities employ 1.8 million.[5]

Combining pensions, health care, and education totaled nearly $2.4 trillion in 2005, which accounts for more than six out of every ten dollars the government spends and one out of every five dollars of the national economy.

## RETIREMENT, HEALTH CARE, AND EDUCATION
## REPRESENTED 61 PERCENT OF ALL
## GOVERNMENT SPENDING IN 2005

|                                        | RETIREMENT | HEALTH CARE | EDUCATION | TOTAL   |
| -------------------------------------- | ---------- | ----------- | --------- | ------- |
| Spending ($Billions)                   | 862.3      | 780.6       | 730.7     | **2373.6** |
| % of Total Gov't Spending              | 22.1%      | 20.0%       | 18.7%     | **60.9%** |
| % of Gross Domestic Product            | 6.9%       | 6.3%        | 5.9%      | **19.1%** |

These numbers are huge. The Takings Coalition has worked long and hard to make millions of Americans see themselves as dependent on the government for their retirement, their health care, and their children's education.

Common sense and the lessons of the last fifty years of elections inform us that we will never "cut" government spending on education, retirement benefits, or health care. There have been brave and well-meaning efforts to trim back Social Security benefits in 1986—that cost the Republicans control of the Senate. Freshman Republicans in 1995 ran around talking about abolishing the federal Department of Education. A fine idea, but the American people heard not an attack on bureaucracy, but lack of interest in their children's education.

What then is to be done? Some have thrown up their hands and proclaimed that Americans should come to grips with the inevitability of big government. The economist Bruce Bartlett has suggested that a value-added tax, or VAT, is the least destructive way to raise massive amounts of money to fund an inexorably growing state. Fred Barnes, who wishes for small government, sees no hope and suggests that conservatives try and manage the larger government in service of conservative goals. It is not, however, our task to fund their government spending. We are not reduced to answering the "question" or "choice" offered Gary Gilmore.

The Ghost of Big Government Yet to Come should scare us into action, not panic, and certainly not paralysis and surrender.

We can and must dramatically reduce the amount of taxpayer dollars spent on the big three—pensions, health care, and education—if we are to bring the cost of government down to a level consistent with a free society. But we will accomplish that through reforming the big three, not cutting them.

## REFORM ONE: MAKE ALL PENSIONS INDIVIDUALLY OWNED AND PORTABLE

President Bush's entire presidency can be justified in the seriously brave work he did in reaching out and touching the "third rail of American politics," Social Security reform. Before the Bush campaign in 2000, politicians *knew* that Social Security as presently structured was an insupportable Ponzi scheme. Politicians *knew* that Social Security taxes—FICA taxes—were not saved or invested by the government for your retirement when you hit sixty-five. The politicians have *always* known that every single dollar you pay in FICA taxes is immediately turned around and spent on your parents' or grandparents' Social Security or just spent on the federal budget somewhere else.

There is no Social Security surplus. No savings. No security. The federal government in 2006 has promised future retirees $12 trillion more than they have promised to take from their children and grandchildren. Spending promises outpace taxation threats by $12 trillion over the next seventy-five years.[6] (And if the Earth is not hit by a meteor in seventy-five years, then we are really screwed.)

But Bush erred in saying that Social Security was in crisis because it would go broke in 2018 or 2042, The crisis is not that the Social Security system's bookkeeping will be out of kilter in the near future.

The crisis of Social Security is *now* for every young American. Social Security makes every young American poorer every day. Not in the future. Now.

Social Security (FICA) taxes are immediately spent by the government. They are not invested in the stock market. No interest is paid on Social Security taxes collected from you in your name. If the government is going to pay you more in retirement than it took from you when you were twenty-five it is going to have to take more from your children and grandchildren than it took from you. A lot more.

Today, a single twenty-five-year-old earning the median wage is promised a rate of return on Social Security of less than 1 percent per year. Yet even to provide those benefits, Social Security taxes will have to be raised 50 percent, further lowering that person's rate of return. Conversely, a balanced portfolio of stocks, corporate bonds, and treasuries would generate an annual return seven times greater than what Social Security promises (but cannot even pay without massive future tax hikes that would significantly damage the economy).[7]

Today, Social Security forces every young American to put money into a "program" that promises a 1 percent return and keeps them from investing those dollars in real investments that have consistently

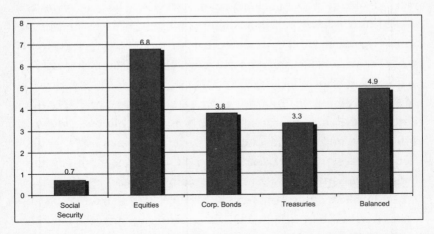

Real Rates of Return for Median Wage 25-Year-Old. *Source: CBO, ASA.*

returned 7 percent. This government program makes young people poorer. It turns gold into lead.

President Bush was elected in 2000 and 2004 arguing that all young Americans should have the opportunity to choose to leave the present pay-as-you-go unfunded Social Security system and move to one where they set aside part—and eventually all—of their Social Security taxes and invest them in a personal savings account that they control. That way every year they would earn interest on their Social Security "contribution."

Any reform, Bush promised, would protect those already retired and those near retirement by keeping the promises made by the government. Demagogues have always attacked Social Security reform by trying to scare older Americans into thinking that reform of the system for their children and grandchildren would take away their own Social Security checks. (We remember that Lyndon Johnson lied in 1964 about his plans for the Vietnam War. He also lied in attacking Barry Goldwater by claiming that reforming Social Security to protect younger Americans would tear up the Social Security checks of their grandparents.)

Bush promised in 2000 and 2004 that he would oppose any cut in benefits to those collecting Social Security or near retirement. He promised that he would not raise taxes on younger Americans. The establishment has always "fixed" Social Security by raising taxes and cutting benefits. This happened in 1983 with the bipartisan Social Security Commission that raised Social Security taxes and delayed retirement to age sixty-seven for those born after 1960, which is a significant benefit reduction (particularly if you die at age sixty-seven). The Clinton folks did the same in 1993. They decided to increase taxes on your Social Security benefits, which is both a tax hike and a benefit cut.

In past elections Democrats threatened older Americans by claiming that Republicans wanted to take away their Social Security benefits. This helped win many elections.

But in 2000 and 2004, something changed. First, many older Americans had grown weary of the Democrats and AARP crying "wolf." Bush's vow to protect promised benefits helped. Second, increasing numbers of younger Americans understood that Social Security was a bad deal for them. There was the famous poll that showed that Americans under thirty were more likely to believe in UFOs than that Social Security would be there for them.[8] In the past, Democrats would yell "Social Security" in a crowded theater and the old folks would get terrified and the younger Americans would be bored. Now, when "Social Security" is screamed, the younger Americans get angry and older Americans are not as easily scared.

As more Americans realized there was a problem, that Social Security was a bad deal and even that bad deal was not sustainable, the tables turned. Bush had a solution: personal accounts. The Democrats had and have no "solution" except raising taxes and cutting benefits.

Bush's solution—allowing younger Americans to invest their FICA taxes in personal savings accounts—made sense to Americans who were increasingly familiar with IRAs, 401(k)s, and mutual funds. Bush was not asking Americans to imagine an alternative to Social Security. They had been living with the alternative since the late 1970s.

Polls in 2000 and 2004 showed that Americans, particularly younger Americans, wanted the option of a personal savings account to replace all or part of Social Security.[9] The issue was a winner rather than a liability for Republicans for the first time since Social Security was created in 1938. President Bush was a visionary. Karl Rove was a genius.

After the 2004 elections, when Bush was reelected and Republicans won a total of 55 Senate seats and 232 House seats, the president said he intended to "spend" some of his political capital on promoting his Social Security reform. This was a failure. If the Bush administration had thought about the nature of the Takings Coalition behind the Democrat Party they would have realized that you cannot create personal savings accounts as an alternative to Social Security until you have sixty Republicans in the Senate.

Giving every young American the opportunity to save, say, 10 percent of his or her income every year and accumulate bonds or a mutual fund with bonds and stocks changes America. It changes a twenty-one-year-old if you say: "When you hit sixty-five you will have more than one million dollars in your personal savings account."[10]

In an America where every young person looks to the stock market and the business community to create his personal retirement wealth, the party and movement run by and for trial lawyers, labor unions, and government workers is a dead man walking. Trial lawyers sue companies and reduce stock prices. Every trial lawyer is a potential parasite damaging your personal retirement accounts. Labor unions inflict above-market costs on companies. Union bosses siphon off $500 per worker. Union work rules make unionized workers less productive. Unions damage your retirement portfolio. Government workers living off high property taxes, sales taxes, and corporate income taxes are looting your personal savings account every day. All taxes on businesses are taxes on your retirement.

When every American has the option of investing his or her FICA taxes in a personal savings account, the party of trial lawyers, labor unions, and government workers is over. Finished. Done. RIP Takings Coalition.

Make no mistake: There will always be two political parties in the United States. The non-Republican party could become the tree-hugger party, the peace party, or the weird-sex party. But in a world where every American is in the stock market watching his retirement income grow each year, there is no future for the trial-lawyer, labor-union, government-spending party. The first thing every American will want left alone is his retirement wealth.

When the 2004 election produced fifty-five Republican Senators we knew that Social Security reform was stillborn in 2005 and 2006. All efforts should have gone into winning sixty Senate seats in 2006 or 2008. Then and only then can reform happen.

The White House believed they could talk six Democrats into voting for personal accounts. They cited that eight or nine Democrats had been willing to discuss or even vote for Social Security reform that entailed tax hikes and benefit cuts. Yes, Democrats will always be willing to cut the benefits to retired Republicans and to raise taxes on working Republicans to continue to run an unreformed Social

Security system. They voted to allow IRAs and 401(k)s for, they thought, higher-income Americans. But they regret that now a majority of Americans have such retirement accounts. They will never agree to give every American a large, self-controlled retirement savings plan.

The White House thought they could talk the Democrats into committing political suicide. They were not that good. The Democrats were not that stupid. There is the memorable scene in *The Silence of the Lambs* when Anthony Hopkins playing Hannibal Lecter tells of talking the guy in the next cell into swallowing his own tongue and killing himself. Karl Rove couldn't do this with the Democrats.

Instead we were treated to the spectacle of the president of the United States conducting imaginary conversations with imaginary Democrats about an imaginary compromise: *Harvey* on a national scale. Social Security reform was dead the minute there were fewer than sixty Republicans in the Senate. It was not Bush's fault that it was dead. But it would have been more dignified if he had held a quick vote in the House and Senate on whether they supported the principle of personal savings accounts for all Americans, and lost the vote to a Democrat-led Senate filibuster. This would have pointed out to voters that the Reagan Republicans did not control the Congress, despite their majorities, and put everyone on record. Instead Bush traveled around the country for six months, dragging Social Security reform alongside him as in the movie *Weekend at Bernie's* and Bush periodically poked the reform and claimed that it moved and was still alive. It wasn't.

Social Security reform will happen. It will be the legacy of George W. Bush. But it will not happen until there are sixty Republican Senators and that cannot happen until after the 2008 or 2010 or 2012 election. Maybe longer.

Ronald Reagan's legacy is that he won the Cold War. When did he win it? In December 1991, when the Soviet Union ended. That was three years after Reagan left the presidency. But everyone knows that Reagan won the Cold War. George Herbert Walker Bush was physically in the Oval Office when the Soviet Union ended, but no one, not even an immediate family member, has ever said that Bush "41" won the Cold War. Reagan explained the goal. He set the strategy. He didn't negotiate for less than victory, and his game plan—peace through strength, the Reagan doctrine, and cutting off loans—worked.

If Reagan had in 1986 said to himself, "I have two more years in my presidency and I must now—to ensure my anti-Soviet legacy—negotiate the best deal we can with the Soviet Union before I leave office," he would have negotiated a deal that left the Soviet Union in place.

George W. Bush's legacy will be the creation of an ownership society where every American owns a personal savings account and has personal security in their retirement. Independent control of their wealth. Not dependent on the promises of politicians. This may not happen until after the election of 2010 or 2012. But it will happen, and fifty years from now schoolchildren will learn about "W" accounts and how George W. Bush changed America into the ownership society—as great a revolutionary change as universal suffrage.

The next several years are clear. The Leave Us Alone Coalition simply needs to remind Americans of the benefits of personal savings accounts and the costs of the Democrat Party's alternatives: tax hikes and spending restraint.

This is an easy sell on both ends.

If we only moved halfway to personalizing Social Security for a new worker, and only the employee's *half* of his or her payroll tax (6.2 percent) was invested in the balanced portfolio (50 percent equity/30 percent corporate bond/20 percent treasuries), that worker would retire with $400,000 or more. In contrast, that same worker with a normal life expectancy is set to receive a total benefit stream of just $160,000 (in today's dollars) from the current Social Security system. Removing treasuries from the equation and making the account 60 percent equity/40 percent corporate bonds generates even greater retirement income for workers.[11]

If every young American was able to invest *all* of his Social Security taxes into his personal account, the average wage earner would retire with nearly $800,000 in today's dollars. This compares with Social

Security's present promise of $160,000 dollars in income (all in 2006 dollars).[12] Assuming an average life span.

Oh yes, moving from a defined-benefit program that is under-funded to the tune of $12 trillion to a fully funded individually held personal retirement system would "save" the Social Security system. But our goal is not to "save the system" but to protect and improve your retirement finances.

Republicans can talk about how their reform will make you richer and more secure while the Democrats are left offering to raise your taxes and cut your benefits to make the system happy.

The Democrats have always been willing to "save" the system at your expense. Again and again the federal government has "saved" Social Security by raising your taxes and/or by reducing your benefits. What if your bank announced its goal was to "save" the banking sys-tem and to do so they would reduce your interest payments to keep the mismanaged bank solvent and periodically demand you "invest" more in the bank? Sure, you get less. But the key point here is that "the bank-ing system" is saved. That is what the politicians have done year after year with Social Security. Every tax increase raises the forced invest-ment you put into Social Security. This reduces the rate of return you get on each dollar. More tax dollars invested for the same return. At the other end the politicians cut or tax your promised benefits to re-duce the amount you get from Social Security, to "save" the system.

The two dangers for the Leave Us Alone Coalition are first that politicians will attempt to negotiate a compromise that leads to tax hikes and benefit cuts rather than personal accounts, and second that the reform debate will be turned into a conversation of how to "save the system" rather than how to give younger Americans the best rate of return on their Social Security investment.

If we focus on the rate of return on each American's Social Security investment, we see that Social Security is a lousy deal now. An Amer-ican of age sixty-five will receive a rate of return of 2.5 percent on his/her Social Security "investment" or "contribution" (aka taxes). Meaning if the sixty-five-year-old had invested his Social Security taxes in a bank account and received a 2.5 percent rate of return, it would be the equivalent of what the Social Security system promised him. This number declines as you get younger and a twenty-year-old today will receive a negative rate of return. This is what Social Security promises and cannot pay without raising taxes 50 percent.[13]

Any alternative to privatization must be challenged to answer the question "And how would your reform affect the return on investment on my Social Security tax contribution/investment?" Increasing the Social Security tax increases the investment without increasing the benefit and thereby reduces my return. Cutting or delaying benefits also reduces the rate of return. Only personal accounts protect younger Americans.

The other nonnegotiable in reforming Social Security is that the reform be sustainable. Liberals have advocated increasing taxes and/ or reducing promised benefits, which only delays the time when the system collapses. They do not make the system stable. Watch for statements such as: "This will save the system for the next seventy-five years." Why do they give a time limit? Because their "fixes," as with the 1983 "permanent fix," only kick the can down the road.

Only personal accounts make the Social Security system solvent permanently into the future. As long as the Leave Us Alone Coalition insists that any reform increase the rate of return for Social Security contributions and that any reform be sustainable and fix the system permanently, any reform moves toward full personalization.

*Federal, State, and Local Government Pensions.* There are 14.1 million state and local employees and 6.9 million retirees receiving pensions from taxpayers. Over the years politicians have found it easier to promise higher retirement pay in the future. Some later mayor or governor would deal with finding the money to pay those bills. This is bad for taxpayers and it puts "golden handcuffs" on government workers who are unlikely to feel free to change jobs when so much of their compensation comes in retirement.

A number of states and local governments have begun to provide their workers a portable pension system like a 401(k) or IRA in addition to or in place of traditional defined-benefit (DB) plans. Michigan made it mandatory for all new state employees beginning in 1998. Florida allows any state or local employee to leave the state's traditional defined-benefit plan and take all his accumulated savings with him in a portable plan.[14] Then if the worker wants to move to Alabama or a different job, the portable pension goes along.

State and local governments are required to set aside enough money to cover the costs of retirement for all their employees. There is about $3 trillion set aside in such accounts now.[15] That money should be divided up among all present government workers and put in portable personal accounts for each one. This will protect their pension money from being spent by politicians or used for political purposes by "investing" it in socially responsible ways that lose money.

Republicans who speak to state and local workers too often are understood to be saying, "I wish there were fewer of you and we paid you less." A more cheerful conversation can now be had where a Republican state legislator or mayor says, "I want you to control your own retirement and to retire rich." State and local workers have all the time in the world for that conversation. They know that across the nation previous politicians have underfunded their pensions (by some $400 billion in 2006).[16] Leaders who move them to defined-contribution pensions are not only treating them as adults, giving them control over their retirement wealth, but they are also protecting them from the present and future politicians who may use their retirement as a piggy bank.

When every civilian and military government employee owns shares of stock directly through his or her personal retirement accounts, it will greatly increase the size and intensity of the Leave Us Alone Coalition. Taxes on business are now a threat to those employees' retirement. Trial lawyers are suing not some nameless corporation, but their nest egg. Labor-union featherbedding will be as popular as Conrad Black's art gallery in "his" corporate jet.

In the real economy, where looting your workers' pensions gets you into jail rather than reelected, the reform is well under way. Today there are seventy-six million American workers in the private sector with a pension. Twenty-one million workers are in the old-style defined-benefit plans.[17] The DB pensions tend to be in unionized old industries, and those pensions and those industries are in trouble. Microsoft and other newer companies have defined-contribution (DC) plans. Fifty-five million Americans have defined-contribution plans similar to 401(k)s or individual retirement accounts.[18]

In 2007, nearly 60 percent of all private-sector retirement dollars are held in defined-contribution plans, up from just 30 percent twenty-five years ago.[19] The trend has moved toward defined-contribution plans, and it is always easier for the government to follow the reforms already under way in the real economy.

How can we pay for the transition of Social Security? State and local governments and private-sector companies have set aside money to pay the retirement benefits of their present employees. True, they sometimes underfund their workers' pensions. But the state and local governments are saints compared to the federal government.

The federal government had a completely unfunded pay-as-you-go pension plan, the Civil Service Retirement System that was replaced for employees hired after 1984 by the Federal Employees Retirement System that has a large defined-contribution component. There remains a large unfunded liability for the older system: In 2006 alone, the federal government spent $190 billion on federal civilian and military retirement benefits. This compares with $540 billion that year for all of Social Security.

To shift Social Security and all federal retirement to a defined-contribution system, we would start with allowing new entrants to the workforce to have in effect a 401(k) and allowing present employees to shift over if they wish. For present retirees or those close to retirement, it would be necessary to float a bond to cover the expected value of those future requirements. Transition costs could be reduced by phasing in the move to defined-contribution pensions. Social Security expert Peter Ferrara estimates that the federal government would need to borrow $2 trillion to cover the transition costs for Social Security. This is a lot of money, until you compare it with the unfunded liability of $12 trillion over the next seventy-five years if we keep on the present path. And the $2 trillion "investment" solves the problem. Paying the $12 trillion in higher taxes doesn't even fix the problem. It just pays the bills without making the system sustainable or providing over the next decades a good rate of return for young Americans.[20]

*The Example of Chile.* On November 4, 1980, the day Ronald Reagan was first elected president of the United States, the nation of Chile passed a law to allow every citizen the option of moving from the Chilean Social Security system to a personal retirement account similar to that proposed by President Bush in his 2005 State of the Union Address.

The law took effect on May 1, 1981, Labor Day, a day chosen by the plan's author, Secretary of Labor and Social Security Jose Pinera, to celebrate the day workers in Chile would also become owners.[21]

Ninety-five percent of the total eligible work force joined the new portable retirement accounts plan. To pay for the transition costs, Chile floated a bond equal to 37 percent of the Chilean GDP. Today those personally held savings accounts total $106 billion or 76 percent of the entire Chilean GNP. This would be the equivalent of $10 trillion in America. The average Chilean's retirement account is now $25,000. And as the average monthly salary in Chile is $800, this $25,000 in savings is equivalent to 31 times his monthly wage. He has more than two and a half years' salary in savings.[22]

The annual growth of the Chilean accounts for twenty-seven years has averaged 10 percent—above inflation. And the personal accounts are so popular that Chile's most recent president, Bachelet, a socialist and an admirer of Che Guevara in her youth, does not dare to dismantle the "third rail" of Chilean politics.

Just as Massachusetts shows that a left-of-center electorate will not move away from a flat-rate income tax, Chile shows that even a socialist government knows that its voters oppose moving away from personal portable savings accounts for retirement.

As more and more Americans own stock directly, and eventually when every single American is a shareholder, it will change the American electorate permanently. There will be no going back. Socialists in Chile cannot take back stock from their citizens. The Labor Party in Britain could never take back the council homes that Thatcher privatized. Let Americans become savers and owners, and the politicians will never take that independence and self-control away from them again.

## REFORM TWO: MAKE HEALTH INSURANCE INDIVIDUALLY OWNED AND CONTROL COSTS THROUGH COMPETITION

The second large sector of government spending is health care. Medicare was enacted in 1965 and was originally estimated to cost just $26 billion in 2003:[23] The actual cost was more than ten times higher, coming in at $274 billion. In 2006, Medicare cost taxpayers $374 billion.

While the $12 trillion unfunded liability of Social Security over the next seventy-five years sounds like a lot, and it is, it's dwarfed by the Medicare unfunded liability of $61 trillion. State and local governments have an unfunded liability for their employees' health-care costs of $1.4 trillion.[24]

As with Social Security, permanent reform requires moving from a pay-as-you-go system to a fully funded individually controlled system where you save each year into a health savings account that will accumulate enough money to buy an annuity to pay for your health insurance from retirement to death.

The economics and the politics of fixing Medicare and the promised health-care benefits for retired state and local government workers is the same. Medicare will require a phased-in transfer from pay-as-you-go to a fully funded individually held health-care retirement fund. For Medicare, young Americans will be required to "save" their Medicare taxes to a health savings account that will accumulate real savings so that on retirement each American can buy a health-insurance plan for the rest of his life. No American would be without health care and no one would be dependent on the government to provide their care. They would have been required to save enough to buy such insurance. The transition will be expensive. It will be less expensive than not making the reform.

Over time this reform of Medicare will move roughly 25 percent of the federal budget out of the government's hands and into a forced-savings plan held by Americans. It is a massive transfer of resources and power and control from Washington to individuals.

Medicaid is a welfare program and the best way to reform Medicaid is to replicate the success of welfare reform—put present levels of federal funding into a block grant to the states and allow each state to experiment with various ways to keep costs down. At present, the states put all their ingenuity into getting more federal funds and little into controlling costs. This would have the benefit of getting fifty states looking for good ideas. We have learned over the centuries that monopolies serve themselves rather than their customers, and only competition can force reform in a monopoly.

A number of general reforms will help reduce the overall costs of heath care and this will also reduce the hockey-stick spending curves that threaten to bankrupt the federal government and the taxpayers.

*Tort Reform.* First, tort reform in medicine will significantly reduce the cost of medicine across the board. The Pacific Research Institute estimates that our present abusive medical malpractice system adds $124 billion to the cost of health care in America through defensive medicine and that this higher cost causes 3.4 million Americans to lose their health-care insurance.[25] One ob-gyn in Rhode Island, Kate Cassin, saw her insurance premiums jump from $28,000 to $90,000 in 2004 and she had never been sued.[26] Imagine how much that adds to the cost of every baby delivered. As bad as tort law is for industrial America, the medical liability costs have increased an average of 11.7 percent each year since 1975, even more than the general tort costs' growth of 5.9 percent each year. One can also compare California, which passed mild malpractice reform through the initiative process and has seen its medical malpractice costs grow one-third as rapidly as the rest of the nation's between 1976 and 2003: up 282 percent rather than up 920 percent.[27]

*Health Savings Accounts.* Second, moving private and government workers from traditional third-party payment for health care to medical savings accounts would have a tremendous downward competitive pressure on all health-care costs.

The present mess was brought to us courtesy, no surprise, of a previous government smart move. During World War Two, the federal government imposed wage and price controls (so our economy would more closely mirror our opponents'? Only sporting, I guess). But Americans do not take well to such heavy-handed government control over their lives, and businesses offered health-care benefits as a way to compete for workers in lieu of "illegal wage increases."

As this continued, employers eventually started paying not just for insurance against catastrophic medical costs, but for first-dollar coverage. So if all health care is "free" because it is paid for by the company, how much effort would rational Americans put into shopping around for the best deal? Somewhere between very little and none. Think about how much time in your own experience you put into looking at the prices of goods in the grocery store to save a few pennies or at most a few dollars. Or how much time you spend price shopping for a television, washing machine, stereo system, or automobile. Compare that to what time, if any, you put into looking at how much different doctors or different hospitals charge for health care. Why should you, if your insurance company or your employer will pay for all of it? And when there is a modest co-pay, it increases the price sensitivity, but only to the size of the co-pay rather than the true total cost.

A new study by Amy Finkelstein of MIT argues that half of the growth of health care—from 6 percent of GDP to 16 percent of

GDP—was caused by third-party payments for health care, both through government programs and health-insurance companies.[28]

Health care has increased in cost by an average of 7 percent each year for the past decade. But there have been two health-care procedures that have not had such increases in cost: cosmetic surgery and laser eye surgery. Insurance usually does not cover either, and patients shop around. If every American shopped around for all health care it would greatly reduce the health-care inflation we all pay for in higher doctors' bills and higher taxes.

Health savings accounts (HSAs) were liberalized in the 2003 legislation that also expanded Medicare. HSAs allow you and your employer to set up an account of, say, $2,000 for you to spend on the first $2,000 of health-care costs. That is attached to a catastrophic coverage plan that will pick up costs of any expenses beyond the $2,000. So if you have little in the way of health costs in one year and you spend only $500 on checkups and medicine, you get to save the $1,500. This is a very real incentive to shop around and get the best price. It is your money you are working with, not the insurance company's. And you are protected by the catastrophic health-insurance policy against the cost of getting badly hurt or seriously ill. Truly unexpected costs are insured against, just as they are with your home or automobile. Day-to-day costs such as preventative health care and annual checkups are paid out of the personal account that you control just as you pay for the routine costs of your home and gas for your car. Home-heating costs are not part of your homeowners insurance. Nor is an oil change paid for by your auto insurance.

The number of Americans with HSAs increased to one million in 2004 and three million by 2006, and is expected to hit ten million in 2008 and twenty-five million by 2025.[29]

*Limit State Mandates: Through Competition.* One of the greatest pressures driving health-care costs is the tendency of state governments to mandate that all insurers cover various diseases. You may want a simple health-insurance plan that does not include coverage for drug rehabilitation or hair transplants or sex-change operations. But some "health-care providers" have gone to state legislators and "gold-plated" insurance coverage. There were 1,900 such mandates in the fifty states in 2007. The chiropractor lobby has been very busy. Forty-six states make it illegal to sell insurance that does not cover chiropractors' bills. It is illegal in New Jersey to sell insurance that does not cover specific mandates benefits regardless of whether you want such coverage. The more corrupt the legislature, the more such mandates are put in to please campaign contributors.[30]

Legislation sponsored by Representative John Shadegg of Arizona would allow you to buy your health insurance from a company in any of the fifty states regardless of where you live. You could live in a high-mandated-cost state such as New Jersey and buy your health insurance from a company based and regulated in Iowa. This alone would save the average single person hundreds of dollars each year. Consumers would always be free to insure for any amount they wish. There would not be a mandated minimum cost with mandated benefits. The fifty states would compete to provide desired regulations of the insurance industry, like making sure they are financially sound, rather than pimping for various interest groups. Passing the Shadegg bill alone and allowing such competition would reduce the cost of health insurance by 12 percent according to the Council of Economic Advisers, 5 percent according to the Congressional Budget Office (CBO), and 20 percent according to the Council for Affordable Health Insurance (CAHI).[31]

Health-care costs are inflated in America because the government has taken much of the health-care industry out of the private competitive market and taken consumer sovereignty away.

The creation of HSAs parallels the creation of IRAs in the 1970s. A growing number of Americans are now familiar with the option of consumer-controlled health care. Americans who control their own health-care dollars will not have to beg the government or their insurance company or HMOs for care and protection. They will be in control of their decisions and their resources. And as with retirement-income security, the more independent Americans are, the closer we come to where every American is a charter member of the Leave Us Alone Coalition.

Americans are never more vulnerable than when they fear for their health or the health of their family members.[32] These reforms will put Americans back in charge of their own health-care decisions, not the government rationing or their employer choosing. The politicians who feed on fear to lock Americans into dependence will have lost one of their most powerful tools of control.

## REFORM THREE: GIVE PARENTS REAL CHOICE IN EDUCATION

America in the third millennium runs its public-school system as a cross between the Soviet Union's steel industry—a monopoly—and Socrates chatting with a handful of students under a tree, which is by definition 2,000-year-old technology.

Ignoring technological change in communications is inexplicably silly. Running something as important as the education of our children though a monopoly bureaucracy that since the 1960s is also subject to labor-union rules is difficult to understand.

Albert Shanker, the former president of the American Federation of Teachers, confessed, "It's time to admit that public education operates like a planned economy, a bureaucratic system in which everybody's role is spelled out in advance and there are few incentives for innovation and productivity. It's no surprise that our school system doesn't improve: it more resembles the communist economy than our own market economy."[33]

Steve Jobs, the CEO of Apple, sees from the outside what Shanker saw. "I believe that what is wrong with our schools in this nation is that they have become unionized in the worst possible way. This unionization and lifetime employment of K–12 teachers is off-the-charts crazy."[34]

The good news is that the solution is quite simple. Allow every tax dollar that is pledged to "education" to follow each child. Today we fund the school system and pass a compulsory school-attendance law forcing parents to deliver their child six hours a day to whatever the local school board produces.

In 2003–2004, the government paid $443 billion to educate children in kindergarten through high school. This is an average of $9,052 per child. If that money was given as a tuition grant to every parent, the parents themselves could judge which schools and which teachers they wished to invest that scholarship with.[33] Homeschoolers could fund their own children's education without being taxed to provide for others a benefit they don't themselves receive. Those in private schools would no longer be paying twice for education.

The wall keeping children out of the schools their parents want them to attend has begun to crack. Many states now allow some public-school choice. There are now more than 3,000 charter schools that give some independence and choice to teachers and parents. An estimated 2 million students are homeschooled and 6.5 million attend private schools already.[34]

The public-school industry responds with horror the idea of parental choice. They suggest that any voucher or scholarship plan would result in an exodus of students from their schools to private schools. These "defenders" of government-monopoly education remind one of the old joke where the wife of the dictator of East Germany asks her husband to open the Berlin Wall. Honecker is taken aback by this request, but quickly understands and says to his wife, "Oh, you romantic woman, you just want to be alone with me."

If the government-school monopoly believed they were putting out a quality product, they would welcome school choice. Everyone would want to go to their school. Opponents of school choice believe they are producing a shoddy product that empowered parents and students would flee.

The movement to parental school choice has been slowed by the power of the teachers unions. They own a great number of state politicians—Republican and Democrat. George Wallace used to stand in the schoolhouse door and tell black children they could not go *in* because it would offend his racist supporters. Ted Kennedy

stands in the schoolhouse door and tells children in failing schools
that they cannot leave because it would embarrass and defund his
labor-union backers in the teachers unions.

Reform will be hastened by the stunning hypocrisy of the left. Bill
and Hillary Clinton sent their own precious daughter to an elite private school, Sidwell Friends School. Bill then vetoed a Republican bill
that would have given poor families in D.C. vouchers to attend private
schools. Al Gore spelled out the left's different rules for those who
govern and their subjects. "If I was a parent of a child who went to an
inner-city school that was failing, I might be for vouchers, too." Gore
sent his children to elite private schools.[35] As did then-Senator John
Edwards, who proclaimed that D.C. schools were "deeply troubled."
Edwards voted against school choice for the little people who evidently do not mind "deeply troubled" schools for their children of a
lesser God.[36]

Holding the education of children hostage to the needs of unions
and bureaucracies will not last forever. Segregation was beaten down.
The government monopoly and those who profit from it will go into
the dustbin of history.

Parents with a scholarship worth $9,000 for each child will be em-
powered. When they enter a school they will be treated the way you
are treated when you enter an automobile showroom: You are a cus-
tomer with cash. They want your business. Parental choice in education will create a next generation with a stronger education and more
self-respect as kids see their parents treated better by their teachers.
The present monopoly teachers union tells us that they have to take
care of our kids and need to be paid extra because parents do not care
enough about their children's education. At the same time they refuse
to allow those parents to have any say in what and how and where the
child is taught. Having kept parents out of every single decision about
their child's education they have the nerve to damn the parents for
not being involved.

It is easy to see the benefits of school choice for children and parents. But there are great rewards to competent teachers and education
managers. Those teachers who teach and respect parents and students

and those managers who can deliver a great education will be rewarded with "customers" flocking to their doors. They will figure out how to use television, computers, iPods, and other modern technology to expand their reach. We are not legally bound to listen only to the music of our neighborhood garage band. We can listen to the Beatles and the Rolling Stones and to Jim Morrison, who is dead, for crying out loud. We are not forced to see only plays performed by the local theater troupe. We can see films made in Britain, France, and Italy by the world's best directors and actors. Why cannot great teachers be similarly recorded and reach a nation and the world?

With parental choice good teachers and good schools will be greatly rewarded. Teachers who cannot teach will not be protected by tenure or labor-union work rules. Bad schools should and will go bankrupt. It is estimated that roughly 57 percent of restaurants started in America go belly-up within the first three years.[37] That is why the restaurants that stay in business are quality. Government-run schools do not close. They do not go bankrupt when customers find them failures. They pass laws forcing parents to send their children as the Athenians fed the Minotaur. The failure to fire bad teachers and bad schools does not mean there are no bad teachers and bad schools—it means they never leave. They never improve.

The growth in parental choice in education, however slow, is a one-way movement. Parents will never surrender the power they attain. Every small step in this direction will be an example to other states and cities and fuel the demand for more and total parental choice.

Imagine turning the present government monopoly K–12 system with 3 million teachers and 5.6 million total employees into a competitive educational marketplace with teachers and schools competing to provide the best product at the lowest cost.[38] What if we treated education as seriously as we treat every other industry in America and freed it up to serve consumers and respect providers? We would have the best education system in the world. And we cannot say that today. What are we waiting for, another betrayed generation?

In a world where every child of every parent is empowered with a scholarship, the teachers and school administrators that create successful schools will themselves be successful professionals and businessmen. They will leave the teachers-union seat at the Takings Coalition and join the Leave Us Alone Coalition as businessmen and -women, professionals in the free market fighting against the unions, the trial lawyers, and the tax collectors.

## REFORM FOUR: COMPETITIVE SOURCING

The fourth reform is simple and revolutionary. Every single government service administered by federal, state, or local government that can be provided by the private sector should be contracted out. There should be no monopolies claimed by the government outside of running the military and arresting and punishing criminals. There is no reason that government workers should collect trash in cities, cut the grass in parks, or serve food in school cafeterias or statehouses. If the job appears in the yellow pages it is inherently private sector. There is no reason the U.S. Postal Service should have a monopoly on delivering mail. If you want to start a first-class-mail delivery service in your hometown or nationwide, why should the police arrest you?

Even under Bill Clinton the federal government did a review of its employment and found eight hundred thousand jobs that could be done by the private sector.[39] When nongovernmental contractors have bid for the jobs done by government workers, taxpayers have historically saved one-third of the cost of that service. This was true whether the contract went to the private bidder or was won by the government workers. Government workers can often reorganize themselves to compete, if they know that keeping their job requires being competitive. This should be done in all federal agencies and in all state and local governments. This will squeeze out the monopoly rents in government work and government pay, and benefits will more closely approximate work, pay, and benefits in the real economy. Reason Foundation did a study showing that such competitive sourcing at the state level would save $10 billion each year for California taxpayers.[40] A government worker will not contribute money or his vote to a politician to "protect" his job and pay if they are the same as everywhere else in the economy. Private-sector workers don't pay off politicians to allow them to work at the mall or a factory.

## REFORM FIVE: TRANSPARENCY

The four preceding reforms have moved on to the political agenda over decades. Moving from defined-benefit pensions to portable defined-contribution pensions has been a thirty-year process in the private sector. It has been the central part of the Social Security debate for six years, and state and local pensions have begun to move in that direction for eight years. School choice was forecast by Milton Friedman in the 1960s and the scholarship programs passed in Wisconsin in 1990, Florida in 1999, and Arizona in 1997. Health savings accounts were legalized in 1996 and made universally available in the 2003 legislation. Competitive sourcing or privatization of government services was promoted by the Reason Foundation back in the 1970s and went worldwide with the Thatcher revolution. Competitive sourcing at the federal level became routine in the 1990s. Block-granting federal programs to create the opportunity for fifty states to innovate burst on the national scene with welfare reform in 1996.

The next big thing driving limited government and expanding citizen empowerment is transparency. Real transparency was made possible by the Internet and advanced search engines. Newt Gingrich got the ball rolling by insisting that all legislation be put on the Worldwide Web so that every American could read any bill before Congress, not just the lobbyists. The system was called "THOMAS" after Thomas Jefferson. Transparency got a leg up in 2006 with the passage of the Coburn-Obama legislation requiring all federal grants and contracts to be made available on the Web by January 2008. A limited government group, Downsize DC, has begun a campaign to pass legislation to require any bill before Congress to appear for seven days on the Internet so that every citizen can see what is being voted on and no last-minute deals can be made in the dark.

Texas governor Rick Perry began the future of state and local government transparency when in the fall of 2006 he put the governor's office's quarterly expenditures online. No law required this. He just did it. The Texas comptroller, Susan Combs, did the same for her agency and many other departments. Legislation to require this of the entire state government of Texas enjoyed bipartisan support and was signed into law on June 15, 2007.

Indiana governor Mitch Daniels placed the actual wording of state contracts on the Web for all citizens to see. Kansas and Oklahoma passed transparency legislation putting comprehensive information on government expenditures online in a searchable format. Hawaii and Minnesota passed laws increasing government transparency in grants and contracts.

Governor Matt Blunt of Missouri decreed an executive order on July 11, 2007, to put the comprehensive information on government spending on a website called the Missouri Accountability Portal, http://mapyourtaxes.mo.gov, which was launched the same day. The website received more than 1.77 million hits within the first four months. Other states noticed that Missouri accomplished transparency without appropriating an additional penny. Those accounting for state spending just placed the information on the Web with existing staff and resources.

Fifty-eight local school districts in Texas with 22 percent of the schoolchildren in the state have voluntarily put their check registers on the Internet. Parents can look up every dollar spent by their children's schools and see how their tax dollars are being allocated. In Florida, legislation has been prepared to require every school district, town, city, and county to make their spending and contracts completely transparent and searchable on the Internet.

You see your credit card statement each month. Why shouldn't you see the government credit card statements of those who spend your money—the mayor, his staffers, the school principal?

Transparency reform is as inevitable as the other four reforms, but I believe it will move even faster. Many liberals who would oppose school choice, portable pensions, block grants, and competitive sourcing are strong advocates of transparency. Ralph Nader doesn't mind the government taking your money in the first place, but he recognizes that transparency makes it less likely that tax dollars will be stolen a second time.

Imagine a future where every check written by your school and every contract signed by the school is public information available at all hours on the Web. This will generate tens of thousands of serious candidates for school board. Today, too many parents who are concerned about their children's schools cannot articulate what they want changed. They have too little information on what goes on at school. Now a challenger for the school board would have his opposition research done for him or her. The speech to the local chamber of commerce, Kiwanis club, or church group would be a slide show of "the 25 checks that would not have been written if I were on the school board." Knowing that every check, credit-card invoice, and contract would be truly open for public scrutiny would immediately change the behavior of local government and public school officials.

Complete fiscal transparency for government will make it easier for competitive sourcing or contracting out to expand. The understandable fears that sweetheart contracts would be let at the expense of the public good are best protected by the disinfectant of public scrutiny.

A second wave of transparency will sweep the government when parents realize that they can work best with their children and their teachers if they have full information on what goes on in their child's classroom. C-Span has shown Americans that they can watch their congressmen and senators and be immediately informed as to what is happening in their name. For most Americans what happens with their child at school is more important than congressional debates.

Technology now makes it possible for every parent to come home at the end of the day and go online and punch in his child's name and be able to access a video of his child's math class with all the homework and class exercises done that day. Mom or Dad could follow their child through the day, seeing exactly what their child saw in classroom instruction and what he or she received as handouts and homework. How much more preparation would go into each day's class presentation when teachers know that parents will be dropping in to watch—not in school but on the Internet. Teachers unions will find it tougher to defend teachers who cannot spell or add. Parents can best help their children when they can follow their child's education day to day rather than learn at the end of the semester that Johnny has failed.

*Forward to America, Not Backward to Europe.* These five reforms will cut the cost of government in half over the next generation. Pensions will move from defined-benefit to portable-defined-contribution personal savings accounts for private-sector workers, government employees, and all Americans through Social Security. Health care will move away from third-party payer to allow consumer-driven decisions and eliminate politically motivated gold-plating of health insurance. Tort reform will reduce the cost of health care. Parental choice in education will end a government monopoly and create tens of millions of empowered parents and millions of teachers free to teach and innovate. And competitive sourcing of all government services will end the stagnation of monopoly and create a government workforce as innovative and flexible as that of America's best industries. Transparency will bring the disinfectant of sunlight to all government spending, reducing waste and corruption.

Every step of this movement will be supported by the Leave Us Alone Coalition and opposed by the leaders of the Takings Coalition. Every step toward a society where each individual is independent, self-reliant, and needs nothing from the state but the equal protection of his life and property strengthens the center-right.

In Europe men and women are dependent on the government for their pension, their health care, their children's education, and, for many, their very jobs. Many of us left Europe through the decisions of our ancestors. But we all left Europe as Americans who own the history of our Revolution and Constitution. The Takings Coalition would drag us back across the Atlantic to dependency. Rather, we will seize back control of our lives, our incomes, our property, and our families from the intrusions of officious government at all annoying levels.

The Leave Us Alone Coalition is determined to continue its progress toward Jefferson's vision of the self-reliant, independent American—toward a free society where everyone lives off the earnings of no man but himself.

# AFTERWORD

What will America look like in 2050?

Until then and beyond, the Leave Us Alone Coalition and the Takings Coalition will face off every two years. They offer completely different visions of the future.

The Takings Coalition will try to move more decisions, more industries, more jobs under government control—either direct control or hidden control through regulation and litigation. If they win, taxes will be higher. Fewer choices will be made by parents. More by the state. America will become a European welfare state.

In past elections pundits not happy with the two visions have called for a third party. Bill Clinton and Britain's Tony Blair have spoken of a "third way" between freedom and statism. But there is *no* third way. No alternative to the two contestants now in the ring.

After the 2006 election Sebastian Mallaby of the *Washington Post* suggested a possible coalition between liberals and libertarians. The economic libertarians now in the Leave Us Alone Coalition are, the theory runs, tired of hanging in the party with all the guys who go to church all the time. Okay. Is a libertarian who wants his taxes lowered and is an absolutist on free trade and freedom of contract going to leave the party that fights for lower taxes, free trade, and tort reform, and join the party of government spenders and higher taxes, union bosses against trade and trial lawyers?

There is nowhere for a free-market advocate to go. No deal to be made with the Takings Coalition. On his primary vote-moving issue he cannot move. A Milton Friedman economic libertarian will stay in his coalition and simply choose not to have dinner and drinks with the churchgoers.

From time to time there are self-proclaimed "social conservative" leaders who get their only press attention when they threaten to bolt.

To where? What home will the party of radical feminists, radical secularists, and environmentalists who have an alternative faith they wish the state to impose offer to a traditional-values conservative?

A trial lawyer who wanted lower taxes cannot knock on the door of the Leave Us Alone Coalition and find a party willing to tax him less and yet allow him to loot the countryside with lawsuits.

*Huis Clos.* No exit. There is no alternative structure for the two competing coalitions. Some suggested that "everything changed" after September 11. Actually nothing changed in the two parties and coalitions. One prominent conservative said that if the Republicans were insufficiently enthusiastic about occupying Iraq he would be comfortable hanging with the "liberal hawks." Connecticut's Lieberman is one. Where did he get the plural "hawks"? Even an event as dramatic as September 11 and the subsequent wars and occupation in Afghanistan and Iraq have not led to a single congressman or senator, governor, state legislator, or party official switching sides. That suggests a certain stability in the American divide. One's opinion of the war is more likely to be shaped by one's existing view of George Bush. Republicans supported the war because Bush recommended it. Democrats opposed it for the same reason. It is the flip side of how Americans reacted to Clinton's wars in Yugoslavia and Somalia.

The two competing coalitions will win or lose as presently structured. This book has outlined a number of trends that overall favor the Leave Us Alone Coalition. Will they give our coalition enough strength, soon enough, to avoid the fiscal crack-up threatened by midcentury? I intend to work hard to make that true.

*Quo Vadis?* We will know which direction America is heading before 2050. If nothing changes, if the two parties simply fight to a stalemate, the demographic reality of an aging population and automatic spending on entitlement programs will bring government spending to European levels. We will become a social democracy.

But if the Leave Us Alone Coalition is successful in winning majority status in the House and sixty votes in the Senate, it can cut taxes to increase American income and wealth. That will give us the possibility to reform the government programs that will otherwise bankrupt America. And every government program that is reformed to reduce dependency and provide individual control will strengthen the Leave Us Alone Coalition. Yesterday's liberal with a growing 401(k) is tomorrow's taxpayer advocate. A parent formerly blackmailed into paying higher property taxes by the demands of the public school system will, given parental control, wield that voucher or scholarship to demand a real future for his or her child.

We see the Takings Coalition future in old Europe as it recedes with a standard of living falling farther and farther behind America today. The task of the Leave Us Alone Coalition is to keep America away from that path of decline and turn it to the bright and high road of individual liberty and limited government that our Constitution promised and that our grandchildren can win.

If the Leave Us Alone Coalition wins, we will have dramatically lower taxes and lower government spending.

If we win, every American will have the widest possible set of choices. Transparency will let all of us know exactly how our tax dollars are spent by the federal, state, and local governments and by the public schools.

If we win, every American will have a personal savings account to save tax free for their retirement. We will have complete choice on where to educate our children, at home, in a private or government school of our choosing, not the government's. More of us will be self-employed. None will be forced to pay union dues. No one will be sued by greedy trial lawyers out to make a buck regardless of personal fault. Americans of all religious faiths will be free to practice their religion and share it with their children.

If we win, the death tax will be abolished and those foolish enough to die will not surrender half their lives' savings to the government.

If we win, America will be freer. America will be richer, more mobile, with new jobs, new industries and new technologies, and without the dead weight of government.

The limited tasks assigned to government will be done more competently because we will no longer be asking government to do many things it is not equipped to accomplish. We'll be able to compensate fairly the government workers that a free society needs—the strongest military in the world, serious police and courts—without crushing taxpayers.

If we win, America will dominate the planet through example, not force. We will be the most competitive nation in the world.

If we win, America wins.

# NOTES

## Introduction

1. The 22 years include: 1875–1881, 1883–1889, 1891–1895, and 1911–1917. Office of the Clerk, Party Divisions of the House of Representatives (1789 to Present), United States House of Representatives, http://clerk.house.gov/art_history/house_history/partyDiv.html#1 (accessed Sept 18, 2007).
2. Analysis performed by Americans for Tax Reform using Bureau of Economic Analysis data.
3. Bureau of Economic Analysis, Income and Employment by Industry, US Department of Commerce, http://www.bea.gov/national/nipaweb/SelectTable.asp?Selected=N (accessed September 1, 2007).
4. Office of the Clerk, Party Divisions of the House of Representatives (1789 to Present), United States House of Representatives, http://clerk.house.gov/art_history/house_history/partyDiv.html#1 (accessed September 18, 2007).
5. The twelve years were: 1931–1933, 1947–1949, 1953–1955, and 1981–1987. Senate Historical Office, Party Divisions in the Senate, 1789–Present, US Senate, http://senate.gov/pagelayout/history/one_item_and_teasers/partydiv.htm (accessed September 23, 2007).
6. Nicholas Hoffman, "The Third Man Theme," *New York Times,* 28 September 1980, sec. 6.
7. Federal Election Commission, "Election Results" (Washington, D.C.: 2007) http://www.fec.gov/pubrec/electionresults.shtml (accessed September 24, 2007).

# PART ONE

1. Full Greta Garbo quote: "I never said, 'I want to be alone.' I only said, 'I want to be left alone.' There is all the difference."

## Chapter 1

1. IRS, All Returns: Tax Liability, Tax Credits, and Tax Payments, by Size of Adjusted Gross Income, Tax Year 2004, http://www.irs.gov/pub/irs-soi/04in02ar .xls (April 26th, 2007).
2. Census Bureau, U.S.—all industries—by Employment Size of Enterprise, http://www.census.gov/epcd/susb/latest/us/US–.HTM (accessed April 23, 2007).
3. Direct Selling Association, U.S. DIRECT SELLING IN 2005, http://www.dsa .org/pubs/numbers/calendar05factsheet.pdf (accessed September 24, 2007).
4. TechBytes, "It's eBay or the Highway" (Washington, D.C.: Institute for Policy Innovation, 2006) http://www.ipi.org/ipi/ipipressreleases.nsf/70218ef1ad92c4 ad86256ee5005965f6/b1b755df02ba1bb8862571400063727d?OpenDocument (accessed September 24, 2007). Entry cites ACNielsen International Research done for eBay.
5. Bureau of Labor Statistics, May 2005 National Occupational Employment and Wage Estimates, United States, U.S. Department of Labor, http://www.bls.gov/ oes/current/oes_nat.htm (accessed May 14, 2007).
6. The Pew Forum on Religion and Public Life, "Religious Demographic Profile: United States" (Washington, D.C.: Intuit, 2007). http://pewforum.org/ world-affairs/countries/?CountryID=222 (accessed September 21, 2007).
7. "Largest denominations/denominational families in U.S.," adherents.com http://www.adherents.com/rel_USA.html (accessed November 12, 2006).
8. CNN, U.S. PRESIDENT NATIONAL EXIT POLL, http://www.cnn.com/ ELECTION/2004/pages/results/states/US/P/00/epolls.0.html (accessed August 31, 2007).
9. CNN 2004 Presidential Exit Poll.
10. Ibid.
11. Binyamin L Jolkovsky, "Orthodox Jews as New Evangelicals?" *Jewish World Review*, January 19, 2005.
12. Weyrich brought Adoph Coors to support the Heritage Foundation that now stands as the largest conservative think tank in Washington. Weyrich founded and runs the Committee for a Free Congress, and in 1971 organized the Kingston Group meeting that weekly brought together the broad conservative activist base and staff and members of Congress. Weyrich, the godfather of the new right, witnessed or midwifed the creation of almost every successful conservative group spawned in the 1970s and 1980s.
13. Investment Company Institute, *2007 Investment Company Factbook* (Washington, D.C.: ICI, 2007), http://www.icifactbook.org/ (accessed August 25, 2007).
14. Elizabeth Drew, *On the Edge: The Clinton Presidency* (Rockefeller Center: Touchstone, 1994), 91.

15. Statistical Information Analysis Division, Active Duty Military Strength for December 31, 2006, Department of Defense. http://siadapp.dior.whs.mil/personnel/MILITARY/ms1.pdf (accessed May 1, 2007).

16. Brian DeBose, "Military Survey 3-to-1 for Bush," *Washington Times*, October 16, 2004, sec. A.

17. Bureau of Labor Statistics, Protective Services Occupation, Department of Labor, http://www.bls.gov/oes/current/oes_nat.htm (accessed May 1, 2007).

18. Mathee Imbert, "Tough Stance Towards China Favored in Polls," *Seattle Post-Intelligencer*, February 23, 1996, A2.

19. Federal Election Commission, *2000 Presidential General Election Results* (Washington, D.C.: FEC, 2000), http://www.fec.gov/pubrec/fe2000/2000presge.htm (accessed September 23, 2007).

20. Federal Elections Commission, 1996 Presidential Primary Election Results, http://www.fec.gov/pubrec/fe1996/presprim.htm (accessed August 31, 2006).

21. Chris W. Cox, Election Day 2006, NRA-ILA. http://www.nraila.org//Issues/FactSheets/Read.aspx?ID=207 (accessed September 20, 2007).

22. Log Cabin Republicans, Chapters, http://online.logcabin.org/chapters/ (accessed April 29, 2007).

23. Pink Pistols, Find a local Pink Pistols Chapter, http://www.pinkpistols.org/local.html (accessed April 29, 2007).

## Chapter 2

1. Calculations by Scott Rasmussen, "If you own $5,000 of stock you are more likely to be a Republican," Data from Rasmussen Research, 1998.

2. Chris Edwards, "Federal Pay Outpaces Private-Sector Pay," *Tax & Budget Bulletin*, May 2006, http://www.cato.org/pubs/tbb/tbb-0605-35.pdf (May 1, 2007).

3. Americans for Tax Reform analysis of data from National Income and Product Accounts, Bureau of Economic Analysis, U.S. Department of Commerce.

4. Charles Cowan, interview by Grover Norquist, September 14, 2006.

5. U.S. Bureau of Labor Statistics, Table A-1. Employment status of the civilian population by sex and age, Department of Labor, http://www.bls.gov/news.release/empsit.t01.htm (accessed April 29, 2007).

6. BLS, Union Members in 2006, ftp://ftp.bls.gov/pub/news.release/union2.txt (accessed September 1, 2007).

7. Linda Chavez and Daniel Gray, *Betrayal: How Union Bosses Shake Down Their Members and Corrupt Americans Politics* (New York: Crown Forum, 2004).

8. Opensecrets.org, "Republican National Committee: 2003–2004 Election Cycle," *The Center for Responsive Politics* (Washington, D.C.: 2006), http://www.opensecrets.org/parties/total.asp?Cmte=RNC&cycle=2004 (accessed September 15, 2007).

9. Presentation by Foley & Lardner LCC, http://www.foley.com/ (accessed August 15, 2007).

10. Union Members in 2006, ftp://ftp.bls.gov/pub/news.release/union2.txt (accessed September 1, 2007).

11. Presentation by Foley & Lardner LCC, http://www.foley.com/ (accessed August 15, 2007).

12. Steve Malanga, "The Real Engine of Blue America," *City Journal* (Winter 2005), http://www.city-journal.org/html/15_1_blue_america.html (accessed August 22, 2007).

13. Compiled by Americans for Tax Reform using State Election Board Data.

14. TaxBytes, "Labor over TABOR" (Washington, D.C.: Institute for Policy Innovation, 2006).

15. Steven Malanga, *New New Left: How American Politics Works Today* (Chicago: Ivan R. Dee, 2005).

16. Ibid., 12.

17. Ibid., 13.

18. Ibid.

19. Bureau of Economic Analysis, "Table 6.5D. Full-Time Equivalent Employees by Industry," Department of Commerce.

20. Daniel J. Flynn, *Deep Blue Campuses* (Clarendon: Leadership Institute, 2005). http://www.bea.gov/national/nipaweb/TableView.asp?SelectedTable=183& FirstYear=1947&LastYear=1948&Freq=Year (accessed July 2, 2007).

21. Flynn, http://www.leadershipinstitute.org/resources/?pageid=dbc.

22. AAJ, About AAJ, http://www.atla.org/about/index.aspx (accessed April 29, 2007).

23. Council of Economic Advisors, "Who Pays for Tort Liability Claims? An Economic Analysis of the U.S. Tort Liability System," 2002 (Washington, D.C.), 10.

24. Lawrence J. McQuillan et al., *Jackpot Justice: The True Cost of America's Tort System* (San Francisco: Pacific Research Institute, 2007), 15.

25. Center for Legal Policy, *Trial Lawyer Inc.,* Manhattan Institute (New York: 2003), 6.

26. Julie Defalco, *The Deadly Effects of Fuel Economy Standards: CAFE'S Lethal Impact on Auto Safety* (Washington, D.C.: CEI, 1999), 3.

27. Division of Parasitic Diseases, Frequently Asked Questions about Malaria, National Center for Infectious Diseases, http://www.cdc.gov/malaria/faq.htm (accessed April 29, 2007).

28. McQuillan, 40.

29. Research from U.S. Senate Historical Office.

30. Mark Wahlgren Summers, *Rum, Romanism, and Rebellion: The Making of a President 1884* (Chapel Hill: University of North Carolina, 2000).

31. William B. Prendergast, *The Catholic Voter in American Politics: The Passing of the Democratic Monolith* (Washington, D.C.: Georgetown University Press, 1999).

## Chapter 3

1. 2007 Investment Company Book, http://www.icifactbook.org/ (accessed August 25, 2007).

2. Tax Almanac, *Internal Revenue Code:Sec. 408. Individual retirement accounts* (Washington, D.C.: Intuit, 2007), http://www.taxalmanac.org/index.php?title=

Internal_Revenue_Code:Sec._408._Individual_retirement_accounts&oldid= 195317 (accessed July 16, 2007).

3. Ibid.

4. Investment Company Institute, *2006 Investment Company Fact Book* (Washington, D.C.: ICI, 2006).

5. Investment Company Institute, *401(k) Plans: A 25-Year Retrospective* (Washington, D.C.: ICI, 2006), http://www.ici.org/stats/res/arc-ret/per12-02.pdf (accessed June 13, 2007).

6. Calculations by Scott Rasmussen, "People who work for the government are more likely to be Democrats," Data from Rasmussen Research.

7. John Zogby, New Zogby "American Values" survey, Zogby International, http://zogby.com/search/ReadNews.dbm?ID=287 (accessed May 1, 2007) and David Lambro, "Social Security plan backed in new poll," *Washington Times*, May 31, 2005.

8. John Zogby, John Bruce, and Rebecca Wittman, *Report on the Political Outlook of American Investors* (Washington, D.C.: Zogby International, 2000).

9. An analysis performed by American Shareholders Association using Federal Reserve Flow of Funds data.

10. Ibid.

11. Americans for Tax Reform analysis using data from the Department of Labor.

12. Michigan's Offices of Retirement Services, *About the State Employees' Retirement System* (Lansing: Department of Management and Budget, 2007), http://www.michigan.gov/orsstatedc/0,1607,7-209-34710-109542-,00.html (accessed September 24, 2007).

13. Office of the Governor, Governor Corzine's Budget Address, Assembly Chambers, February 22, 2007, As prepared for delivery (Trenton: Office of the Governor, 2007), http://www.state.nj.us/governor/news/news/approved/20070222.html (accessed September 20, 2007).

## Chapter 4

1. Kathryn Jean Lopez, "Not Your Father's Labor Union: Labor Unions Are More Michael Moore than George Meany," *National Review Online*, August 5, 2004, http://www.nationalreview.com/interrogatory/chavez200408050802.asp (accessed September 27, 2007).

2. Opensecrets.org, THE BIG PICTURE 2000 & 2004 Cycle, http://opensecrets.org/bigpicture/blio.asp?display=Total&Cycle=2000, http://opensecrets.org/bigpicture/blio.asp?display=Total&Cycle=2004 (accessed April 29, 2007).

3. Executive Council Report, *For Every Worker, A Voice* (Washington, D.C.: AFL-CIO, 2005), http://www.aflcio.org/aboutus/thisistheaflcio/convention/2005/upload/execcouncil_report.pdf (accessed September 20, 2006).

4. Ron Nehring (Member, San Diego County School Board), Interview by author, September 26, 2006.

5. The Joint Center for Political and Economic Studies, "African American, Hispanics Less Optimistic than Whites about Local Public Schools," http://www.jointcenter.org/pressroom1/PressReleasesDetail.php?recordID=16 (accessed May 1, 2007).

6. Wendell Cox Consultancy, Us Private Sector Trade Union Membership, http://www.publicpurpose.com/lm-unn2003htm (accessed March 23, 2007).

7. Ibid.

8. BLS, Union Members in 2006, ftp://ftp.bls.gov/pub/news.release/union2.txt (accessed September 1, 2007)

9. Fast Stats AtoZ, Deaths/Mortality, Center for Disease Control, http://www.cdc.gov/nchs/fastats/deaths.htm (accessed April 29, 2007).

10. Answer, Affirmative Defenses and counterclaims of Education Association Defendants, *State v. WEA*, 1997 and Estimated from Washington Education Association reports.

11. Heather Reams (Director of Communications at Association of American Educators), interview by author, September 27, 2007.

12. William T. Wilson, Ph.D., *The Effect of Right-to-Work Laws on Economic Development* (Midland: Mackinac Center for Public Policy, 2002), 13.

13. Opensecrets.org, "Labor: Long-Term Giving Trends," http://opensecrets.org/industries/indus.asp?Ind=P (accessed September 25, 2007).

14. David Denholm (President of the Public Service Research Foundation), interview by author, 29 September 2006.

15. United States House of Representatives, Letter to the Junta Local de Conciliacion y Arbitraje del Estada de Pueblo (Washington, D.C.: Office of Representative George Miller, 2001.).

16. Zogby International Release, "Disorganized Labor," *Zogby International*, August 10, 2005.

17. Erik Reece, "Harlan County Blues," *The Nation*, June 28, 2006, http://www.thenation.com/docprem.mhtml?i=20060717&s=reece.

## Chapter 5

1. Professor Arthur Brooks, "The Fertility Gap: Liberal politics will prove fruitless as long as liberals refuse to multiply," Opinionjournal.com, http://www.opinionjournal.com/editorial/feature.html?id=110008831 (accessed March 27, 2007).

2. Brooks, http://www.opinionjournal.com/editorial/feature.html?id=110008831 (accessed March 27, 2007).

3. Ed Kilgore, "Expand the Base! To build a majority coalition, Democrats must appeal to more voters outside cities," *Blueprint Magazine*, http://www.dlc.org/ndol_ci.cfm?contentid=253984&kaid=127&subid=173 (accessed July 18, 2007).

4. Ibid.

5. Ibid.

6. Steve Sailer, "Baby Gap: How birthrates color the electoral map," *American Conservative*, http://www.amconmag.com/2004_12_06/cover.html.

7. Steve Sailer, "Beyond the Baby Gap: Marriage Drives the Red-Blue Divide," VDare.com, http://www.vdare.com/sailer/041212_secret.htm.

8. The American National Election Studies, Age Cohort of Respondents 1948–2004., http://www.electionstudies.org/nesguide.toptable/tabla_1.htm (accessed August 2006).

9. Ibid.

10. CNN, Exit Polls 2000. CNN, Exit Poll 2004. and CNN, Exit Poll 2006, http://www.cnn.com/ELECTION/2006/pages/results/states/US/H/00/epolls.0.html (September 16, 2007).

11. Larry L. Eastland, "The Empty Cradle Will Rock: How abortion is costing the Democrats—literally," Opinionjournal.com, http://www.opinionjournal.com/extra/?id=110005277(April 29, 2007).

## Chapter 6

1. Amanda Hydro (Former Executive Director of the College Republican National Committee), Interview by Author, June 8, 2007.

2. Scott Stewart, *The College Republicans—A Brief History* (Washington, D.C.: CRNC, 2002), http://www.crnc.org/images/CRNChistory.pdf (accessed August 2006), 1–3.

3. Ibid.

4. Amanda Hydro (Former Executive Director of the College Republican National Committee), Interview by Author, September 28, 2007.

5. Morton Blackwell (President of the Leadership Institute), interview by the Author, June 28, 2006.

## Chapter 7

1. William Clinton, *My Life* (New York: Random House, 2004), 629–630.

2. Senate: 1993 Vote #394 on HR 1025 passed 63–36. House: 1993 Vote #564 on HR 1025 passed 238–189.

3. Ibid.

4. Ibid.

5. Zogby International, "New Zogby "American Values" Poll reveals: NRA represents America's views more than the AFL-CIO or the Religious Right; Majority says Supreme Court decisions unbiased," http://zogby.com/search/ReadNews .dbm?ID=319 (accessed September 12, 2007).

6. National Rifle Association, "NRA Life and Five-Consecutive Year Membership Growth" (Fairfax: NRA, 2006).

7. U.S. Sportmen's Alliance, "Families Afield: An Initiative for the Future of Hunting," Families Afield, http://www.familiesafield.org/pdf/FamiliesAfield_Report .pdf (accessed May 15, 2007).

8. Florida Department of Agricultural and Consumer Services, Concealed Weapon / Firearm Summary Report, October 1, 1987–November 30, 2006 (http://licgweb .doacs.state.fl.us/stats/cw_monthly.html). See also More Guns, Less Crime (2000).

9. ArgusLeader.com, http://www.argusleader.com/apps/pbcs.dll/article?AID=/20061217/ NEWS/612170334/-1/DATABASE01 and Mark Nichols, John R. O'Neill, "300,000 Hoosiers have Gun Permits," *Indy Star*, July 11, 2004, http://www2.indystar. com/articles/1/161649-4651-092.html.

10. Division of Licensing, Concealed Weapon / Firearm Summary Report October 1, 1987–March 31, 2007, Florida Department of Agriculture and Consumer Services, http://licgweb.doacs.state.fl.us/stats/cw_monthly.html.

11. John R. Lott, Jr., *More Guns, Less Crime: Understanding Crime and Gun Control Laws* (Chicago: University of Chicago Press, 2000).

12. Ibid.

13. Ibid.

14. See Fla. Stat. ch. 776.013 (2005).

15. House Committee on Government Reform Subcommittee on National Security, Emerging Threats and International Relations, Statement of Michael D. Gulledge, Director, Evaluation and Inspections Division, U.S. Department of Justice Office of the Inspector General Concerning Homeland Security: Surveillance and Monitoring of Explosive Storage Facilities, Part II (Washington, D.C., October 31, 2005) http://www.usdoj.gov/oig/testimony/0510/final.pdf (accessed September 25, 2007).

16. John R. Lott, Jr., *The Bias Against Guns* (Washington, D.C.: Regnery, 2003), chapter 8.

17. Estimated number of guns based on research in Gary Kleck, *Targeting Guns* (Hawthorne, N.Y.:, de Gruyter, 1997), 63–70. Number of gun owners is based on studies described by Kleck, applied to projected data from 2000 Census.

## Chapter 8

1. Daniel J. Mitchell, Ph.D., *Fiscal Policy Lessons from Europe* (Washington, D.C.: The Heritage Foundation, 2006).

2. Ibid.

3. Ibid.

4. Statistics Canada (1991). General Social Survey-Health. Public-use microdata file.

5. Administration for Children and Families, "ACF News: Statistics," Department of Health and Human Services, http://www.acf.hhs.gov/news/stats/6090_cht .htm (accessed April 29, 2007).

6. David Rousseau (Principal Policy Analyst of the Kaiser Family Foundation), Interview by Author, March 23, 2007.

7. "Food Stamp Program Participation and Costs" (Washington, D.C.: Department of Agriculture, 2007), http://www.fns.usda.gov/pd/fssummar.htm (accessed November 16, 2007).

8. Mark Trumball, "As US tax rates drop, government's reach grows," *Christian Science Monitor*, April 16, 2007, http://www.csmonitor.com/2007/0416/p01s04 -usec.html (accessed September 25, 2007).

9. President George H. W. Bush, *Remarks at the Swearing-in Ceremony for Jack F. Kemp as Secretary of Housing and Urban Development* )Washington, D.C.: White House, 1989), http://www.presidency.ucsb.edu/ws/print.php?pid=16665 (accessed September 26, 2007).

10. Robert Rector, The Impact of Welfare Reform: Testimony before Committee on Ways and Means U.S House of Representatives, July 19, 2006, The Heritage Foundation, http://www.heritage.org/Research/Welfare/tst 071906a.cfm.

## Chapter 9

1. Michael Farris (Cofounder of the Home School Legal Defense Association), interview by author, June 28, 2006.
2. Ibid.
3. Ibid.
4. Ibid.
5. Dr. Brian Ray, "Research Facts on Homeschooling," *National Home Education Research Institute*, July 10, 2006, http://www.nheri.org/content/view/199/ (accessed January 27, 2007).
6. Michael Farris (Cofounder of the Home School Legal Defense Association), interview by author, June 28, 2006
7. Ibid.

## Chapter 10

1. Chris Edwards, "Number, Cost of Government Workers Growing Fast, Study Says," *Budget and Tax News*, April 2006, 17.
2. Bureau of Economic Analysis, http://www.bea.gov/national/nipaweb/SelectTable .asp?Selected=N (accessed June 12, 2007).
3. Edwards, Number, Cost of Government.
4. Wendell Cox, *Public vs. Private Compensation: A Comparison of Public and Private Compensation in Alabama's Workforce* (Birmingham: Alabama Policy Institute, 2006).
5. Ibid.
6. Chris Edwards and Jagadeesh Gokhale, "Unfunded State and Local Health Costs: $1.4 Trillion," *Tax and Budget Bulletin*, October 2006.
7. Office of Personnel and Management, *Retirement Projections* (Washington, D.C.: OPM), http://www.opm.gov/feddata/retire/rs2004_projections.pdf (accessed September 25, 2007).
8. Chris Edwards, "State Bureaucracy Update," *Tax and Budget Bulletin* (Washington, D.C.: Cato Institute, 2006), http://www.cato.org/pubs/tbb/tbb-0601-29 .pdf (accessed September 26, 2007).

## Chapter 11

1. U.S. Census Bureau, "American FactFinder" http://factfinder.census.gov/servlet/ SAFFFacts?_event=&geo_id=01000US&_geoContext=01000US&_street=& _county=&_cityTown=&_state=&_zip=&_lang=en&_sse=on&ActiveGeo-Div=&_useEV=&pctxt=fph&pgsl=010&_submenuId=factsheet_1&ds_name =ACS_2005_SAFF&_ci_nbr=null&qr_name=null&reg=null%3Anull&_key-word=&_industry= (accessed April 29, 2007).
2. David Leip. *Dave Leip's Atlas of U.S. Presidential Elections.* http://www.uselectionatlas.org (accessed July 22, 2006).

3. David Leip, http://uselectionatlas.org/RESULTS/index.html (accessed December 15, 2006).

4. Ibid.

5. Tom Hamburger and Peter Wallsten, *One Party Country: The Republican Plan for Dominance in the 21st Century* (Hoboken: John Wiley & Sons, 2006).

6. Edward Kilgore, *Growing the Vote: The Political Challenges and Opportunities in Fast-Growing Areas* (Washington, D.C.: DLC, 2006), http://www.dlc.org/ndol_ci.cfm?kaid=127&subid=173&contentid=253890 (accessed September 27, 2007).

7. Ibid.

8. Ibid.

9. Ibid.

10. Tom Hamburger and Peter Wallsten, *One Party Country: The Republican Plan for Dominance in the 21st Century* (Hoboken: John Wiley & Sons, 2006).

11. Lauren E. Glaze, and Seri Paila, Probation and Parole in the Unites States, 2004, Bureau of Justice Statistics (November 2005).

12. The Sentencing Project, Felony Disenfranchisement Laws in the United States, http://www.sentencingproject.org/Admin%5CDocuments%5Cpublications%5Cfd_bs_fdlawsinus.pdf (accessed April 30, 2007).

13. Jeff Manza, Christopher Uggen, Marcus Britton, The Truly Disenfranchised: Felon Voting Rights and American Politics, http://www.northwestern.edu/ipr/publications/papers/manza.pdf. For completed work, see: Jeff Manza and Christopher Uggen, *Locked Out: Felon Disenfranchisement and American Democracy* (Studies in Crime and Public Policy) (USA: Oxford University Press, 2007).

14. Kate Zernike, "Iowa Governor Will Give Felons the Right to Vote," New York *Times*, June 18, 2005, A8.

15. John R. Lott, Jr., "The Criminal Constituency," *Baltimore Sun*, February 16, 2006, http://www.aei.org/publications/filter.all,pubID.23901/pub_detail.asp (accessed September 25, 2007).

16. The Sentencing Project.

17. Federal Bureau of Prisons, *Quick Facts about the Bureau of Prisons* (Washington, D.C.: DOJ, 2007), http://www.bop.gov/news/quick.jsp (accessed September June 17, 2006).

18. Editorial, "Louisiana purchased again—need to investigate the 1996 Louisiana Senate election," *National Review*, May 5, 1997.

19. Bob Williams, "Reforming Elections for the Preservation of Liberty," Imprimis: The National Speech Digest of Hillsdale College 34 (2005).

20. Ibid.

21. U.S Election Assistance Commission, Election Crimes: An Initial Review and Recommendations for Future Study, 2006 (Washington, D.C.).

22. John Fund, *Stealing Elections: How Voter Fraud Threatens Our Democracy* (San Francisco: Encounter Books, 2004), 4.

23. Larry J. Sabato and Glenn R. Simpson, *Dirty Little Secrets: The Persistence of Corruption in American Politics* (New York: Times Books 1996).

24. "The Acorn Indictments," *Wall Street Journal*, November 3, 2006.

25. John Fund, "How to Run a Clean Election: What Mexico can teach the United States," *Wall Street Journal 's Opinion Page*, July 10, 2006 (http://www.opinion-journal.com/diary/?id=110008630 (accessed July 15, 2006).

## Chapter 12

1. David Van Biema, "Kingdom Come," *Time Magazine,* August 4, 1997.
2. CNN Exit Polls 2004 and CNN, Exit Polls 1996, http://www.cnn.com/ALLPOL-ITICS/1996/elections/natl.exit.poll/index1.html (accessed September 1, 2007).
3. CNN Exit Polls 2004.
4. Maisel and Forman, 153, and The American-Israeli Cooperative Enterprise, Jewish Vote in Presidential Elections, http://www.jewishvirtuallibrary.org/jsource/US-Israel/jewvote.html (September 17, 2007).
5. CNN Exit Polls 2006.
6. Anna Greenberg and Patrick McCreesh, Presidential Vote 2004—Jewish Voters, Greenberg Quinlan Rosner Research, http://www.greenbergresearch.com/index.php?ID=1941(accessed April 28, 2007).
7. North American Jewish Data Bank, National Jewish Population Survey 1990, Mandell L. Berman Institute, http://www.jewishdatabank.org/NJPS1990.asp and North American Jewish Data Bank, National Jewish Population Survey 2000-01, http://www.jewishdatabank.org/NJPS2000.asp.
8. Bulletin Correspondent, "Demographic time-bomb could decimate Jewish life as we know it," *Jewish News Weekly of Northern California*, October 6, 1995, http://www.jewishsf.com/content/2-0-/module/displaystory/story_id/2141/edition_id/34/format/html/displaystory.html (August 19, 2006).
9. North American Jewish Data Bank, National Jewish Population Survey 1990, Mandell L. Berman Institute, http://www.jewishdatabank.org/NJPS1990.asp and North American Jewish Data Bank, National Jewish Population Survey2000-01, http://www.jewishdatabank.org/NJPS2000.asp.
10. Ibid.
11. Jeff Ballabon, interview by author, April 1, 2007.
12. George J. Marlin, *The American Catholic Voter: 200 Years of Political Impact* (South Bend Ind.: St. Augustine's Press, 2004), xiv.
13. Ibid., xvii.
14. CNN Exit Poll 2000.
15. Report to *Crisis Magazine* on the American Catholic Vote (Washington, D.C.: QEV Analytics, 1996), http://www.qev.com/Final_rpt.pdf (accessed August 18, 2006).
16. Ibid.
17. Grover Norquist, "The Catholic Vote," *American Spectator*, August 2000, http://www.atr.org/press/editorials/tas/tas0800.html.
18. Samuel G. Freedman, *The Inheritance: How Three Families and the American Political Majority Moved from Left to Right* (Rockefeller: Touchstone, 1996).
19. *2002 Report on Anti-Catholicism* (New York: Catholic League for Religious and Civil Rights, 2002), http://www.catholicleague.org/annualreport.php?year=2002 (accessed June 22, 2007).

20. Randy Hall, "Abortion Causing 'Black Genocide,' Activists Say," CNSNews.com February 7, 2005, http://www.cnsnews.com/ViewSpecialReports.asp?Page=%5CSpecialReports%5Carchive%5C200502%5CSPE20050207a.html (accessed July 2, 2007).

21. Kenneth C. Jones, "Vatican II Renewal: Myth or Reality?" *The Latin Mass: A Journal of Catholic Culture* 12, no. 4 (Fall 2003): 10–16.

22. *Democrats More Eager to Vote, but Unhappy with Party* (Washington, D.C.: Pew Research Center for the People and the Press, 2006), http://people-press.org/reports/display.php3?ReportID=279 (accessed July 29, 2007).

23. *Religious Demographic Profile: United States* (Washington, D.C.: The Pew Forum on Religion and Public Life, 2007), http://pewforum.org/world-affairs/countries/?CountryID=222 (accessed September 27, 2007).

24. CNN Exit Polls 2004.

25. Michael Beschloss, "FDR's Auschwitz Secret," *Newsweek,* October 14, 2002, 37.

26. Michael S. Hamilton and Jennifer McKinney, "Turning the Mainline Around: New sociological studies show that evangelicals may well succeed at renewing wayward Protestantism," *Christianity Today,* August 1, 2003, http://www.christianitytoday.com/ct/2003/august/1.34.html (accessed August 24, 2007).

27. The Institute for Religion and Democracy, "Chart of Mainline Church Membership Decline," http://www.ird-renew.org/site/apps/nl/content2.asp?c=fvKV-LfMVIsG&b=470745&ct=1571507 (July 21, 2006).

28. Carol Bender of Christian Booksellers Association, interview by the author, April 9, 2007.

## Chapter 13

1. Project for Excellence in Journalism, 2006 Annual Report on the State of the News Media, Journalism.org, http://www.stateofthenewsmedia.org/2006 (October 14, 2006).

2. Ibid.

3. "The Top Talk Radio Audiences," *Talkers Magazine,* http://www.talkers.com/main/index.php?option=com_content&task=view&id=17&Itemid=34 (accessed September 13, 2007).

4. Ibid.

5. N. Z. Bear, "The TTLB Blogosphere Ecosystem," The Truth Laid Bear, http://truthlaidbear.com/ecotraffic.php?start=1 (accessed May 2, 2007).

6. Dan Balz and Mike Allen, "Election Is Now for Bush Campaign: Early Efforts Aim to Amass Voters," *Washington Post,* November 30, 2003, sec. A.

7. "U.S. Newspaper Employment," *The Source- Newspapers by the Numbers,* (Arlington, Va.: Newspaper Association of America, 2006), http://web.naa.org/the-source/24.asp (accessed August 4, 2007).

8. Price History, New York Times, http://phx.corporate-ir.net/phoenix.zhtml?c=105317&p=irol-stocklookup&t=HistQuote.

9. The Associated Press, "Circulation at the Top 20 Newspapers," Associated Press,

April 30, 2007, http://biz.yahoo.com/ap/070430/newspapers_circulation_list .html?.v=1&printer=.

10. Audit Bureau of Circulation, US NEWSPAPER - SEARCH RESULTS, http://abcas3.accessabc.com/ecirc/newstitlesearchus.asp (accessed April 29, 2007).-pg 195 line 5

11. S. Robert Lichter, Stanley Rothman, and Linda S. Lichter, *The Media Elite* (Winter Park, Fl.: Hastings House, 1990).

12. Lichter and Rothman, 30.

13. Lichter and Rothman.

14. Ken Dautrich and Chris Barnes, *Press Freedom in the U.S.: A National Survey of Journalists and the American Public* (West Hartford: University of Connecticut School of Public Policy, 2005), http://importance.corante .com/archives/UCONN_DPP_Press_Release.pdf (accessed September 25, 2007).

15. Ken Dautrich and Chris Barnes, http://importance.corante.com/archives/ UCONN_DPP_Press_Release.pdf (accessed September 25, 2007).

16. Grover Norquist, "McCain's Big Backers: Who needs public financing if the media love you?" *American Spectator*, December 1999/January 2000, 78–79.

17. Ibid.

18. Ibid.

19. Nielsen Media Research, Weekday Competitive Program Ranking for December 2006, Obtained from Media Bistro (www.mediabistro.com).

20. "Evening News Viewership, All Network," State of the Media 2007 (Washington, D.C.: Project for Excellence in Journalism, 2007), http://www.stateofthemedia .org/2007/chartland.asp?id=211&ct=line&dir=&sort=&col1_box=1# (accessed September 28, 2007).

## Chapter 14

1. David Hogberg and Sarah Haney, *Funding Liberalism with Blue-Chip Profits: Fortune 100 Foundations Back Leftist Causes* (Washington, D.C.: Capital Research Center, August 2006).

2. Charles E. Wilson, confirmation hearing, January 15, 1953. Nominations, hearings before the Committee on Armed Services, United States Senate, 83d Congress, 1st session, p. 26 (1953).

3. Brooks Jackson, *Honest Graft: Big Money and the American Political Process* (Washington, D.C.: Farragut Publishing Company, 1990).

4. Research performed upon request of author by The Center for Responsive Politics.

5. Opensecrets.org, http://opensecrets.org/industries/indus.asp?Ind=D (accessed September 22, 2007).

6. Jonathan D. Salant, "Boeing, Banks Give to Democratic Candidates after Election Wins," Bloomberg.com, http://www.bloomberg.com/apps/news?pid=ewsarchive &sid=aT7EeUujXdw4 (accessed April 29, 2007).

7. Opensecrets.org, http://opensecrets.org/industries/indus.asp?Ind=K (accessed August 4, 2007).

## Chapter 15

1. Roberto Suro, Richard Fry, and Jeffrey Passel, Hispanics and the 2004 Election Population, Electorate and Voters, Pew Hispanic Center, http://pewhispanic.org/reports/report.php?ReportID=48 (accessed January 18, 2007).
2. CNN Exit Polls 2006.
3. National Health Center for Statistics, Preliminary Births for 2004, Center for Disease Control, http://www.cdc.gov/nchs/data/hestat/prelimbirth04_tables.pdf (accessed November 1, 2006).
4. Richard Cizik, personal interview with executive director of National Association of Evangelicals.
5. S. G. Liaugminas, "Catholicism with a Latin Beat," *Crisis*, September 2001, http://www.crisismagazine.com/september2001/cover.htm (accessed September 24, 2007).
6. "Religion and the Presidential Vote: Bush's Gains Broad-Based" (Washington, D.C.: The Pew Research Center for the People and the Press, 2004), http://people-press.org/commentary/display.php3?AnalysisID=103 (accessed June 6, 2006).
7. Suro, Fry, and Passel, 19.
8. Ibid., 18.
9. Richard Nadler, *Border Wars: The Impact of Immigration on the Latino Vote* (Overland Park, Kan.: America's Majority Foundation, 2007).
10. Benn J. Wattenberg, *Fewer: How the New Demography of Depopulation Will Shape Our Future* (Chicago: Ivan R. Dee), 77.
11. Claudette E. Bennett, We the American People: Blacks, U.S. Census Bureau, http://www.census.gov/apsd/wepeople/we-1.pdf (accessed May 15, 2007).
12. Major Features of the Civil Rights Act of 1964 from the Dirksen Congressional Center.
13. Ibid.
14. "Election Results September 2003," *Ballot Initiative Strategy Center,* http://www.ballot.org/index.asp?Type=B_BASIC&SEC=%7B230884C4-B76B-4542-A914-A5EBFA7DFFE4%7D&DE=%7B606C9306-FE7D-4DC4-888B-640321DF3EAC%7D#al (accessed August 26, 2007).
15. Analysis done by author using Census Bureau data.

## Chapter 16

1. Analysis performed by American Shareholders Association using Flow of Funds Data, http://www.federalreserve.gov/releases/z1/Current/z1r-5.pdf (accessed July 14, 2007).
2. Demian S. Brady, *Committee Control in the 110th Congress: Who Will Be Left Sitting?* (Washington, D.C.: National Taxpayers Union Foundation, 2006), 1.
3. Tim Kaine, "Global U.S. Troop Deployment, 1950–2005." The Heritage Foundation. http://www.heritage.org/Research/NationalSecurity/cda06-02.cfm (accessed November 26, 2006).

4. John Kenneth White, Daniel M. Shea, *New Party Politics: From Jefferson and Hamilton to the Information* (Boston: Bedford/St. Martin's, 2000), 93.

## Chapter 17

1. Tax Foundation, "State and Local Tax Burdens Compared to Other U.S. States," http://www.taxfoundation.org/files/burden_by_year_all_states-2007-04-04 .pdf (accessed September 20, 2007).
2. Analysis of IRS data by Americans for Tax Reform Foundation.
3. Ibid.
4. There are a handful of states that are seeing a net loss of residents but a net gain in income or vice versa. Although this may seem counterintuitive, these apparent inconsistencies are due to the IRS data's inclusion of all income included in the adjusted gross income calculation. The inclusion of sole proprietorship business income, IRA distributions, dividends, and other types of income explain the variations in the pattern of individuals and their incomes moving from one state to another.
5. Office of Economic and Demographic Research, General Revenue Fund Financial Outlook Statement, State of Florida, http://edr.state.fl.us/conferences/generalrevenue/groutl.pdf (accessed April 30, 2007).
6. Wendell Cox Consultancy, U.S. Private Sector Trade Union Membership http://www.publicpurpose.com/lm-unn2003.htm (accessed March 23, 2007).
7. Analysis performed by Alliance for Worker Freedom using Census Bureau data.
8. Ibid.
9. ATR Foundation Study Using IRS Statistics of Income Data.
10. Americans for Tax Reform Foundation analysis using 2005 U.S. Census data and IRS data.
11. Thomas Geoghegan, "Take It to the Blue States: Maybe Labor Should Give Up on Washington in Favor of Friendlier Terrain," *The Nation*, November 29, 2004, 14–17.
12. Americans for Tax Reform Foundation analysis of data from the Internal Revenue Service.
13. Ibid.
14. U.S. Census Bureau. Web: www.census.gov. For 1900–2005 population estimates, see Population of the 20 Largest U.S. Cities, 1900–2005.

## Chapter 18

1. Tax Policy Center, Tax Facts: Individual Income Tax Brackets, 1945–2007, http://www.taxpolicycenter.org/taxfacts/Content/PDF/historical_parameters .pdf (accessed August 1, 2007).
2. Scott Cummings, "May 10, 1773: Parliament passes the Tea Act; December 16, 1773: Boston Tea Party," *The Patriot Resource*, http://www.patriotresource.com/ events/bostontea.html (accessed August 28, 2007).

3. Internal Revenue Service, Brief History of the IRS, http://www.irs.gov/irs/article/0,,id=149200,00.html (accessed August 7, 2007).

4. Ibid.

5. U.S. Department of State, *Smoot-Hawley Tariff, 1930* (Washington, D.C.: State, 2007), http://www.state.gov/r/pa/ho/time/id/17606.htm (accessed September 3, 2007).

6. Democratic Party Platform of 1932, *The American Presidency Project*, July 27, 1932, http://www.presidency.ucsb.edu/ws/print.php?pid=29595 (accessed August 15, 2007).

7. See Bureau of Economic Analysis, Table 6.5A and B. Full-Time Equivalent Employees by Industry.

8. Amity Shlaes, *The Forgotten Man* (New York: HarperCollins Publishers, 2007), 127–28.

9. Dwight D. Eisenhower, "84—Special Message to the Congress Recommending Tax Legislation," *The American Presidency Project*, http://www.presidency.ucsb.edu/ws/index.php?pid=9856 (accessed June 27, 2007).

10. BEA data, http://www.bea.gov/national/nipaweb/TableView.asp#Mid.

11. Herbert Stein, "Why JFK Cut Taxes," *Wall Street Journal*, May 30 , 1996, http://www.msjc.edu/econ/jfk022502.htm (accessed September 23, 2007).

12. BEA data, http://www.bea.gov/national/nipaweb/TableView.asp#Mid.

13. "Rationale for Kennedy's Tax Cut," *New York Times*, September 18, 1984, http://query.nytimes.com/gst/fullpage.html?res=9505E2D6163BF93BA2575AC0A962948260&sec=&spon=&pagewanted=print (accessed April 23, 2007).

14. "New Treasury Data Confirm ACCF Analysis of Thirty Years Ago," *ACCF Capital Formation Newsletter*, January–February 2005, Vol. 30, No. 1.

15. CBO, *Capital Gains Taxes and Federal Revenues* (Washington, D.C.: CBO, 2002), http://www.cbo.gov/ftpdoc.cfm?index=3856&type=0 (accessed August 13, 2007).

16. Mark Simon, "Buffett's Prop. 13 comments cause stir," *San Francisco Chronicle*, August 16, 2003, and Stephen Moore, "Voters Say No to New Taxes . . . even on the Left Coast," *National Review Online*, March 5, 2004, http://www.nationalreview.com/moore/moore200403051114.asp (accessed August 10, 2007).

17. Election Atlas, http://uselectionatlas.org/RESULTS/ (accessed April 15, 2007).

18. President Ronald Reagan, Address before a Joint Session of the Congress Reporting on the State of the Union (Washington, D.C.: 1984), http://reagan2020.us/speeches/state_of_the_union_1984.asp (accessed June 2, 2007).

19. Tax Policy Center, Tax Facts: Individual Income Tax Brackets, 1945–2007, http://taxpolicycenter.org/TaxFacts/TFDB/Content/PDF/individual_rates.pdf (accessed August 1, 2007).

20. Michael Barone, Grant Ujifusa, *The Almanac of American Politics 1990*, 10th ed. (Washington, D.C.: National Journal, 1989), 737, p. 275, line "shifted permanently to Bush."

21. George H. W. Bush, "1988 Republican National Convention Acceptance Address," *American Rhetoric*, http://www.americanrhetoric.com/speeches/georgehbush1988rnc.htm (accessed April 16, 2007).

22. Dave Leip's election atlas, http://www.uselectionatlas.org/RESULTS/.

23. Tax Policy Center, Tax Facts: Individual Income Tax Brackets, 1945–2007, http://taxpolicycenter.org/TaxFacts/TFDB/Content/PDF/individual_rates.pdf (accessed August 1, 2007). Tax Policy Center, Tax Facts: Historical AMT Legislation, http://taxpolicycenter.org/TaxFacts/Tfdb/TFTemplate.cfm?DocID=195 &Topic2id=30&Topic3id=36 (accessed August 1, 2007).

24. Michael Barone and Grant Ujifusa. *The Almanac of American Politics 1982* (Washington, D.C.: Barone & Company, 1981), xv–xix.
Michael Barone and Grant Ujifusa. *The Almanac of American Politics 1986* (Washington, D.C.: National Journal Inc., 1985), lii.
Michael Barone and Grant Ujifusa. *The Almanac of American Politics 1994* (Washington, D.C.: National Journal Inc., 1993), xxix.
Grant Ujifusa and Michael Barone. *The Almanac of American Politics 1990* (Washington, D.C.: National Journal Inc., 1989), xxxii.

25. House History. Office of the Clerk, U.S. House of Representatives http://clerk .house.gov/art_history/house_history/index.html (accessed August 10, 2007).

26. March Fong Eu, "Statement of the Vote: General Election November 3, 1992 (Sacramention: Secretary of State, 1992), http://www.sos.ca.gov/elections/sov/1992 _general/statement_of_vote_general_1992.pdf (accessed September 1, 2007).

27. Ibid.

28. Secretary of State, "1992 Election," (Massachusetts Board of Elections, 1992), http://www.sec.state.ma.us/ELE/elebalm/balmpdf/balm1992.pdf (September 10, 2007).

29. Tax Policy Center, http://taxpolicycenter.org/TaxFacts/TFDB/Content/PDF/ individual_rates.pdf (accessed August 1, 2007).

30. "Line in the sand against new taxes: Legislative Republicans could block new levies, if they stick together," OC Register, http://www.ocregister.com/ ocregister/opinion/homepage/article_1646827.php (accessed August 9, 2007), April 10, 2007.

31. Scott Riley, "Sweet Home Alabama: 2006 Preview," *Election Projection 2006* August 11, 2005, http://www.electionprojection.com/archives110105.html (accessed August 15, 2007).

32. John J. Miller, "America's Best Governor: For Republicans, a Rocky Mountain high," *National Review* Vol. LIV, No. 16 (2002).

## Chapter 19

1. Internal Revenue Service, 2007 Federal Tax Rate Schedules, http://www.irs.gov/ formspubs/article/0,,id=164272,00.html (accessed August 8, 2007).

2. Neal Boortz and Congressman John Linder, *The FairTax Book: Saying Goodbye to the Income Tax and the IRS* (New York, N.Y.: HarperCollins, 2005).

3. Elections Division, Massachusetts Statewide Ballot Measures: 1919–2004, Secretary of State's Office, http://www.sec.state.ma.us/ele/elebalm/balmidx.htm (accessed August 9, 2007).

4. Darien B. Jacobson, Brian G. Raub, and Barry W. Johnson, "The Estate Tax: Ninety Years and Counting," Internal Revenue Service, http://www.irs.gov/ pub/irs-soi/ninetyestate.pdf (accessed September 27, 2007).

5. Ibid.
6. Leonard E. Burman, William G. Gale, and Jeffrey Rohaly, "Options for Reforming the Estate Tax," *Tax Analysts Tax Break,* Tax Policy Center, http://www.taxpolicycenter.org/UploadedPDF/1000780_Tax_Break_4-18-05.pdf (accessed June 11, 2007).
7. Internal Revenue Service, SOI Tax Stats- Collecting Revenue, http://www.irs.gov/taxstats/compliancestats/article/0,,id=97168,00.html (accessed June 11, 2007).
8. U.S. Department of the Treasury, *Summary of H.R. 1836—The Economic Growth and Tax Relief Reconciliation Act of 2001 (Conference Report),* http://www.policyalmanac.org/economic/archive/taxes-2001-05-25.shtml (accessed August 9, 2007).
9. California Secretary of State, *A History of California Initiatives: 2002,* http://www.sos.ca.gov/elections/init_history.pdf (accessed June 1, 2007).
10. Ibid.
11. Nancy Gibbs and Michael Duffy, "Two Men, Two Visions; Now comes the choice. Each man holds a core belief that invites a case study in who is for real: Bush and his big tax cut? Gore and his populist battle cry? We look at how they decided where to make a stand," *Time,* November 6, 2000, 48.
12. Karlyn Bowman, *Public Opinion on Taxes* (Washington, D.C.: American Enterprise Institute, 2007), 64.
13. Analysis done by author using the IRS code.
14. "Social Security: Prosperity Through Ownership," *The Heritage Foundation,* 2007, http://www.heritage.org/Research/features/socialsecurity/SSCalcWelcome.asp (accessed June 4, 2007).
15. U.S. Department of Treasury Office of Public Affairs, *U.S. Assistant Treasury Secretary Pam Olson Remarks to the Federal Bar Association at 27th Annual Tax Conference,* http://www.treas.gov/press/releases/js96.htm (accessed July 10, 2007).
16. Daniel Clifton and Eric Wong, *LSA's and RSA's: The Keys to Economic Prosperity* (Washington, D.C.: ATR, 2003), http://www.atr.org/content/pdf/pre2004/111803rept-LSA.pdf.
17. Sarah Holden and Jack VanDerheil, *The Influence of Automatic Enrollment, Catch-Up, and IRA Contributions on 401(k) Accumulations at Retirement* (Washington, D.C.: Investment Company Institute, 2005).
18. Cynthia G. Fox, "Income Tax Records of the Civil War Years," *Prologue Magazine.*
19. *Federal Taxation of Earnings versus Investment Income in 2004* (Washington, D.C.: Institute on Taxation & Economic Policy, 2004), http://www.itepnet.org/earnan.pdf (accessed August 21, 2007).
20. American Shareholder Association analysis of U.S. Market Capitalization.
21. Office of Tax Analysis, *Capital Gains and Taxes Paid on Capital Gains for Returns with Positive Net Capital Gains, 1954–2004* (Washington, D.C.: Treasury, 2007), http://www.treas.gov/offices/tax-policy/library/capgain1-2006.pdf (accessed July 12, 2007).
22. Ibid.
23. Ibid.
24. Ibid.
25. Daniel Clifton, "2003 Tax Cut: Updated Charts and Data," *American Sharehold-*

*ers Association Blog,* February 12, 2007, http://www.americanshareholders.org/2007/02/2003-tax-cut-up.html (accessed August 4, 2007).

26. Leon Lazaroff, "Despite cash hoard, companies wary of dividends," *Chicago Tribune,* June 4, 2006, http://www.chicagotribune.com/business/yourmoney/sns-yourmoney-0604dividends,0,195934.story (accessed August 29, 2007).

27. Gary Robbins and Aldona Robbins, *What's the Most Potent Way to Stimulate the Economy?* (Washington, D.C.: Institute for Policy Innovation, 2001), http://www.ipi.org/ipi%5CIPIPublications.nsf/PublicationLookupFullText/CF8A52ECDCAF9A2986256AE1007BCF7D (accessed September 20, 2007).

28. Congressional Record, Making Further Continuing Appropriations for the Fiscal Year 2007 (Washington, D.C.: Govtrack.us, February 14, 2007), http://www.govtrack.us/congress/record.xpd?id=110-s20070214-16&person=300048 (accessed June 21, 2007).

29. Analysis done by author using the IRS code.

30. Federal Reserve Statistical Release, Flow of Funds Accounts of the United States, Federal Reserve, http://www.federalreserve.gov/releases/z1/current/default.htm.

31. Joint Committee on Taxation, Estimated Budget Effects of the Conference Agreement for H.R. 4520, The "American Jobs Creation Act of 2004, Fiscal Years 2005–2014," http://www.house.gov/jct/x-69-04.pdf (accessed August 10, 2007).

32. Flow of Funds, http://www.federalreserve.gov/releases/z1/current/default.htm.

33. Daniel Mitchell, "Iceland Joins the Flat Tax Club," *Tax and Budget Bulletin,* (Washington, D.C.: Cato Institute, 2007), http://www.cato.org/pubs/tbb/tbb_0207-43.pdf (accessed September 15, 2007).

34. Don Feder, "Here Come the Massachusetts Democrats," *Front Page Magazine,* July 5, 2004, http://www.frontpagemag.com/Articles/Read.aspx?GUID=D7EAC5F5-1C3A-42A8-82EA-E9C898F5A480 (accessed April 9, 2007).

35. Daniel J. Mitchell, "Corporate Taxes: America Is Falling Behind," *Tax and Budget Bulletin* (Washington, D.C.: Cato Institute, 2007), http://www.cato.org/pubs/tbb/tbb_0707_48.pdf (accessed August 2, 2007).

36. James Tisch, Statement of James Tisch, President and Chief Executive Officer, Loews Corporation, New York, New York, *Testimony Before the Subcommittee on Select Revenue Measures of the House Committee on Ways and Means* (Washington, D.C.: Congress, 2006), http://waysandmeans.house.gov/hearings.asp?formmode=view&id=4941 (accessed September 24, 2007).

## Chapter 20

1. BEA, http://www.bea.gov/national/nipaweb/TableView.asp#Mid (accessed September 26, 2007).

2. CBO, http://www.cbo.gov/ftpdocs/35xx/doc3521/125RevisedJuly3.pdf (accessed September 24, 2007).

3. BEA, http://www.bea.gov/national/nipaweb/TableView.asp#Mid (accessed September 25, 2007).

4. Calculations performed by Americans for Tax Reform using Bureau of Economic Analysis data.

5. ATR calculations based on data from the CBO and BEA.
6. Trude B. Feldman, "Former President Bush at 80," *World Tribune*, September 11, 2004, http://www.worldtribune.com/worldtribune/WTARC/2004/ss_ghwbush_08_18.html (accessed September 23, 2007).
7. Analysis performed by Americans for Tax Reform Foundation using BEA data.
8. Joshua Bolten, *Testimony of OMB Director Joshua B. Bolten Mid Session Review of the President's FY 2006 Budget Request Committee on the Budget United States House of Representatives* (Washington, D.C.: White House, 2005), http://www.whitehouse.gov/omb/legislative/testimony/director/071405bolten.pdf (accessed September 20, 2007).
9. President George W. Bush, *State of the Union Address* (Washington, D.C.: 2004), http://www.whitehouse.gov/news/releases/2004/01/20040120-7.html (accessed September 21, 2007).
10. President Bush, Press Conference in the Rose Garden (Washington, D.C.: White House, October 11, 2006).
11. Brady, 1.

## Chapter 21

1. Congressional Budget Office, Historical Budget Data, http://www.cbo.gov/budget/historical.xls (accessed September 21, 2007).
2. Americans for Tax Reform analysis of data from Office of Management and Budget, Congressional Budget Office, Bureau of Economic Analysis, and Census.
3. Data compiled by Americans for Tax Reform Foundation using Bureau of Economic Analysis, National Economic Accounts. http://www.bea.gov/national/nipaweb/TableView.asp#Mid (accessed September 21, 2007), Office of Management and Budget, Fiscal Year 2008 Budget, http://www.whitehouse.gov/omb/budget/fy2008sheets/hist16z1.xls (accessed September 21, 2007), U.S. Government Spending, United States Federal, State, and Local Government Spending, Fiscal Year 2005. www.usgovernmentspending.com (accessed September 21, 2007).
4. Andrew T. LeFevre, *Report Card on American Education: A State-by-State Analysis* (Washington, D.C.: American Legislative Exchange Council, 2006), 74.
5. Ibid.
6. Office of the Chief Actuary, Social Security, *Actuarial Resources* (Baltimore: 2007), http://www.ssa.gov/OACT/ (accessed July 16, 2007).
7. "Social Security: Prosperity Through Ownership," The Heritage Foundation, 2007, http://www.heritage.org/Research/features/socialsecurity/SSCalcWelcome.asp (accessed June 4, 2007).
8. Lawrence R. Jacobs, "UFO stories: more Social Security bunk. (Cynicism about the future of Social Security benefits)," *The New Republic*, 1998, http://www.clas.ufl.edu/users/kenwald/pos3233/socsec.htm (accessed September 17, 2007).
9. "Archived Polls," Project on Social Security Choice: Cato Institute, http://www.socialsecurity.org/congressional/polls.html (accessed December 15, 2006).

10. Peter Ferrara, *Social Security: The Inherent Contradiction* (Washington, D.C.: Cato Institute, 1980).

11. Ibid.

12. Heritage Social Security Calculator, http://www.heritage.org/Research/features/socialsecurity/SSCalcWelcome.asp (accessed May 14, 2007).

13. Peter Ferrara and Michael Tanner, *A New Deal for Social Security* (Washington, D.C.: Cato Institute, 1998).

14. EBRI Databook on Employee Benefits, http://www.ebri.org/publications/books/index.cfm?fa=databook (accessed July 6, 2007).

15. Ibid.

16. Ibid.

17. Ibid.

18. Ibid.

19. Facts from the EBRI, http://www.ebri.org/pdf/publications/facts/0902fact.pdf (accessed September 20, 2007).

20. Peter Ferrara, *Personal Accounts and Social Security: A New Progressive Proposal for Reform* (Washington, D.C.: Institute for Policy Innovation: Policy Report #176, 2003).

21. Jose Pinera (Co-chairman, Project on Social Security Choice), interview by author, September 20, 2007.

22. Revised edition of "Empowering Workers: The Privatization of Social Security in Chile" published in 1996 as Cato's Letter No. 10. Originally published in the *Cato Journal*, Vol. 15, Nos. 2–3 (Fall/Winter 1995/96). Copyright © 2002 Cato Institute. http://www.josepinera.com/pag/pag_tex_empowering.htm and the website of the Superintendency of AFP www.safp.cl.

23. Steven Hayward and Erik Peterson, "The Medicare Monster: A Cautionary Tale," *Reason Online*, January 1993, http://www.reason.com/news/show/29339.html (accessed September 28, 2007).

24. Social Security Office of the Chief Actuary, http://www.ssa.gov/OACT/ (accessed July 16, 2007).

25. McQuillan, 19–20.

26. American Medical Association, *Medical Liability Reform—Now!: A compendium of facts supporting medical liability reform and debunking arguments against reform* (Chicago: 2006), http://www.ama-assn.org/ama1/pub/upload/mm/-1/mlrnow.pdf,21.

27. *Trial Lawyers Inc., California* (New York: Manhattan Institute, 2005), http://www.triallawyersinc.com/TLI-ca.pdf (accessed September 21, 2007).

28. Amy Finkelstein, *The Aggregate Effects of Health Insurance Evidence from the Introduction of Medicare* (Cambridge: National Bureau of Economic Research, 2006), http://www.nber.org/~afinkels/papers/Finkelstein_Medicare_April06.pdf.

29. Center for Research and Policy, January 2006 Census Shows 3.2 Million People Covered By HSA Plans, America's Health Insurance Plans, http://www.ahip.org/content/default.aspx?docid=15302 (accessed September 1, 2007).

30. Victoria Craig Bunce, J. P. Wieske, and Larry Siedlick, *Health Insurance Mandates in the States 2007* (Alexandria: CAHI, 2007), http://www.cahi.org/cahi_contents/resources/pdf/MandatePub2007.pdf (accessed June 6, 2007).

31. Council for Affordable Health Insurance, Letter Urges Consideration of the

Health Care Choice Act Legislation Will Help Uninsured Get Coverage, http://www.cahi.org/article.asp?id=807.

32. "National Education Testing: A Debate," *Cato Policy Report*, July/August 2001, 6.

33. Leander Kahney, "Steve Jobs, Proud to Be Nonunion," *Wired*, February 20, 2007, http://www.wired.com/techbiz/people/news/2007/02/72754 (accessed September 28, 2007).

34. Dr. Brian Ray, "Research Facts on Homeschooling," National Home Education Research Institute, July 10, 2006, http://www.nheri.org/content/view/199/ (accessed January 27, 2007).

35. Samuel Freedman, "As a parent, Gore abandons public schools," *USA Today*, September 20, 2000, sec. A.

36. Clint Bolick, "Selective School Choice," *Wall Street Journal*, March 2, 2007, http://www.allianceforschoolchoice.org/more.aspx?IITypeID=4&IIID=3233 (accessed June 7, 2007).

37. Rhonda Adams, "Focus on success, not failure," *USA Today*, May 6, 2004, http://www.usatoday.com/money/smallbusiness/columnist/abrams/2004-05-06-success_x.htm (accessed August 10, 2007).

38. LaFevre, 60.

39. The Office of Management and Budget is required to collect this data under the Federal Activities Inventory Reform (FAIR) Act, http://www.whitehouse.gov/omb/procurement/fair-index.html (accessed June 26, 2007).

40. Carl Demaio et al., *Citizens' Budget 2003–2005* (Los Angeles, Ca.: Reason Foundation and the Performance Institute, 2003).

41. Sandra Fabry, *State, Federal, and Local Efforts to Increase Transparency in Government Spending* (Washington, D.C.: ATR, 2007).